Motion Graphics with Adobe
Creative Suite 5
STUDIO TECHNIQUES

Richard Harrington and Ian Robinson

The CD/CD-ROM has been removed from this item due to Copyright restrictions.

Adobe

Motion Graphics with Adobe® Creative Suite® 5 Studio Techniques

Richard Harrington and Ian Robinson

Copyright © 2011 Richard Harrington and Ian Robinson

This Adobe Press book is published by Peachpit. For information on Adobe Press books, contact:

Peachpit
1249 Eighth Street
Berkeley, CA 94710
(510) 524-2178
Fax: (510) 524-2221

To report errors, please send a note to errata@peachpit.com

Peachpit is a division of Pearson Education
For the latest on Adobe Press books, go to www.adobepress.com

Senior Editor: Karyn Johnson
Development and Copy Editor: Anne Marie Walker
Production Editor: Tracey Croom, Myrna Vladic
Technical Editor: Todd Kopriva
Proofreader: Elizabeth Welch

Composition: Danielle Foster
Indexer: Valerie Haynes Perry
Cover design: Peachpit Press/Charlene Will
Cover illustration: Regina Cleveland

Notice of Rights

Notice of Liability

The information in this book is distributed on an "As Is" basis, without warranty. While every precaution has been taken in the preparation of the book, neither the authors nor Peachpit shall have any liability to any person or entity with respect to any loss or damage caused or alleged to be caused directly or indirectly by the instructions contained in this book or by the computer software and hardware products described in it.

Trademarks

Adobe, Creative Suite, After Effects, Premiere Pro, Photoshop, Illustrator, Flash Professional, Soundbooth, Bridge, OnLocation, Encore, Flash Catalyst, and Device Central are registered trademarks of Adobe Systems Incorporated in the United States and/or other countries. Many of the designations used by manufacturers and sellers to distinguish their products are claimed as trademarks. Where those designations appear in this book, and Peachpit was aware of a trademark claim, the designations appear as requested by the owner of the trademark. All other product names and services identified throughout this book are used in editorial fashion only and for the benefit of such companies with no intention of infringement of the trademark. No such use, or the use of any trade name, is intended to convey endorsement or other affiliation with this book.

ISBN 13: 978-0-321-71969-0
ISBN 10: 0-321-71969-7

9 8 7 6 5 4 3 2 1

Printed and bound in the United States of America

Contents at a Glance

Contents

Additional chapter on broadcast package design available for download
on the web at www.peachpit.com/mgcs5st

About the Authors

Richard Harrington has had a long relationship with media. When he was seven, he was grounded for using magnets to rearrange the picture tube on the family's 13-inch color TV (it works, but don't try it). He has since gone on to many more interesting adventures as the founder of RHED Pixel, a visual communications company in Washington, DC.

Rich was first exposed to Adobe Photoshop and Adobe After Effects while working in a television newsroom. In those early days, computers were slow (very slow). Rendering projects often took days. When he was not creating graphics for broadcast, Rich worked on early websites, published a music magazine, was a concert photographer, and worked on the first nonlinear editing systems. A master's degree in Project Management fills out Rich's broad spectrum of experience.

Rich is also a certified instructor for Adobe and regularly speaks at industry events like the NAB conference, DV Expo, IBC conference, Photoshop World, and more. He has been the Program Manager and a Technical Chair for the Post|Production World Conference at the National Association of Broadcasters since 2003.

Rich is an internationally published author. His book *Photoshop for Video* was the first of its kind to focus on Photoshop's application in the world of video. He is also the coauthor of *After Effects for Flash / Flash for After Effects*, *Broadcast Graphics on the Spot*, and *From Still to Motion: A Photographer's Guide to Creating Video with Your DSLR*.

If you're looking for video training, Rich has created thousands of tutorials, which you'll find on Adobe TV and Creative COW, and as podcasts in the iTunes Store.

Rich believes that we live in a world that is getting increasingly cluttered with confusing messages. His personal philosophy is communicate, motivate, create. He's a firm believer that media can have powerful results.

When he's not working, Rich spends as much time with his wife Meghan as he possibly can. Rich enjoys traveling and digital photography, as well as teaching his kids the joys of science fiction, video games, and comic books.

You can find more information about Rich on his blog at www.RichardHarringtonBlog.com. Follow him on Twitter at @rhedpixel. Answers to technical questions are provided via www.CreativeCOW.net.

Ian Robinson started creating motion graphics in the days before real-time playback. Having patience for a render was never his strong suit. Fortunately, after he spent years learning how to multitask, Ian's designs have appeared on many networks, including the Discovery Channel, Animal Planet, and National Geographic International.

As an instructor, Ian enjoys teaching online as well as in the classroom. As an author for Lynda.com, Ian provides courses in motion graphics and 3D. In the classroom, Ian teaches video game design and animation at George Mason University.

Ian also likes to step away from the computer and keep his traditional art skills sharp as a photographer. He enjoys shooting events with his wife Lisa as a part of SoftBox Media Photography.

Acknowledgments

This book is the direct result of our love for Adobe After Effects and Adobe Photoshop. These two tools have been the foundation of our entire professional careers. Thank you to the product teams at Adobe for continuing to grow and evolve these tools. Each new version unlocks thoughtful tools that save us time and inspire creativity. A special thanks to Todd Kopriva, Michael Coleman, and Michelle Gallina at Adobe for answering our questions and helping us to discover the bigger picture that is the Creative Suite.

A big thanks to those who gave us our first starts. Rich would like to thank Larry Hawk, Jack Tow, and Eric Fishback, who challenged him to learn broadcast graphics in the first place. Ian would like to thank Henry Holdren, Joyce Peifer Forbes, and John Woody for inspiring a career. Both authors also owe a debt of gratitude to the coworkers, employees, clients, and students who've challenged them with tough questions and difficult requests.

A big thanks to the talented motion graphics community who've shared their knowledge with us through the years. In no particular order we'd like to thank Angie Taylor, Chris and Trish Meyer, Jayse Hansen, Rod Harlan, Jeff Foster, Ron Lindebloom, Brian Maffit, Mark Christiansen, Bob Donlon, Marcus Geduld, Jim Kanter, Paul Tuersley, Mark Coleran, Alex Lindsay, Mark Spencer, Michele Yamazaki, Rob Birnholz, and Stephen Kilisky.

Thanks to the great team at Peachpit Press who put this book together. Karyn Johnson, our patient and determined editor, brought the project together. Anne Marie Walker made any of our jumbled thoughts coherent (and made up for time spent doodling during English class). A big thanks to Todd Kopriva from Adobe who scrutinized our techniques and writing to ensure the best experience for you, the reader.

Introduction

Why This Book?

In the beginning, there was After Effects—and it was good (so good that a graphics company from California bought it). Once inside the Adobe fold, After Effects grew immensely with new features and capabilities. The most important in our opinion has been integration.

Sure, there are lots of sexy features in After Effects, and we love them. But what truly helps us get the job done is that After Effects enables us to import graphics files, photos, illustrations, and footage, and create compelling animation. These features have existed for a long time (layered Adobe Photoshop and Adobe Illustrator support has been around for ages).

But Adobe hit upon a true need when it started bundling applications together. Although the logic has taken a while to seep into the pores of designers, there indeed is power in numbers when it comes to software. Being able to see After Effects as the center point in the Creative Suite empowers a designer to be more productive.

A few years back, Rich asked an Adobe exec why he had to use Photoshop to bring 3D models into After Effects (instead of direct support to just import models). The answer was eye opening. It turns out that designers, medical-imaging professionals, and 3D animators all need to use Photoshop. By condensing the support for 3D models and formats into one tool, the development could be more feature rich. You see, it's easier to put money toward new features to benefit a bigger group of users.

This is why killer features like Dynamic Link exist, for the seamless exchange of media between After Effects and Adobe Premiere Pro. Photoshop features like Vanishing Point, 3D Layers, and Camera Raw can work effortlessly with After Effects. The Creative Suite has evolved into a true toolbox; one that has a coordinated approach to working seamlessly while getting the job done.

Unfortunately, most After Effects artists are afraid to venture outside their comfort zone. For us, a love of Photoshop motivated us to explore new ways of making these two applications work together. What we found encouraged us and eventually led us to Illustrator, Premiere Pro, and Encore. Newer additions like the Adobe Media Encoder and Flash also play an important role.

We're not advocating for you to go back to school and learn every application at the same level that you know After Effects. Rather, we offer compelling reasons and practical techniques that let you get more from Creative Suite. Whether you use only a few applications or want to explore the entire suite, you'll find time-saving and inspirational techniques that help you get more done.

Organization of This Book

Motion Graphics with Adobe Creative Suite 5 Studio Techniques is organized into three sections:

- ▶ Section I, "Working Foundations," discusses the approach to modern motion graphics projects. You'll explore the tools contained within the Creative Suite as well as enabling technologies like Dynamic Link and the Open in Editor command. You'll also learn how to organize your project for cross-application (and even multiplatform) workflows. Don't skip these two chapters, because you'll learn some core technology that will save you time and reduce your stress.

- ▶ Section II, "Design Essentials," explores the core tasks we face as motion graphics artists. You'll learn how to use applications like Photoshop, Illustrator, and Adobe Premiere Pro to enhance After Effects projects. You'll also learn about new After Effects tools and overlooked commands that are truly essential. The whole gamut of tasks is covered, from logos, type, and vectors to footage, audio, and 3D.

- ▶ Section III, "Design Exploration," examines real-world projects and techniques. We often pick up a camera and break into the world of production as well. Here you'll investigate new ways to apply your motion graphics knowledge to produce creative output. You'll find three chapters in this section and a bonus chapter on creating a broadcast package design for download at www.peachpit.com/mgcs5st.

What's on the DVD?

To see the techniques in the pages come to life, we've included hands-on projects and source files. Although space limitations have meant some compression and trimming, you'll still find completed shots and source materials so you can understand how we accomplished the results.

As you read this book, you'll encounter specific advice and techniques. But if you lift the curtain and jump right into the project and source files, you'll see the duct tape and bubble gum that holds everything together. We're not calling our techniques flimsy; rather, we're guiding you through real-world projects where nothing is ever perfect. Footage can be poorly shot, assets can be lacking, and the like, yet the job still gets done.

We're results-oriented people. The assets and materials on the DVD will show you just how we completed the project. Be sure to copy the appropriate folder to your computer's hard drive for each lesson. Due to speed issues and an inability to save your progress, you should not work directly off the disc.

SECTION I

Working Foundations

1

The Motion Graphics Toolbox

An architect's most useful tools are an eraser at the drafting board, and a wrecking bar at the site.

—Frank Lloyd Wright

The Motion Graphics Toolbox

Chances are you've picked up this book because you want to master Adobe After Effects. Well, it turns out that the path to mastery is a bit windy. We see many motion graphics artists limit themselves by being too narrowly focused. They come to rely on Adobe After Effects for everything. Don't get us wrong, After Effects has powerful motion graphics capabilities, but it is part of a bigger ecosystem, the Adobe Creative Suite.

Our philosophy is simple. If you were a carpenter, you could do all your work with a hammer. But things would get tough when it came time to tighten a screw in a board. Sure, you could force it through, but seasoned pros know that using the right tool for the job makes the job easier and produces better results.

It's difficult to create motion graphics without the graphic component (hence the need for Adobe Photoshop, Adobe Illustrator, and Adobe Flash). Likewise, you may want to utilize video in your After Effects work, which means using Adobe OnLocation and Adobe Premiere Pro. This chapter looks at the Production Premium bundle of tools and identifies ways in which they'll help your After Effects workflow.

Adobe Creative Suite 5 Production Premium

Many users have moved to the Production Premium edition of Creative Suite because it's a natural progression. For less than the cost of After Effects and Photoshop, you can add a powerful suite of tools to your workflow. Several of the applications in the suite may be just sitting on your computer, rarely being launched. We'd like to change that and make your job easier.

The Production Premium toolset offers a complete solution for motion graphic design. Once you become familiar with the entire suite, you'll see how seamlessly the tools intersect. All the applications share a similar user interface, and you'll find that technologies like Dynamic Link and the Edit Original command workflow can make the entire process of sharing projects and assets effortless. Let's explore the support role each application plays when you're working with After Effects. The Production Premium toolset allows you to output your final project to multiple formats for viewing on air, online, and on device.

Adobe Premiere Pro CS5

 The presence of video in After Effects projects has become commonplace. The use of Premiere Pro enables you to capture, organize, edit, and output video more efficiently than any other tool in the Creative Suite. Premiere Pro shares many similarities with After Effects, so if you are familiar with After Effects, you should be comfortable using Premiere Pro.

Using Premiere Pro allows you to professionally polish your video footage. By creating a sequence, you can assemble shots in the correct order, trim away any unwanted portions, seamlessly blend audio, adjust color and volume, and then add transitions. Premiere Pro is an efficient and powerful, yet clear-cut solution. Once the video is edited, you can import it into After Effects in several ways. We'll explore this workflow later in this chapter.

TIP

After Effects is rarely used for its audio capabilities. Typically, the audio track is exported from Premiere Pro, Audition, or Soundbooth and re-synced with the final composition.

Photoshop CS5 Extended

 Photoshop is the leading choice for editing raster graphics such as photos. The current version of Photoshop significantly extends its nondestructive editing capacities, allowing for even greater control.

Many designers also choose to build their initial designs in Photoshop. With its powerful type controls and precise alignment and scaling tools, you can quickly build prototype designs. Photoshop's layered file format also imports seamlessly into After Effects with nearly every feature intact, including blending modes, layer grouping, and even layer styles.

The Production Premium bundle includes the additional capabilities of Photoshop Extended. This allows for easier video file integration and also provides advanced options like Vanishing Point Exchange and 3D objects when working with After Effects. With Adobe Photoshop CS5 Extended, you can even use the new Repoussé command (**Figure 1.1**) to create 3D objects, which you can then import into After Effects.

Figure 1.1 The Repoussé command is a powerful graphics creation tool that is included with Photoshop CS5. The 3D models you create can be imported as Live 3D objects into After Effects.

Illustrator CS5

As Photoshop is to raster graphics, Illustrator is to vector graphics. Vector graphics can be infinitely scaled and often have very small file sizes. For After Effects, vector files offer the flexibility of scaling to any size without pixelization. They can also be used as design elements or vector masks. In addition, After Effects can import a layered Illustrator file, which makes animation tasks painless.

We'll explore vector tools in depth in Chapter 10, "Designing with Vectors."

Flash Professional CS5

Flash Professional has a long history of being the tool of choice for developing rich interactive content. On its own, it offers sophisticated tools for animation, video delivery, and interactive design. When combined with the other tools in the Creative Suite, its power truly shines.

The latest version of Flash also sports powerful animation tools, including inverse kinematics. This robust animation style uses a series of linked objects to create relationship-based animation. Additionally, a single shape can be distorted or animated using the new Bones tool. Flash now has an easier-to-use animation model for creating animations in its Timeline for use in multimedia projects or for export to After Effects.

Soundbooth CS5

Adobe Soundbooth represents a significant evolution in approaching audio tasks (**Figure 1.2**). The software is designed to simplify essential audio tasks like mixing audio tracks, sweetening sound, and creating music or sound beds. It is designed to be intuitive since much of the complexity of other audio tools has been removed.

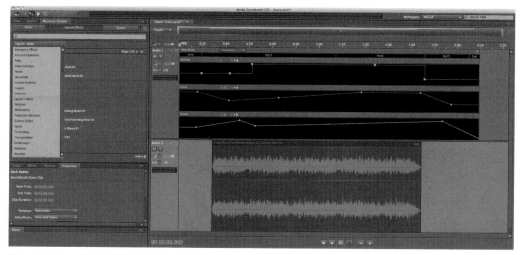

Figure 1.2 Soundbooth offers several scores to choose from. You can customize these scores in duration and intensity. Several sound effects can also be used to sound design your animations (such as glints and impact effects). Be sure to visit Resource Central (Window > Resource Central) to browse and download more elements.

Be sure to visit the extensive Adobe TV online learning center at tv.adobe.com for more on Soundbooth. You should also check out the official page at www.adobe.com/support/soundbooth.

After Effects recognizes six audio file formats. If your source file is not on the following list, you might be able to use Soundbooth to convert it:

- ▶ Adobe Sound Document (ASND)
- ▶ Advanced Audio Coding (AAC, M4A)
- ▶ Audio Interchange File Format (AIF, AIFF)
- ▶ MP3 (MP3, MPEG, MPG, MPA, MPE)
- ▶ Video for Windows (AVI)
- ▶ Waveform (WAV)

If you need to add a custom score or perform sound design for an After Effects composition, remember the value of Soundbooth. In Soundbooth just choose File > Adobe Dynamic Link > Import Adobe After Effects Composition. This makes it very easy to create custom music or add sound effects because you can adjust to match the video.

Soundbooth even allows you to mix multiple audio tracks together to create complex sound beds. These mixes can be saved using the Adobe Sound Document (ASND) format. You can then bring an ASND file into After Effects, which results in making your timelines cleaner without sacrificing the ability to make adjustments.

Many users bypass Soundbooth and miss out on significant features. Some mistake its ease of use for a lack of functionality; others avoid it due to past experiences with the complexity of other audio tools. However, we recommend you take a closer look because Soundbooth offers a truly useful toolset that works well with After Effects. We'll explore its uses in Chapter 9, "Designing with Audio."

Bridge CS5

Adobe Bridge is a command center for the entire Creative Suite. The most useful functions of Bridge include its ability to visually manage media. This includes moving, copying, and renaming files. Bridge can also facilitate tasks that involve multiple applications within the Creative Suite (like creating contact sheets or websites for client review). We'll explore Bridge more in Chapter 2, "Organizing Your Project."

Adobe OnLocation CS5

If you need to acquire new footage for your motion graphics projects, OnLocation can help. OnLocation is a direct-to-disk recording and monitoring solution. By using OnLocation during the preproduction and production stages of a project, you can accelerate the pace of postproduction.

During the planning of a video project, OnLocation allows you to create interactive shot lists or shooting plans that you can check off as you acquire shots. You can also use this organization to improve logging and note taking during the video shoot. If you use Adobe Story, an online tool you have access to through CS Live services, you can even integrate your script and footage directly.

While shooting, OnLocation offers several valuable features. It provides powerful calibration tools—including waveform and vectorscopes—to set up your camera accurately. You can also compare multiple shots for continuity in lighting and exposure. The shots you record can be written directly to a hard drive, which means the footage is organized and ready for After Effects or Premiere Pro for rapid import.

One unique feature that animators will like is that OnLocation provides support for the stop-motion style of animation. This traditional approach uses a series of stills to create fluid motion. OnLocation makes the frame recording options simple and even allows for a split-screen overlay view with opacity control. This precise control makes it easy to position objects from frame to frame.

Encore CS5

 What began its life as a powerful tool to create DVDs has evolved into a multiformat authoring tool. Adobe Encore is a suite of tools that allows video and photos to be authored for deployment as a DVD, Blu-ray Disc, and SWF file. Encore accepts video files as well as photos, music, and sound.

NOTES

We'll explore Adobe Encore in greater depth in Chapter 13.

Flash Catalyst CS5

 Adobe Flash Catalyst is a new addition to the Production Premium toolset. Like Encore, it is not a graphics creation tool. Rather, it's a simple-to-use authoring solution for creating interactive Flash content using Photoshop and Illustrator files. You can also import rendered video that you create with After Effects or Premiere Pro to use in your projects. Flash Catalyst is an excellent way to build interactive projects such as portfolios, training modules, and entertainment websites.

Device Central CS5

 Adobe Device Central is designed to simplify the production of content for mobile phones and consumer electronic devices. At its heart is an extensive and frequently updated database that profiles many devices. There are several options as to how you can use Device Central to streamline your design process.

The primary use of Device Central is as a launching pad. Because it knows what size and type of files work best on each device, it can create template projects for Flash or After Effects.

Once a project is built, you can test it on a virtual device (even simulating different viewing conditions and connection speeds). Device Central works closely with Bridge and makes it straightforward for multimedia designers to create, test, and deploy their work to consumer electronic devices and phones.

Adobe Media Encoder CS5

 Adobe Media Encoder is a robust application that offers a wealth of output options. You can use it to transcode files between formats or optimize files for delivery via Web or optical media (such as Blu-ray). You can use Media Encoder to optimize the video you create in After Effects for delivery to a broader audience. Be sure to check out the watch folder feature of the Adobe Media Encoder. You can create a set of rules so when After Effects outputs a file, the Adobe Media Encoder can process it to multiple formats in the background.

Improving Your Workflow with the Creative Suite

Now that you've learned about the diverse suite of applications at your fingertips, let's focus on your workflow. Motion graphics has become a broad term. Ten years ago, motion graphics design meant you were only targeting a few screens for standard definition television or film.

Oh, have times changed! The number of devices that can play back motion graphics has grown immensely—from smart phones and tablet computers to digital signage and websites. Let's explore three general scenarios in which motion graphics are in demand.

> **TIP**
>
> You can import a Premiere Pro sequence or After Effects composition directly into the Adobe Media Encoder without rendering.

Traditional Uses

Motion graphics continue to be a requirement in nearly all video and film projects. Whether you're designing for a news broadcast, a film title sequence, or a marketing video, clients want motion graphics.

In these situations, the Creative Suite excels. Programs like Photoshop and Illustrator allow you to create graphic assets. Additionally, you can easily convert existing assets for print and Web projects for motion graphics use because Adobe's tools are used across design fields.

The rich video toolset provided makes integrating your motion graphics into a traditional postproduction pipeline stress-free. Premiere Pro lets you import and organize video assets. It can even exchange media and projects with Final Cut Pro and Avid users.

Interactive Uses

Many motion graphics projects are becoming a key ingredient in interactive experiences. The Production Premium toolset offers several approaches to building interactivity. You can easily import video created by After Effects into Flash Catalyst for interactive content. For more robust interactive design, Flash Professional offers a complete toolset. Making this migration process simpler, you can even harness the XFL exchange format to import a layered After Effects file into Flash.

If optical media is more your approach, there's Encore. Both Blu-ray and DVD have come to depend on motion graphics for their menu systems. You can easily design menus in After Effects and even use individual compositions for menus without intermediate rendering thanks to Dynamic Link. If you plan your project with some foresight, you can even reuse your graphics across multiple mediums. With an Encore project, you can publish a standard DVD, a Blu-ray Disc, and a Flash version.

Mobile Screens

The world of mobile video and motion graphics is a vast wilderness. There truly is a lack of standards when it comes to designing for mobile devices like phones, game systems, and media players. Fortunately, there's Device Central, which offers a rich database of profiles for several devices (**Figure 1.3**).

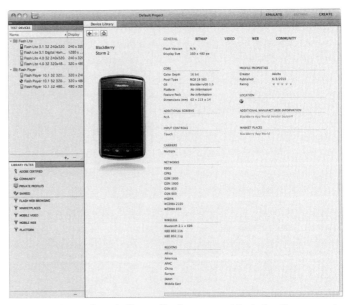

Figure 1.3 Device Central offers profiles for many mobile devices. You can create custom After Effects compositions that match the pixel dimensions and frame rates for the intended device.

You can browse for a particular device that supports video or Flash content in the Device Library. Once you've found the desired platform, drag it into the Test Devices panel and select it. You can then create a new After Effects composition by choosing File > New Document In > After Effects. If it's not visible, click the Create workspace, examine the selected settings to make sure they meet your needs, and click the Create button (**Figure 1.4**) to launch After Effects and create a composition with the newly specified settings. If After Effects is already running, a new composition will be added to a folder called Device Central Comps.

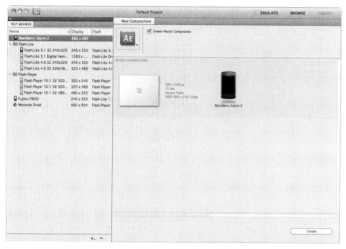

Figure 1.4 If a device supports video playback, you'll often find that Device Central offers After Effects composition settings that you can use.

Making Integration Trouble-free

A major focus of the Creative Suite is to eliminate wasted steps. Instead of constantly rendering or exporting media assets, you'll find support for exchanging media through Dynamic Link as well as layered graphics. On first use, linking may seem a little confusing, but you'll find that the flexibility and speed benefits are enormous. Being able to copy and paste or send assets between applications is a huge time-saver (rendering and exporting are avoided until final render or output). Disk space is also conserved (no need for intermediate files).

Working with Image Files

Using After Effects is a great way to animate images. Whether it's a vector logo or a still photo, it's easy to import and apply effects and transformations. Throughout this book we'll use sources created or manipulated in Photoshop and Illustrator. Although Photoshop is traditionally thought of as a raster-editing program and Illustrator as a vector-editing program, you can actually work with both types of graphics in either application.

Supported Image File Types

After Effects can import several graphic formats. If you have a source image that is not on the list, you can often convert it using Photoshop or Illustrator. If you have a series of still images, you can import them as a sequence. Here are the formats After Effects supports:

Photoshop CS5 discontinued support for PICT graphics. This format was previously widely used by many Macintosh-based video tools. We recommend you switch to other formats like TIFF or PSD to preserve a flexible editing workflow with Photoshop.

- ▶ Adobe Illustrator (AI, AI4, AI5, EPS, PS; continuously rasterized)
- ▶ Adobe PDF (PDF; first page only; continuously rasterized)
- ▶ Adobe Photoshop (PSD)
- ▶ Bitmap (BMP, RLE, DIB)
- ▶ Camera Raw (TIF, CRW, NEF, RAF, ORF, MRW, DCR, MOS, RAW, PEF, SRF, DNG, X3F, CR2, ERF)
- ▶ Cineon/DPX (CIN, DPX; 10 bpc)
- ▶ Discreet RLA/RPF (RLA, RPF; 16 bpc; imports camera data)
- ▶ EPS
- ▶ GIF
- ▶ JPEG (JPG, JPE)

- ▶ Maya camera data (MA)
- ▶ Maya IFF (IFF, TDI; 16 bpc)
- ▶ OpenEXR (EXR, SXR, MXR; 32 bpc)
- ▶ PICT (PCT)
- ▶ Portable Network Graphics (PNG; 16 bpc)
- ▶ Radiance (HDR, RGBE, XYZE; 32 bpc)
- ▶ SGI (SGI, BW, RGB; 16 bpc)
- ▶ Softimage (PIC) *(After Effects can also read ZPIC files corresponding to imported PIC files.)*
- ▶ Targa (TGA, VDA, ICB, VST)
- ▶ TIFF (TIF)

Edit Original Command

The Edit Original command is a great way to update a graphic file. When working in After Effects, we find a continuous need for graphic assets. Although After Effects can import nearly any graphics file format, it's best to stick with layered Adobe formats such as Photoshop (.psd) and Illustrator (.ai).

Both graphic formats can be imported as compositions into After Effects. The major benefit here is the flexibility that layers provide. We'll explore animation techniques throughout the rest of the book.

Although the Edit Original command can be run on any image format, it really shines when you're working with native Adobe files with layers.

1. Select any footage item in the Project panel, Composition panel, or Timeline panel.

2. Choose Edit > Edit Original or press Command+E (Ctrl+E).

3. Make edits to the graphic in its original application, and then save the changes.

4. Return to After Effects, and the source updates automatically.

NOTES

If the graphic you're updating uses an alpha channel, be sure to modify or update it before saving. If you're using the native transparency of layered Photoshop or Illustrator files, there's nothing to update.

Working with Footage Files

There's a good chance your motion graphics project uses footage. If you have more than a few clips, using Premiere Pro to organize, arrange, and trim the footage is essential. With its real-time performance, you can mix and match footage and edit without RAM previews. As an experienced After Effects user, you'll find Premiere Pro fairly intuitive.

Supported Footage File Types

After Effects can import several footage, or motion, formats. The challenge, however, is that footage clips are often much longer than you need. The following formats can be imported directly, although we usually prefer to edit or trim the footage to just what we need in Premiere Pro first.

- ▶ Animated GIF (GIF)
- ▶ DV (in MOV or AVI container or as containerless DV stream)
- ▶ Electric Image (IMG, EI)
- ▶ FLV, F4V
- ▶ Media eXchange Format (MXF)
- ▶ MPEG formats (MPEG-1, MPEG-2, and MPEG-4 formats)
- ▶ PSD file with video layer (requires QuickTime)
- ▶ QuickTime (MOV; 16 bpc, requires QuickTime)
- ▶ RED (R3D)
- ▶ SWF (continuously rasterized)

▶ Video for Windows (AVI, WAV)

▶ Windows Media File (WMV, WMA, ASF; Windows only)

▶ XDCAM HD and XDCAM EX (MXF and MP4 formats only)

When importing a SWF, it is treated as a vector object. Audio, interactive content, and scripted animations are not retained. Nested animations may also not come across correctly. For more on working with Flash and After Effects, see the book *After Effects for Flash/Flash for After Effects* (Adobe Press, 2009).

When you're working with tapeless sources, be sure to download the latest drivers from the camera manufacturer's website. Otherwise, you may have difficulty mounting media and transferring footage.

CLOSE-UP

Working with Tapeless Sources in Premiere Pro

The use of tapeless acquisition is the new standard. Premiere Pro supports most of the options on the market, including Panasonic P2 (**Figure 1.5**), Sony XDCAM, AVCHD, RED, and DSLR cameras. The rise in tapeless sources has been driven by several factors, including lowered costs and greater flexibility in recording formats. Additionally, the tapeless formats are more likely to have extensive metadata already attached. This information about the shot will automatically come in with the file on import.

Figure 1.5 A Panasonic P2 card is one of the many formats supported natively by Premiere Pro.

The tapeless workflow is pretty straightforward:

1. With tapeless sources you'll want to copy the media to a hard drive first. You can copy the media to your Common Media Folder or use the Project Manager later to consolidate footage. Tapeless sources can transfer much faster than realtime if you use a fast card reader or connection type.
2. In Premiere Pro, activate the Media Browser panel. If it's not visible, choose Window > Media Browser. Drag the edge to make the Browser larger.
3. Browse to the folder containing the media files. The Media Browser will show a thumbnail of the footage if the format supports it and the name of each shot.
4. When you're ready to import, choose File > Import From Browser. Premiere Pro imports the selected footage as single clips.

Organizing Footage with Premiere Pro Sequences

The easiest way to select footage for your After Effects project is to assemble the clips into a Premiere Pro sequence. You can edit footage nondestructively, assembling multiple clips into the correct order. By setting In and Out points on your clips, the trims will come into After Effects (with handles intact).

Table 1.1 shows what you can expect when you import a Premiere Pro sequence into After Effects or use the Copy and Paste feature.

Importing from other Nonlinear Editors

As a motion graphics artist, you may find that you've become dependent on video editors for your footage. As such, you may have little control over which nonlinear editing system is used. Fortunately, Premiere Pro is flexible in its support. You can import both media and sequence files from Avid or Final Cut Pro (**Figure 1.6**).

1. Have the editor use the preferred editing software to media manage the sequence. Final Cut Pro and Avid have their own media management tools that the editor should know how to use. The editor should copy the needed media to a mobile drive or across a network.

2. Have the editor export a sequence file in a converted format.

   ▸ For Final Cut Pro systems, the editor should create an XML file for the selected sequence.

   ▸ For Avid systems, the editor should create AAF files for the selected sequence.

3. In Premiere Pro, choose File > Import and select the Final Cut Pro or Avid sequence. All the related media will also be added.

4. Use Dynamic Link or the Copy and Paste command to move assets into After Effects (more next). You can also import a saved Premiere Pro project directly into After Effects.

Figure 1.6 A Final Cut XML file can be imported into Premiere Pro and then shared with After Effects through Dynamic Link or Copy and Paste.

NOTES

Once you've started capturing media, you'll likely end up with more than you need. When you start editing, you can reduce a Premiere Pro project to include only the footage used in a sequence. This is useful for media management as well as efficiency purposes. Be sure to look up the Project Manager in the Premiere Pro help menu to ensure that you've used the proper steps for reducing, collecting, and moving project assets.

Table **1.1** Importing or Copying from Premiere Pro to After Effects

Adobe Premiere Pro Asset	Converted to in After Effects	Notes
Audio track	Audio layers	Surround sound or tracks greater than 16 bit aren't supported. Mono and stereo tracks are imported as one or two layers.
Bars and tone	Not converted	
Blending modes	Converted	
Clip marker	Layer marker	
Color mattes	Solid-color layers	
Crop filter	Mask layer	
Frame Hold	Time Remap property	
Motion or Opacity values and keyframes	Transform property values and keyframes	Bezier, Auto Bezier, Continuous Bezier, or Hold is retained.
Sequence marker	Markers on a new solid-color layer	To copy sequence markers, you import the entire Premiere Pro project as a composition or copy the sequence.
Speed property	Time Stretch property	Speed and time stretch have an inverse relationship. For example, 50% speed in Premiere Pro becomes a 200% stretch in After Effects.
Time Remapping effect	Time Remap property	
Titles	Not converted	
Universal counting leaders	Not converted	
Video and audio transitions	Opacity keyframes (Cross dissolve only) or solid-color layers	
Video effect properties and keyframes	Effect properties and keyframes, if effect exists in After Effects	After Effects doesn't display unsupported effects in the Effect Controls panel.
Volume and Channel Volume audio filters	Stereo mixer effect	Other audio filters are ignored.

Importing Clips from an OnLocation Project

Premiere Pro can easily import clips captured with OnLocation. If you are using a different machine to edit than the one you used when shooting, you'll need to copy the media to a removable drive or to the new computer.

1. In the Media Browser panel, select the folder with the clips from OnLocation.
2. In the Media Browser, select the clips that you want to import into your Premiere Pro project.
3. Choose File > Import From Browser. Premiere Pro adds the selected clips into the Project panel.

Dynamic Link

With Dynamic Link technology, Adobe has created a way to allow tight integration between its core video applications. It's designed to streamline the moving of assets between After Effects, Premiere Pro, Soundbooth, or Encore. The functionality exists between several applications but behaves a little differently depending on the pair being used.

The primary goal of Dynamic Link is to minimize time lost from rendering or exporting. This means an After Effects composition can be placed into a Premiere Pro sequence without needing to render until final output. Additionally, footage can be edited in Premiere Pro and easily exchanged to After Effects for compositing and motion graphics tasks. You can bring over a series of clips as individual clips or use an entire Premiere Pro sequence as a single video track in After Effects.

Premiere Pro to After Effects

Earlier we discussed how useful Premiere Pro is to a motion graphics artist for assembling and pre-editing video clips. With its robust audio controls, real-time performance, and video capture to After Effects, you'll quickly find it indispensible—especially when you see Dynamic Link (**Figure 1.7**) or Copy and Paste in action.

Figure 1.7 With Dynamic Link you can import a single sequence as a clip into After Effects. Changes to the clip in Premiere Pro are automatically updated in After Effects.

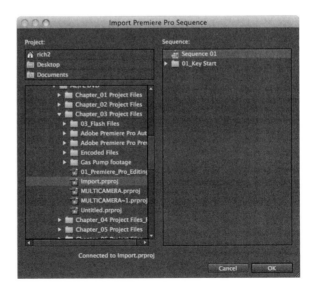

To import a sequence or assets from Premiere Pro to After Effects:

▶ In After Effects, choose File > Adobe Dynamic Link > Import Premiere Pro Sequence. This allows you to use a sequence as a single layer in your After Effects composition. This can all be accomplished without having to render or export from Premiere Pro first. If you make any changes in Premiere Pro, they will be automatically reflected in your After Effects compositions.

▶ If you have desired clips on a Timeline, it's easy to do a precise move. Simply select the clips on your Timeline and choose Edit > Copy. You can then switch to an open composition in After Effects and choose Edit > Paste. After Effects converts all the assets into layers and copies the source footage into its Project panel (**Figure 1.8**). Unlike Premiere Pro, which allows multiple objects on one track, After Effects will convert each item to its own layer. Additionally, any effects or transitions will attempt to be transferred if a close After Effects effect matches.

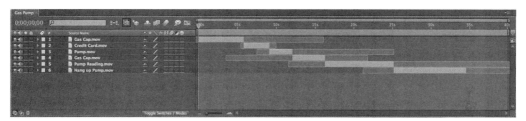

Figure 1.8 Moving assets between Premiere Pro and After Effects is as easy as copy and paste.

After Effects to Other Applications

After Effects compositions can also be imported into other applications within the Creative Suite. It is possible to import without rendering first, which makes it easy to use After Effects compositions in several ways:

In Premiere Pro

▶ Preview a composition in the Source Monitor.

▶ Set In and Out points for a composition, and then add it to a sequence.

▶ Edit a composition with Premiere Pro tools.

NOTES

If you import an After Effects composition with Dynamic Link, Premiere Pro inserts linked video and audio clips into the Timeline. If needed, you can unlink the video from the audio so that the clips can be edited separately.

In Encore

▶ Create a motion menu with a composition.

▶ Insert a composition into an Encore Timeline.

▶ Edit a composition with Encore tools.

XFL Format Exchange

If you want to exchange a project file between After Effects and Flash, it's gotten easier. A newer format, the XFL file, allows you to send layers intact over to Flash. Once in Flash you can add interactivity. When you export a composition from After Effects, all layers and keyframes are preserved.

In After Effects choose File > Export > Adobe Flash Professional (XFL). Choose how you want unsupported effects to be handled and what codec to use for the video assets (**Figure 1.9**). The XFL file can then be converted and exported.

Figure 1.9 The XFL format can export video and graphic assets with layers intact. This makes the process of moving from After Effects to Flash simpler.

For a video tutorial about exporting XFL files from After Effects, see "Importing and exporting XFL files between Flash and After Effects" at www.adobe.com/go/lrvid4098_xp.

The XFL file is essentially a bundle that contains all the pieces in a neat file. When you import the XFL file into Flash, it unpacks the assets and adds them to the FLA file according to the instructions in the XFL file. In Flash choose File > Open and navigate to your XFL formatted file. Flash brings in the media with layers intact and adds it to your current project.

Moving Media in the Creative Suite

The efficiency and versatility of the Production Premium toolset allows you to move files within the Creative Suite quickly. Technologies like Dynamic Link and the Edit Original command save time, effort, and money. **Table 1.2** summarizes how the files are exchanged between applications.

TABLE 1.2 Moving Files Within the Production Premium Toolset

To \ From	PR	AE	SB	EN	PS	AI	FL	AME	OL
Premiere Pro		DL Export	DL Export	DL Export	Export	NA	Export	DL Import	NA
After Effects	DL Export		DL Export	DL Export	Export	NA	Export XFL	DL Export	NA
Soundbooth	Import	Import		Import	NA	NA	Import	DL Export	NA
Encore	NA	NA	NA		Export	NA	Export	DL	NA
Photoshop	Export Import	Export Import	NA	Export Import		Export Import	Export Import	NA	NA
Illustrator	Export	Export Import	NA	Import	Import		Import	NA	NA
Flash	Export	Export	Export	Export	Export	Export Import		Export	NA
Adobe Media Encoder	Export	Export	Export	Export	Export	Export	Export		NA
OnLocation	Export	Export	Export	Export	Export	Export	Export	Export	

DL = Dynamic Link
Export = Export or Save Compatible Files
Import = Import Project File
XFL = XML-based Flash Exchange Format
NA = Not Applicable

2

Organizing Your Project

Talent wins games, but teamwork and intelligence wins championships.

—Michael Jordan

Organizing Your Project

Through the years, we've been called in to clean up some horrendous messes. The scenario is almost always the same. It's the last minute, major deadlines are about to be missed, and the stress level is through the roof. We often find that the project's aesthetics aren't that bad. However, the project's organization usually resembles a car crash.

Creative artists often mistake organization for a lack of creativity. A guiding tenet we always follow is that our projects should be able to be handed off. We're not saying you should make yourself expendable, but don't hold your projects hostage either. Another designer should be able to step in and help out. Otherwise, you'll never be able to take a day off, go on vacation, or even just relax. A little organization goes a long way.

We're not going to force you to clean your desk, but trust us here and open your mind to a little bit of organizational technique.

It's All About Media Management

We know you thought about skipping this chapter. After all, you've gotten this far in your professional career without an organizational strategy. And getting organized does sound pretty boring. You didn't get into this business because you like mundane tasks like setting up folder structures and renaming files. We understand and know that it's tempting to jump to the next chapter.

But don't.

The most experienced pros know that organizing media and assets is crucial (**Figure 2.1**). You can work faster because you'll be able to find your source footage quickly. You can even save time by avoiding unnecessary rendering. These are big claims, we know, but setting up your projects right will pay off in the end.

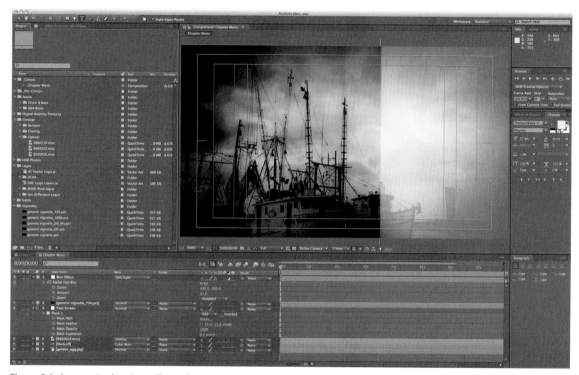

Figure 2.1 An organized project will speed up your design process.

Common Media Folder

When working with your full Adobe toolset, you'll be sharing a lot of media assets. Toss in files from outside applications and you can quickly become overwhelmed by all your project sources. The best approach we've found is to create a Common Media Folder. When properly used, this folder can help you keep all your project files organized.

Here are the top five reasons to use a Common Media Folder:

1. You'll spend less time searching for files.

2. You'll have an easier time backing up and archiving projects.

3. You'll avoid "version control" errors.

4. You'll have an easier time switching between software applications.

5. You'll spend less money on hard drives.

Setting Up the Common Media Folder

How you set up a Common Media Folder for your motion graphics workflow is a personal (or perhaps group) decision. We do offer a starting point, however. On this book's DVD you'll find a starter template for the Common Media Folder shown in **Figure 2.2** in the Chapter_02_Media folder.

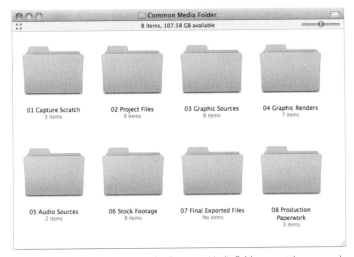

Figure 2.2 Feel free to customize the Common Media Folder to match your needs.

The Common Media Folder contains eight folders, which in turn contain various subfolders for specific tasks. Although this may seem a bit divisive, keeping media organized often means splitting it into isolated and manageable chunks. Here is the folder structure we usually create:

▶ **01 Capture Scratch.** This folder is where you store your Premiere Pro capture folders. All other imported footage from card or disk-based sources should also go here.

▶ **02 Project Files.** You should save all your projects to this folder. Additionally, you should periodically back up this folder to another location. If data loss occurs, a project can be restored in large part due to a backed-up project file.

- ▶ **03 Graphic Sources.** This folder contains all graphic source files (such as logos, fonts, and layered Photoshop files). It should not contain renders or exports. This clean structure makes it simple to enforce version control to avoid errors from minor revisions.

- ▶ **04 Graphic Renders.** All rendered graphic files should end up in the correct directory in this folder. This makes it easy to track which files should get handed off to video editors, Web developers, or clients.

- ▶ **05 Audio Sources.** Place all your audio files here. This includes music scoring projects as well as those files you create when you use Adobe Soundbooth. Keeping audio in one location allows you to track sources, especially since files like stock music and scores lack timecode for recapture.

- ▶ **06 Stock Footage.** We like to put all our stock footage in one folder. This generally refers to two categories: commercially available footage and archived footage that is imported from other projects. Keeping stock elements separate makes expense tracking painless and can simplify archiving at project closeout.

- ▶ **07 Final Exported Files.** We're proponents of keeping all your final exports in one place. This folder can help organize self-contained QuickTime movies as well as any additional compressions you create with the Adobe Media Encoder. Future deliverables to the client are a snap if you keep these exports readily accessible.

- ▶ **08 Production Paperwork.** You'll want to customize this folder so it contains the most important production paperwork. Having essential details like script, storyboard, and budget handy will increase the likelihood of a project's success. We also keep client-provided assets like style guides and white papers accessible for future reference.

Customizing the Common Media Folder

Although we've given you a suggested folder structure, be sure to create your own template. Going forward, you can create a duplicate copy for each new project. Here are a few practical words on how to use this folder:

▶ If the contents of the folder don't match your needs, make adjustments and create a new master folder.

▶ Keep a Zip archive on your drive and unzip a fresh version for each project.

▶ Rename the folder with your current project name followed by _CMF, for example, FOX_Open_CMF.

Targeting the Common Media Folder

An organized folder is useless if you don't direct your Creative Suite projects to it. For most applications this is simple. When you save your project files, target the correct folder on a hard drive (**Figure 2.3**). When rendering in After Effects, be sure to specify the right folder.

When you're happy with your folder structure, create a Zipped copy. Duplicate the folder, and then zip the entire bundle with a compression utility. The archive will be easier to transport.

Figure 2.3 Using a Common Media Folder will cut down on wasted hard drive space.

With Premiere Pro, saving to the Common Media Folder gets a little tougher. Premiere Pro has its own way of setting up folders for preview files, caches, and the like. The best way to direct files to the correct folders is to establish the setup when you make the Premiere Pro project file. Here's how:

1. Choose File > New > New Project or click the New Project button in the Welcome screen.

2. Click the Browse button to choose a location. Navigate to the Common Media Folder > 02 Project Files > 02 Premiere Pro Projects folder and click Choose to identify where to save the file.

3. Name the project in the field labeled Name.

4. Click the Scratch Disks tab to set all of the capture folders (**Figure 2.4**).

Figure 2.4 Make sure that all your Scratch Disk settings are properly assigned to avoid future problems.

5. Click the first Browse button. Navigate to the Common Media Folder > 01 Capture Scratch > 01 Premiere Pro Capture Scratch and click Choose.

6. Click the next Browse button. The same location you set in step 5 is automatically selected, so click Choose to target it.

7. Repeat this procedure for the next two categories, Video Previews and Audio Previews.

8. Click OK. A new dialog box opens for sequence settings.

9. Choose the correct sequence preset that most closely matches your primary footage source (or delivery format). Name the sequence and click OK.

You are now ready to capture media files. Choose either File > Capture for tape-based sources or File > Import for tapeless sources. Remember that when using tapeless sources, you'll want to manually transfer the files to your 01 Premiere Pro Capture Scratch folder on your media drive.

File and Folder Naming

Clarity when naming files and folders is crucial. By assigning unique names to your files, they will be easier to find. You'll also be able to browse through folders and the Project panel and locate your key sources. However, it's possible to create problems in a cross-platform world. Here are some naming suggestions:

▶ Always name files with a descriptive name. Often, stock photos and camera-generated media are named using only a number or a series of nonsensical characters. It's possible to confuse sources or even end up with duplicate names. Assign a new name and simply paste the old name into the file's metadata (this can quickly be done with Adobe Bridge).

▶ As you revise files, consider the use of version numbers for your source files. We've seen instances of shared sources and major problems when one user made modifications to a graphic source.

▶ Be careful not to use illegal characters (**Figure 2.5**). The Mac OS allows you to use characters that can confuse a Windows machine. Projects in After Effects can be used across platforms, so be careful using any of the characters in **Table 2.1** in a file or folder name.

Figure 2.5 If you use illegal characters, you'll get error messages and problem files.

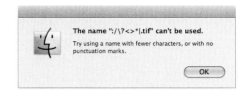

TABLE 2.1 Illegal Filename Characters

Character	Description
:	Colon
/	Slash
\	Backslash
?	Question mark
<	Less than sign
>	Greater than sign
*	Asterisk
|	Vertical line
.	Period (except before file extension)

In your quest for organization, it's possible to become too organized. If you use too many folders and subfolders, the file path can get too long. Keep filenames and folder names short. This problem usually raises its head when you go to collect files or move them to a new folder.

Working with Layered Sources

When you're working with Photoshop or Illustrator, take the time to clean up any layered files (**Figure 2.6**). Sure, you can see great thumbnails in the Layers panel in either graphic application. But when you get to After Effects, you are out of luck. If you get sloppy with your source material, you'll go batty trying to stay organized and might even run into media management issues.

When you're working with layers:

▶ Always use unique and descriptive names for each layer in a layered graphic.

▶ Don't make layer names too long, or you might get file path errors. Long names are also difficult to see in the Timeline.

▶ Avoid using illegal characters in layer names as well, or you'll have compatibility issues.

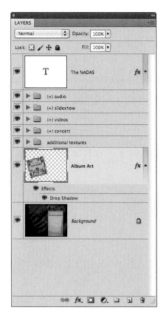

Figure 2.6 This menu designed in Photoshop for Adobe Encore uses layers. These layers will assist in the authoring process when you create buttons. Album cover courtesy Authentic Records (www.thenadas.com)

▶ Try to arrange the stacking order of layers so they match the order you'll need in After Effects.

▶ Use Layer Groups in Photoshop and Illustrator. They will import as precompositions in After Effects.

▶ Make sure you save Photoshop and Illustrator files in the RGB color mode. In Photoshop, be sure to preserve your layers when converting modes.

Once you import a layered source in After Effects, you'll face an important choice on how layers are handled. You'll need to decide if you want layers to be cropped to their source content or to the edge of the document's boundaries (**Figure 2.7**).

If you want to import footage with layers intact (**Figure 2.8**), choose one of these options from the Import As menu:

▶ **Composition.** This brings each layer in at the size of its source composition. All layer anchor points are at the same point. This option works best if you're applying effects that may extend beyond the border of the layer. Most filters can render beyond a layer's crop, but a few old and third-party filters cannot.

NOTES

If you need to replace a merged footage item with a layered source, you can do so in two ways. To change an item for all instances, select it in the Project panel and choose File > Replace Footage > With Layered Comp. If you only want to modify how the footage behaves in a single composition, select the layer in the Timeline panel, and choose Layer > Convert To Layered Comp. Be patient. This process can take a little time to complete.

Figure 2.7 Be sure to specify how you want your layer file imported using the Import As menu.

Figure 2.8 After Effects respects the grouping and layer names of the Photoshop file. Being organized in Photoshop means being organized in After Effects.

TIP

If you're not happy with a layer's anchor point, you can change it. The Pan Behind tool (Y) lets you reposition a layer's anchor point by dragging in the Composition or Footage panel. The anchor point moves, but the layer's visible position remains the same.

▶ **Composition - Retain Layer Sizes.** This option (formerly called Cropped Layers) imports each layer with its dimensions set to a clean crop around the layer's content. The anchor point is set at the center of the cropped graphics object rather than at the center of the composition frame. This option can be useful for animating a multilayered document when the layers are interdependent. This is the easiest way to animate when you'll be rotating, scaling, or animating from the anchor point of a layer.

Fitting a Layer to Your Composition

As you work with layered graphics, you'll quickly discover they're rarely the right size. You might need to scale a vector object full screen. Or, you might want to make a large photo fit your composition. You can remove all the guesswork by using three different stretch commands in After Effects (**Figure 2.9**).

▶ **To stretch a layer to fit,** press Command+Option+F (Ctrl+Alt+F) to scale a layer to fill the entire frame. Note that this option doesn't preserve the footage's original aspect ratio.

▶ **To stretch a layer to fit horizontally,** press Command+Option+Shift+H (Ctrl+Alt+Shift+H). The footage will scale horizontally to the border of the composition. The aspect ratio of the footage is preserved, and you'll likely have an empty area above and below the image.

▶ **To stretch a layer to fit vertically,** press Command+Option+Shift+G (Ctrl+Alt+Shift+G). The footage will scale vertically to the border of the composition. The aspect ratio of the footage is preserved, and you'll likely have an empty area to the left and right of the image.

A

B

C

D

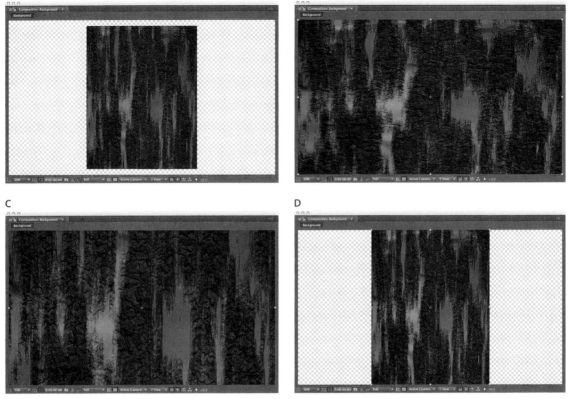

Figure 2.9 The original layer (A) does not fill the composition. The stretch command (B) fills the entire canvas but distorts the image. The stretch to fit horizontally command (C) scales the image until the width matches that of the composition. The stretch to fit vertically command (D) scales the image until it matches the height of the composition. The last two methods can produce a gap, depending on the aspect ratio of the original image.

Organizing Files with Adobe Bridge

 Included with Creative Suite is Adobe Bridge. This application is perhaps the most overlooked tool in the entire suite. Bridge is a media management application that allows for visual organization (**Figure 2.10**). With Bridge, you can quickly browse photos, video, audio, and graphic files. Bridge offers all sorts of capabilities from sorting and ranking to output and conversion.

Here are some reasons to use Bridge:

▶ Import images from camera memory cards.

▶ Rank images using 1–5 stars as well as qualitative rankings like Select and Review.

TIP

Bridge is very useful when designing in After Effects. You can use it to examine After Effects presets by choosing Browse Presets from the Effects & Presets panel submenu.

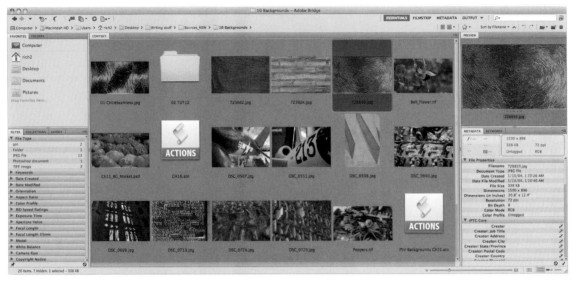

Figure 2.10 Bridge supports several file types, making browsing visually easier.

- ▶ Sort files based on metadata, rankings, and keywords.
- ▶ Rename files individually or in batches.
- ▶ Process raw files with Camera Raw Develop settings.
- ▶ Invoke Automation commands for Photoshop and Illustrator, such as Photomerge, Lens Correction, and Live Trace.
- ▶ Create contact sheets and websites for clients to review project assets.

Keeping an After Effects Project Tidy

Up until this point, we've focused on ways to keep your After Effects project organized using external factors. Truth be told, there's a lot you can do within After Effects. We're continuously amazed at how bloated some projects become. This is due to designers just dragging in every file under the sun and never taking the time to occasionally sort or purge. Think of how your kitchen would get if you never bothered to throw anything away. After Effects offers several easy to use commands that can keep your project streamlined for success.

Importing Folders

A best practice we try to follow is to match the folder structure of our After Effects project to the structure of our
media folder on the hard drive. This simplified approach
makes media management and version control tasks pretty
straightforward, because your project can serve as a virtual
map. It also makes reconnecting to media files easier if you
ever need to.

So, how do you pull this off? It used to be much harder.
In older versions of After Effects you needed to select the
folder at the Finder or desktop level and then hold down
the Option (Alt) key as you dragged it into the Projects
panel. These days it's much simpler. Just choose File >
Import > File, select a folder, and click Open.

After Effects imports the folder and preserves any nested
folders within. There is no limit to the number of folders
you can import, but it is possible to reach a limit based on
the length of the folder names. As we discussed earlier,
there is a limit to the character count used for file paths.
This limit varies by operating system. Typically, the limit is
set to 255 characters for modern versions of both Mac and
Windows operating systems. The secret is to use descriptive
but short filenames.

Internal Folder Organization

Once you have folders in After Effects, be sure to use them.
After Effects provides several useful shortcuts for organizing files. The goal is to use folders in the Project panel
in the same way you would a filing cabinet drawer. Keep
paring things down into small enough categories so they're
easy to find and locate. Remember that it's easy to use a
series of nested folders as well (**Figure 2.11**).

Here is how you can add, use, and remove folders in an
After Effects project:

▶   To add an empty folder to your Project panel, click
    the Create a New Folder button at the bottom of the
    Project panel or press Command+Option+Shift+N
    (Ctrl+Alt+Shift+N).

TIP

Need to import multiple files at
once? Not a problem; just choose
File > Import > Multiple Files
or press Command+Option+I
(Ctrl+Alt+I). You can import them
as footage or compositions. When
you are done importing, click Done
in the Import dialog box.

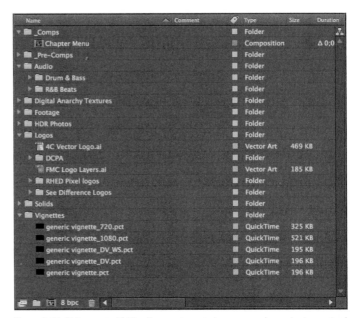

Figure 2.11 Using nested folders is a great way to keep a complex project organized.

▶ Select a target folder, and then invoke the Import command by pressing Command+I (Ctrl+I). The new files will be added to the selected folder.

▶ Select multiple items in an existing folder in the Project panel by Command-clicking (Ctrl-clicking). Then drag them onto the Create a New Folder button. All the items will be moved into a new folder nested within the original.

▶ Select multiple items in folders at different levels in the Project panel. When you drag them onto the Create a New Folder button, a new folder will be added at the same level as the highest folder you selected.

▶ To delete files and folders from the Project panel, select them and press the Delete key. To avoid the warning dialog box, select the files and press Command+Delete (Ctrl+Delete).

Renaming Assets

One of the least standard procedures in After Effects is naming compositions, footage, layers, and folders. Although you're prompted to name them on creation, modifying them after the fact can seem a little tricky. Unlike with your operating system, double-clicking the name doesn't seem to do anything. Sure, you can right-click an item and choose Rename. But the fastest way to rename an item is to highlight it, and then press Return (Enter) to modify its name (**Figure 2.12**).

Figure 2.12 Renaming layers in the Timeline panel can make it much faster to navigate.

In the rush to design, many forget that every Timeline layer has two names. By default, the Timeline panel shows you the name of a source. That's very useful until you start using the same source footage as a fill and matte, or start splitting a long clip into multiple segments. With the layer highlighted you can press the Return (Enter) key and assign a new descriptive name. This name is only displayed to make your job less complicated and won't affect media files or project links. You can toggle between the two names by clicking the Layer Name/Source Name column head in the Timeline.

Swapping Assets

During your design process, you might need to replace footage. This might be due to a new asset becoming available or just a change in the desired design. After Effects offers two ways to replace footage: a global replacement or a localized swap:

▶ **Global.** Select an item in the Project panel and choose File > Replace Footage or press Command+H (Ctrl+H).

You can then navigate to the desired replacement and click the Open button. For best results, choose an item that is identical in frame size and frame rate.

▶ **Local.** If you just want to swap out an item in a single composition, it's simple. Select the footage you want to replace in the Timeline. Then select the file you'd rather use in the Project panel. Hold down the Option (Alt) key and drag the preferred file onto the selected file in the Timeline. Alternatively, select the files and press Command+Option+/ (Ctrl+Alt+/). The new footage will swap places with the targeted layer. Any effects, masks, or keyframes applied to the original will be applied to the swapped content.

Placeholders and Proxies

Sometimes you'll need to start designing even though footage might be missing. You might also find that you want to speed up a project. In both cases you can work with substitute items, either a placeholder or a proxy. The best news is that any masks, attributes, expressions, effects, or keyframes that are applied to the layer are retained after you replace the placeholder or proxy with the final footage item.

Placeholder

A placeholder is shown as color bars (just like when a piece of footage goes missing in a project) (**Figure 2.13**). After Effects can generate placeholders internally without having the footage present. You should use a placeholder when you don't have access to the file you want to animate. For best results, be sure to set the placeholder so it's the same size, duration, and frame rate as the actual footage it's standing in for.

TIP

A placeholder can be truly useful to streamline the render process. For example, you can design an animated background. When you're happy with it, add it to the render queue. Drag the Output Module heading for a queued item from the Render Queue panel to the Project panel.

After Effects will create a placeholder for the composition and set the composition to use the Post-Render Action option for the item to Import & Replace Usage. You can then use the placeholder in other compositions.

When you render the first composition (the one the placeholder was based on), the new file will be brought back into After Effects and will update all other compositions (even if you're in the middle of a render).

Figure 2.13 To replace a placeholder, simply double-click on the color bars in the Project panel.

To create a placeholder:

1. Choose either File > Import > Placeholder to create a new placeholder or select an existing file and choose File > Replace Footage > Placeholder.

2. In the New Placeholder dialog box, specify the placeholder's name, size, frame rate, and duration.

3. Click OK.

When the file becomes available, just double-click the placeholder in the Project panel and navigate to its replacement using the standard file services dialog box.

Proxy

A proxy is essentially a stand-in for an existing piece of footage. The most common uses for a proxy are to replace a high-resolution file with a lower-resolution file or substitute a still frame for a movie (**Figure 2.14**). This is a great way to speed up the previewing or rendering of test movies.

Figure 2.14 An empty box indicates that the full-resolution image is in use (left). A filled box indicates that the proxy is active (right).

To best use a proxy, you'll want it to be exponentially smaller than the original (such as half or quarter the size). For example, you might temporarily replace a piece of footage that is 1280x720 with footage that's 640x360 (this is 50% of the original size and will result in a four times speed boost when previewing). After Effects automatically scales the proxy item to the same size and duration as the actual footage. This adjustment happens internally, so any transformations you apply in the composition will still be accurate when the proxy is replaced with the original footage.

1. Select a footage item or composition in the Project or Timeline panel.

NOTES

If you want to create a still image proxy for a footage item, you'll need to set a poster frame. Open the footage in the Footage panel and drag the current time indicator to the desired frame. When you invoke the Create Proxy > Still command, that is the frame that will be used.

TIP

If you want to save your project but save it as a new version, there's an easy way. The Incremental Save command saves the project using the project name and an incremented numeric identifier (choose File > Increment and Save). For example, rastervector01.aep would become rastervector02.aep. The previous version stores the data from the last time the file was saved; the new version captures the current state of the project.

2. Choose one of the following commands:

   ▶ File > Create Proxy > Still to create a still image proxy.

   ▶ File > Create Proxy > Movie to create a moving image proxy.

3. Switch to the Render Queue panel.

4. Locate the Proxy composition and specify an output destination for the proxy. It's a good idea to target your project folder.

5. Change the Render Settings and set the Resolution output to Half or Quarter.

6. Close the Render Settings window and click Render to create the proxy.

Once the proxy is created, you'll see it indicated in the Project panel. After Effects marks the footage name to indicate whether the actual footage item or its proxy is currently in use:

▶ A filled box next to an item's name indicates that the proxy is in use. The name of the proxy file is also in bold at the top of the Project panel.

▶ An empty box indicates that the original footage item is in use, even though a proxy exists. The name of the original file is also in bold at the top of the Project panel.

Removing Unused Footage

As you design in After Effects, you'll likely import several assets. Often, you'll experiment with different footage until you find the right design. All that extra footage can bog down your project. It means more items to load and more media to manage if you want to bundle up the project. Fortunately, After Effects makes it effortless to remove unused assets (**Figure 2.15**).

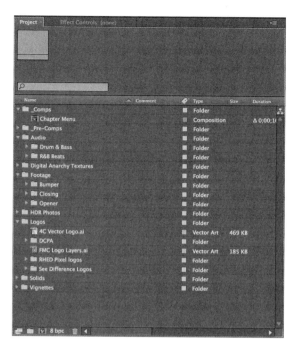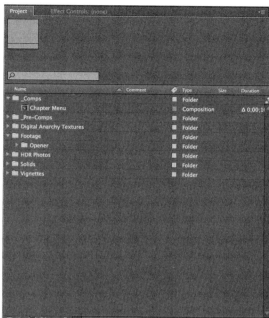

Figure 2.15 Removing unused footage from a project makes it easier to manage. You should run the Remove Unused Footage command when you know you no longer need items that are not a part of a composition (such as when you intend to back up a project).

1. Save your project to capture its current state. You may want to perform a Save As or Incremental Save command in case you change your mind.

2. Choose File > Remove Unused Footage to remove all references to any unused footage in the project. The media on your source drives is unaffected.

   While designing, you might also have brought a footage item into the project more than once. Fortunately, this is a quick fix.

3. Choose File > Consolidate All Footage to remove duplicate footage items from the project. After Effects only consolidates footage items that use the same Interpret Footage settings. The removed items are updated to refer to the remaining copy.

4. Save the project to capture its current state.

Reducing a Project

Another scenario you may face is the need to split a large project. You might want to split off part of a project for a second designer to work on. You might also need to speed up a project by splitting it into smaller parts. This is a possible workaround if a project is so large that you're getting RAM errors (of course you could always add more RAM).

The Reduce Project command is a quick fix:

1. If you only want to keep certain compositions or footage within a project, select them in the Project panel.

2. Choose File > Reduce Project.

   All unselected compositions and files not used in those compositions will be removed.

3. Save the project to capture its current state. You may want to use the Save As command to preserve the original project.

Collecting Files

As you wrap up a project (or reach a critical handoff) it may be time to collect your files. This process is nondestructive in that all collected files are merely copied to a specified destination. This is the simplest way to gather your assets for an archive or a handoff to a team member. Collecting your files can also speed up rendering, especially if files are spread across a network.

1. Choose File > Collect Files (**Figure 2.16**).

   The Collect Files window opens with options on how to gather source files.

2. Choose an option from the Collect Source Files menu:

   ▶ **All.** Collects all footage files in the Project panel. This includes unused footage and proxies. This option works best if you've already used the Reduce Project command.

   ▶ **For All Comps.** Collects all footage files and proxies that are used within any composition in the project. This essentially runs the Remove Unused Footage command first.

NOTES

The Collect Files command cannot gather fonts, plug-ins, or codecs. The command will generate a useful report that identifies the files, effects, and fonts necessary to recreate the project and render the compositions.

Figure 2.16 Be sure to examine all the options in the Collect Files window for precise media management.

▸ **For Selected Comps.** Collects all footage files and proxies used in the currently selected compositions in the Project panel. This essentially runs the Reduce Project command first.

▸ **For Queued Comps.** Collects all footage files and proxies used by any compositions with a Queued status in the Render Queue panel. This is a useful way of collecting files for rendering on another machine or speeding up rendering of a project that has files dispersed across several drives.

▸ **None (Project Only).** Copies the project to a new location without gathering any of the source footage.

3. Click the Comments button to enter custom notes to the generated report. This can include information about the project, contact information for the lead designer, or copyright information about source files.

   You now need to target a drive to store the footage. Be sure the targeted drive has enough space. You can see a size estimate at the bottom of the Collect Files window.

4. Click the Collect button to start the process. Specify a location, name the new folder, and click Save. The folder structure of your project is replicated, and all items (if specified) are copied to the target folder.

TIP

Several additional options are in the Collect Files window. Which ones you can use changes based on the option chosen in the Collect Source Files menu. These include options for handling proxies and targeting a new destination for rendering. You can even target a watch folder if you're using multiple machines to render.

Depending on the size of your project and speed of your drive connections, this command can take awhile.

After you run the Collect Files command, be aware that you will still be working in the original project (not the collected one). Be sure to switch projects if that is what motivated you to run the Collect Files command. Close the current project and switch to the new project.

SECTION II

Design Essentials

3

Typography for the Screen

You never know what is enough unless you know what is more than enough.

— William Blake

Typography for the Screen

One of the greatest tools a motion graphics designer has to communicate ideas and information is type. Unfortunately, creating effective designs with type has become much harder. Gone are the days when an artist could design with one screen resolution in mind. As we continue to ride the edge of technology, it seems that we are in need of some old-school typographic essentials.

An easy way to keep elements aesthetically pleasing on a screen of any size is to go back to the essentials. The type tools that Adobe offers are very powerful with their seemingly endless options for editability. But that power is often wasted without the right knowledge. Some of you had the benefit of learning about typography back in school; others are self-taught. We'd like to revisit some core design theory in this chapter and bring certain technology to life with a few insider tricks. Remember that just because your type might be moving doesn't mean layout, font, and color choices have to fly out the window. Often, it's these little details that help solidify your message across any screen.

Typographic Essentials

Are you (or do you know) an "old-school" designer who remembers what it was like at the start of digital design? Back then, digital artists were commonly viewed as a bunch of unrefined yahoos who didn't know, or worse yet, didn't care about the finer points of design. From setting type to color theory, there was an explosion of "untrained" artists, freely creating without a care in the world.

Although we look back and view that time as an exciting revolution, it did have an everlasting effect on typographic terminology. Many terms, clearly defined for centuries, were beginning to get mixed up and even redefined. Some of this happened through lack of training, but a lot of it had to do with the shift in technology.

Just so we're all designing from the same point of reference, let's take a quick run through some key terms in typography. Who knows; maybe we can pay homage to the "old-school" designers while still staying true to the "untrained yahoo" in all of us.

Font Technology

When talking about setting type digitally, you'll often hear designers discussing fonts. You must install and activate a font, which is a digital file on your system. With it you can view and use a typeface.

Don't confuse the word font with typeface. So we don't get sidetracked, we'll revisit why those terms might cause confusion shortly. As for fonts, there are three different kinds of file formats predominantly in use today: PostScript, TrueType, and OpenType. All three will work with Adobe software.

If you need to convert font technology or make a font cross platform, be sure to check out TransType. This tool from FontLab lets you rebundle Mac OS and Windows fonts as OpenType fonts and make them cross platform. Although it's not cheap, it quickly pays for itself if you need cross-platform fonts.

PostScript

Adobe created PostScript fonts to alleviate common issues when printing text of various sizes on different printers. Before PostScript, each printer would print each font slightly differently, even when printing the same electronic document. PostScript fonts store the shape of each font with Bézier curves to ensure consistency when printing the font. These fonts work with certified printers to communicate exactly how each font should appear regardless of the type of printing technology. The most widely adapted format for PostScript is known as Type 1.

TrueType

TrueType is very similar to PostScript but uses a slightly different and more efficient method for creating the curves that define the fonts' specific shapes. TrueType was created by Apple and later licensed to Microsoft, and was a competitor to PostScript. There are slightly different resources for TrueType fonts on Windows and for Mac OS X, so they are not cross-platform compatible.

OpenType

OpenType fonts hold true to their name in that the format is openly developed by Adobe and Microsoft. Fonts, such as TrueType and Type 1 fonts, may be embedded within an OpenType font. OpenType is based on Microsoft's original TrueType Open format. OpenType fonts use a common wrapper that allows any operating system to decode any OpenType font. There is also a creative benefit to Open-Type fonts. They support far more glyphs within each letter than typical PostScript fonts (**Figure 3.1**). This expanded glyph support also allows for multilingual characters to be embedded within a single font. Adobe OpenType fonts can be identified by the name Pro.

Figure 3.1 This text is Adobe Garamond Pro, and each section is an exact duplicate of the original. The appearance was changed by choosing different glyphs embedded within the OpenType font.

AaBbCcDdEeFfGgHhIiJjKk
LlMmNnOoPpQqRrSsTtUu
VvWwXxYyZz 0123456789
AaBbCcDdEeFfGgHhIiJjKk
LlMmNnOoPpQqRrSsTtUu
VvWwXxYyZz 0123456789
AaBbCcDdEeFfGgHhIiJjKk
LlMmNnOoPpQqRrSsTtUu
VvWwXxYyZz 0123456789
AᵃBᵇCcDᵈEᵉFfGgHʰIⁱJjKk
LˡMᵐNⁿOᵒPpQqRʳSˢTtUu
VᵥWwXxYyZz 0123456789

TIP

For a complete user's guide to OpenType fonts, be sure to check out www.adobe.com/type/browser/pdfs/OTGuide.pdf.

Foundations of Type

Since we mentioned it earlier, we'll clarify the difference between a font and typeface. Basically, a font is the actual computer file that contains the information to display and print a typeface. A typeface is the graphic style of text, often shown with slightly different variations, forming a type family. Now that we're all speaking from the same voice, let's continue on with typography.

Understanding the terms used to describe the stylistic attributes of type can help you solve design problems without having to resort to changing the copy. Because each typeface brings something different to the table, these terms are used to describe exactly why a typeface will or won't work within a given situation.

Did you know it was possible to make a typeface appear larger without changing its point size? Well, you can if you choose a typeface with a tall x-height (**Figure 3.2**). The x-height is literally the height of a lowercase x. This is a good letter to use because it's representative of the relative height of the letters in a typeface. The x-height is used to determine the height of the rest of the lowercase letters within the typeface.

Understanding x-height can save you time while browsing through fonts. If you know the project doesn't allow for a lot of space, you only need to look for a typeface with a tall x-height. Helpful, right?

Here are a few more essential terms you need to know (**Figure 3.3**):

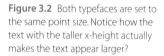

Make text appear larger by choosing a typeface with a taller x-height.

Make text appear larger by choosing a typeface with a taller x-height.

Figure 3.2 Both typefaces are set to the same point size. Notice how the text with the taller x-height actually makes the text appear larger?

cap-height

↕Typographic ↕x-Ray↕

baseline

x-height

Figure 3.3 Some of the core terms used to define character structure.

If you're looking for more information about type in all of its technical and stylistic glory, be sure to visit www.adobe.com/type.

▶ **Baseline.** The baseline is where the bottom of each letter sits. Notice how rounded letters actually sit below the baseline? This helps create the illusion of the rounded letters sitting on the same baseline as the flat letters. If they actually sat right on top of the baseline, the typeface wouldn't look as natural.

▶ **Cap-Height.** The height of a capital letter measured from the baseline to the top of the letter.

▶ **Ascender.** The part of a letter that rises above the x-height (**Figure 3.4**).

▶ **Descender.** The part of a letter that extends below the x-height (Figure 3.4).

▶ **Tangents.** Usually caused by ascenders and descenders, Tangents happen when two lines converge between lines of text that create a distraction for the viewer (**Figure 3.5**).

▶ **Serifs.** The details or marks that appear at the ends of individual letters' main strokes (**Figure 3.6**).

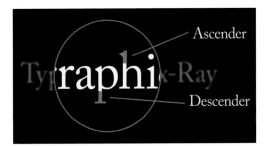

Figure 3.4 Ascenders and descenders are influenced by the x-height. Usually, when a typeface has a short x-height, it has long ascenders and descenders; conversely, when the x-height is tall, they are shorter.

Figure 3.5 Watch your ascenders and descenders when adjusting the leading to avoid creating any tangents.

Figure 3.6 Be aware of serifs with small intricate details when choosing a serif typeface for video. The details can often disappear when viewed on small screens. When you're working with an interlaced project, the fine details will often cause the type to flicker.

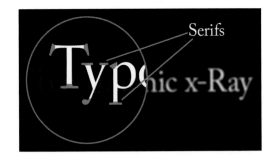

Selecting a Typeface

The Character panel in any of the Creative Suite applications offers two boxes from which to choose a typeface—the Family box and the Style box (**Figure 3.7**). Each font chosen in the Family box determines the fonts that appear in the Style box. Although these choices are intertwined, each option is actually a different font used to create the style variation.

Figure 3.7 Font Family box (A); Font Style box (B).

Font Selection

As a designer, selecting the "right" font can be a bit intimidating. We recommend two techniques that make experimentation easier. The goal is to try new ways of viewing and finding type to move out of your comfort zone.

One trick is to set a block of text in After Effects or Photoshop and then apply the text. Don't make the text too big, because you'll need to accommodate for variations in x-height. In the Timeline or Layers panel, select the text layer. Click inside either the Font Family or Font Style fields, and then use the down and up arrows to cycle through loaded fonts.

Another trick is to access a useful website for font identification. You can load up a JPEG of a type sample and then ask www.WhatTheFont.com to identify it. If it's a font you don't own, the website will of course sell it to you. We find the database to be very accurate and a great time-saver if we're trying to match a design or client asset.

Font Families

A font family is typically a collection of font styles that belong together. For example, Helvetica would be the overarching type family; Helvetica Bold and Helvetica Oblique would be two of the typefaces within the Helvetica type family (**Figure 3.8**).

Figure 3.8 Different typefaces within the Helvetica type family.

Helvetica Regular
Helvetica Bold
Helvetica Oblique
Helvetica Bold Oblique

TIP

Using the variations available in a type family is a way to create a sense of hierarchy within your designs while maintaining one cohesive look.

As you create your projects within any application in Adobe Creative Suite, the delineation between font and typeface can become relatively confusing. We mention this because this is a rare instance where the terms "font family" and "typeface family" can actually be used interchangeably. As you browse through fonts on your system in the Character panel, you are actually directly referencing the font files. So the boxes in the Character panel are labeled "font family" and "font style" accordingly. Although you are technically selecting font families and styles to activate, the results of your choices will be seen in your project as the chosen typeface within a type family (**Figure 3.9**).

Figure 3.9 Because lower-third designs are typically tight on space, we used variations from the Adobe Garamond Pro type family to create the definition between names, eliminating the need for a space.

Different Categories of Typeface

Truth be told, there are literally thousands of fonts in the world. As such, it's become essential to label and describe their unique characteristics (**Figure 3.10**). This makes it easier to better define specific styles of typefaces. It is necessary to subdivide fonts into different categories.

Although more categories exist, these are the categories that are typically used most often:

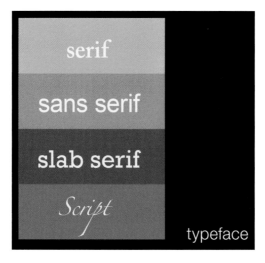

Figure 3.10 It's usually unwise to create a layout using many different typefaces, but we created this so it would be easy to compare the differences in the same composition.

▶ **Serifs.** Serifs are the details or marks that appear at the ends of individual letters' main strokes. Although the true origin of their creation is less than clear, their use is well documented throughout history, across many cultures and languages. Their main function is to assist the eye in identification of each letter for better comprehension.

▶ **Slab serif.** If you want to mix it up with your typographic lingo, expand on your definition of a serif with slab serif. Kind of the "Fred Flintstone" of serifs, slab serifs have very distinct chunky serifs. They don't have to be perfectly squared in their shape, so they can also be identified by the lack of a smooth transition to the serifs.

▶ **Sans serif.** Sans serifs (literally means "without serif") create a clean and modern look because they do not contain serifs. They are commonly used in titles, headlines, and other short lengths of text.

▶ **Script.** If you're looking for a typeface that's a little more expressive—with long flowing strokes and accented curves—scripts are a great place to start.

CLOSE-UP

The Truth About Faux

We're sure you've come across the "faux" font settings in the Character panel menu. We highly recommend that you do not use faux (derived from the French word for "fake") if you have the "real" version of the font. Although the faux setting is fully supported across Photoshop, Illustrator, and After Effects, there's no substitute for the quality of a true font. Most type fanatics would view the use of the faux settings as sacrilege since it often distorts the true design of a typeface. However, there are certain instances where using the faux settings makes sense. If you have a project that requires the use of a font that's way too thin for video, faux bold works well to thicken the lines and remove any flicker. Or if you must create an italic version of a typeface when there really is no italic version, use faux italic.

To recap, the preceding categories help group different typefaces (and their families) together according to general appearance. Then each typeface family has style variations, such as Bold, Italic, Condensed, and so on.

Type Layout

The technical term for placing type on the screen is called setting type. The term "set" refers to letterset printing where each letter is meticulously set in place. Although you won't be using rows of hot metal in After Effects any time soon, we still recommend carefully laying out type. Sloppy design leads to poor results.

The process of setting your type can dramatically change the look and feel of a project. When a strong layout is combined with a dramatic typeface, you can really define the style of a project before you even consider color, texture, and animation speed. Let's start by looking at kerning, leading, and tracking.

Kerning

Kerning is the process of adjusting the space between two characters (**Figure 3.11**). Some fonts have been meticulously kerned by their designers, whereas others are often sloppy (which is often the case with free fonts). The goal here is to create a sense of optical balance (**Figure 3.12**). You want letters to feel interconnected within the word and a sense of visual flow. Kerning is one of those design elements that the average person won't notice when it's done well, and that's a good thing.

Kerning can be quickly done by hand. Once your cursor is in the right place, you can adjust kerning directly in the Character panel or by using the keyboard shortcut Option+left or right arrow (Alt+left or right arrow).

TIP

To move in increments of ten while kerning, press Command+ Option+left or right arrow (Ctrl+Alt+left or right arrow).

When setting type, it makes sense to adjust the kerning of a word first, and then go back and adjust the tracking. That way, once you've set the proper space between individual letters, adjusting the tracking will space out all the letters in proportion, preserving your initial kerning adjustments.

Figure 3.11 If you want to quickly fine-tune kerning in a word, just use your left and right arrow keys to move the cursor through the word between characters. Once the cursor is in the new position, use the kerning key command to adjust the new area.

Figure 3.12 Poor kerning can stick out like a sore thumb. Kerning is not an exact science. It's more about the feeling you create. You want to create the feeling of balance and uniformity, even if the spaces between the letters are technically uneven.

Tracking

Tracking is very similar to kerning. Instead of adjusting the space between two letters, tracking adjusts the space between all the selected letters (**Figure 3.13**). If you plan on animating text, a slightly looser track may be necessary to improve readability. We also track text a little looser to accommodate for strokes or bevels.

To adjust tracking, select all the characters you want to adjust and make changes directly in the Character panel or use the same kerning keyboard shortcuts, Option+left or right arrow (Alt+left or right arrow).

Figure 3.13 Notice as the tracking is performed that the spaces that get adjusted are always to the right of the selected characters.

Leading

Leading is the process of adjusting the space between multiple lines of text on the screen. The term is actually derived from when printers used pieces of lead to control the amount of space between the lines of text in the printing press (**Figure 3.14**).

By default, text leading is set by the point size and internal properties of the font. To use this setting, just leave the Leading field set to Auto. On the other hand, you may need to fit more text on the screen. In this case, you can tweak the Leading size. Just be careful to avoid collisions between the ascenders and descenders, or text will become hard to read.

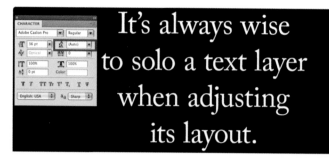

Figure 3.14 You can select one or multiple lines to adjust the leading between the different lines of text. With the text selected, you can adjust the leading in the Character panel or by using the keyboard shortcuts Option+up or down arrow (Alt+up or down arrow).

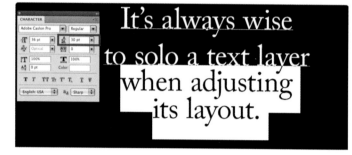

NOTES

Another important option for adjusting kerning and leading automatically is the Adobe Every-line Composer option in the Paragraph panel. This can automatically adjust text properties for the best layout. We'll explore it in depth later in the chapter.

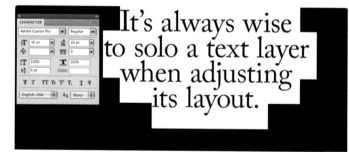

Various designers prefer to set type in different applications. We find that Adobe Illustrator has the most typographic controls (although the essentials are still present in both Photoshop and After Effects). Adobe Illustrator text will import as a vector object (which can be scaled with the Continuously Rasterize switch). You'll need to return to Illustrator to make edits.

We often set text in Photoshop, because it can be easily converted into editable (and animatable) text in After Effects. You'll of course also need to set and work with text right in After Effects.

Controlling Type

One of the most overlooked joys of working with Adobe applications has to be the consistency of the user interface. It doesn't matter if you're used to working in Photoshop, Illustrator, or After Effects. The layout and function of the controls are remarkably similar between each application. When creating type, you'll find the Character and Paragraph panels in each application with many of the same controls and options.

Before we delve into the specifics of each application, let's cover the core features and functions you'll find repeated throughout Photoshop, Illustrator, and After Effects. Learning how to master type in each application produces consistent results in your design, no matter where you start the process.

Entering Type

There are mainly three forms of type found throughout Adobe Creative Suite 5: point type, paragraph type, and type on a path (**Figure 3.15**). Although the method for creating paragraph type and type on a path varies slightly between applications, their function remains the same.

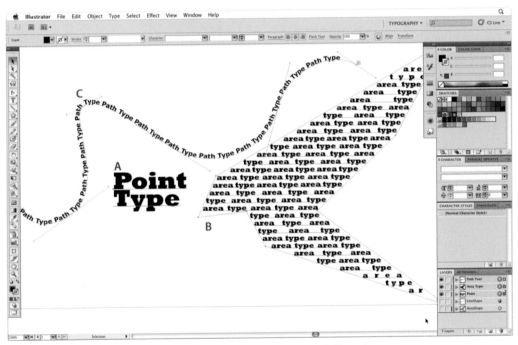

Figure 3.15 Examples of point type (A), paragraph type (B), and type on a path (C) are shown.

▶ **Point type.** If you use the Type tool or the Vertical Type tool and click once in your canvas without dragging, you're creating point type. An actual point will appear exactly where you clicked in the canvas. Once you create the initial placement of your text, point type will keep the text on one line as you continue to type. If you want to have multiple lines of text within one type layer, you must press Return (Enter) for each new line. Point type is useful when you want to align text to a particular area. You can combine it with an alignment command to create a line of text that can literally run off the screen.

▶ **Paragraph type.** Paragraph type is text that resides within a specified area. In Illustrator, it's literally called area type. Click and drag with the Type tool to create a rectangle to define the area for your text. In Photoshop and Illustrator, you can click directly inside a vector path with the Type tool to have text flow inside an irregular shape.

▶ **Path type.** Path type is text that flows along and follows a specific path. A number of parameters control the appearance and placement of the text along the path. The variations are literally endless. Animating path type will give you a whole new level of control via the ability to animate the path as well as the text along the path.

To change the size of the area of paragraph type later, select the Type tool and click inside the paragraph to bring up the Transform controls. Then click on the handles to resize accordingly. You may need to hover your cursor at an edge to access the control handles.

Are You Safe?

When setting type for video, it's important to be aware of title safe and action safe areas. Because the edges of a video screen often get cropped off by the edges of the television, you want to make sure text is inside the title safe area and any important picture in the video stays within the action safe area. Title and action safe are built into Photoshop and Illustrator with the preset project templates for video. To view and hide title and action safe areas in Photoshop, choose View > Show > Guides. The inner guides indicate title safe, and the outer guides indicate action safe. In Illustrator, they are on by default when using a video preset. To turn off safe zones in Illustrator, select the Artboard tool, navigate to the top of the interface, and click the Artboard Options button to access the menu where you can enable and disable the visibility. In After Effects, just Option-click (Alt-click) the Choose Grid And Guide Options button at the bottom of the Composition panel or Layers panel to enable or disable safe zones.

Character Panel Controls

Although each application has slightly different features for type, the majority of the features in the Character panel are the same. In this example we'll look at the Character panel in Photoshop (**Figure 3.16**).

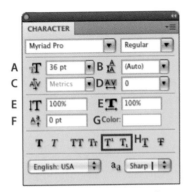

A **Point size.** Controls the size of your type in points (based on Postscript). To change the default measurement for a point, choose Preferences > Units & Rulers > Type.

B **Leading.** Controls the spacing between lines of text.

C **Kerning.** Controls the spacing between two characters. Two options are available:

- **Metrics.** An automatic setting for kerning based on character pairing. This setting works only as well as the information supplied by the font designer.

- **Optical.** Automatically adjusts the kerning between individual letters by analyzing their unique shapes. We generally recommend trying this setting before making manual adjustments to the kerning.

D **Tracking.** Controls the spacing between all selected characters.

E **Text scale.** Controls the scale of type vertically and horizontally independently.

F **Baseline.** Controls the distance above or below the baseline.

G **Color.** Where color is defined for the type selected.

H **Superscript and Subscript characters.** Specify whether a character is a superscript (aka superior) or a subscript (aka inferior). Most commonly used for scientific notation, these settings make quick work of formulas and expressions. Rather than having to change both the point size and baseline of a character, try these settings instead. You're now ready to animate $E=mc^2$ as you drink your H_2O.

I **Anti-aliasing.** Controls the amount and sharpness of anti-aliasing applied to the typeface. Try different settings if you are having a hard time reading smaller type or to smooth edges on extremely large type.

Figure 3.16 The Character panel in Photoshop is similar to those in other Adobe Creative Suite applications. Many controls are available to help precisely set type down to the character.

NOTES

The Superscript and Subscript buttons are not in all the applications in the Adobe Creative Suite, but you can still access these options through the Character panel menu in the upper-right corner of the panel. Even if a font is missing the glyphs, the software will automatically make the adjustments.

Paragraph Panel Controls

Whenever you need to lay out large areas of text, you should pay a visit to the Paragraph panel. We're sure you're familiar with the basic settings: Left, Right, and Center Align. Usually, that's just the start of the process when setting a large block of text. This panel can help you specify exactly when to hyphenate a word; justify all text; set spacing rules for lines, characters, and indents; and more.

Alignment

The Align buttons are grouped in the upper-left corner of the Paragraph panel (**Figure 3.17**). To apply alignment to any text, select a layer to change the entire layer. If you want to affect only a certain area, select the specific lines of text to change and click the appropriate button to apply the alignment.

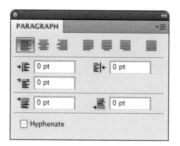

Figure 3.17 When Align is applied, you will always have at least one ragged edge. If you're using vertical text, the buttons will change to Top, Bottom, or Center Align.

Justification

Using Justification on paragraph text will remove the ragged edges in your layout. Choosing Left, Right, or Center really only refers to the last line of type (**Figure 3.18**). To justify the bottom line, click the Justify All button on the right; this is also known as forced justification. If you're unhappy with the results, you can fine-tune the Justification settings in the Paragraph panel menu (**Figure 3.19**).

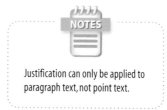

Justification can only be applied to paragraph text, not point text.

Setting type is a process that some designers love, and some loathe. I don't understand the latter, but some days I sympathize.	Setting type is a process that some designers love, and some loathe. I don't understand the latter, but some days I sympathize.	Setting type is a process that some designers love, and some loathe. I don't understand the latter, but some days I sympathize.

Figure 3.18 Examples of Left, Center, and Right justification.

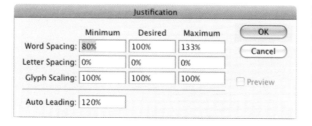

Figure 3.19 Any adjustments made in the Justification menu are applied to the entire paragraph. Use the traditional tracking and kerning adjustments in the Character panel to make changes within specific areas of text.

The Justification settings allow you to adjust three different parameters:

▶ **Word Spacing.** This option literally adjusts the amount of space used for a space, typed in by using the spacebar.

▶ **Letter Spacing.** This option controls the amount of space between each letter including both the kerning and tracking settings.

▶ **Glyph Scaling.** This option controls the amount of width a glyph (individual character) can scale when applying justification.

Every time justification is applied to different text, the settings will be slightly different to account for the various fonts, characters, space, and format settings. That is the reason for Minimum and Maximum and Desired settings. As the justification is applied, the software can adjust for each given situation. To better understand how this works, let's look at the descriptions of the settings:

▶ **Minimum and Maximum.** This option controls the minimum and maximum settings acceptable for justified paragraphs only.

▶ **Desired.** This option specifies the optimum settings for each parameter in both justified and unjustified paragraphs alike.

Adobe Line Composers

Line composers use two different methods to analyze text and decide where to best apply line breaks and hyphens based on the format parameters specified at that time. These methods of analysis are called line composers. To change line composers, click the panel menu in the upper-right corner of the Paragraph panel (**Figure 3.20**):

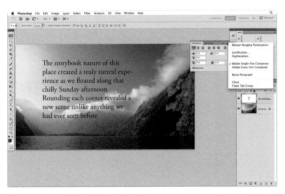 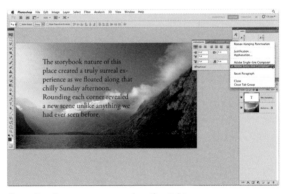

Figure 3.20 Adobe Single-line Composer was used on the left; Adobe Every-line Composer was used on the right. Although the adjustments were minor, the line composers make for a good starting point before delving into the finer points of justification and hyphenation settings.

▶ **Adobe Single-line Composer** is the more traditional and default way of setting type one line at a time. This composer will always try to compress the spacing between characters before increasing space.

▶ **Adobe Every-line Composer** is a more intensive way of setting type where each character and line is analyzed, and different parameters are assigned different values. These values help determine exactly where to best create hyphens and line breaks. First and foremost, it will always try to maintain even spacing between words and characters. This option only works with paragraph text.

Hyphenation

Often, you'll have long words in a sentence that will need to wrap to another line. By breaking a word across lines, large gaps can be avoided. To do this, you'll need to use a hyphen. Found in both Photoshop and Illustrator, Hyphenate can be activated or deactivated by selecting or deselecting its check box at the bottom of the Paragraph panel (**Figure 3.21**). With Hyphenate enabled, there are many options to control exactly when and how a word will be hyphenated. To open the options menu, choose Hyphenation from the Paragraph panel menu (**Figure 3.22**):

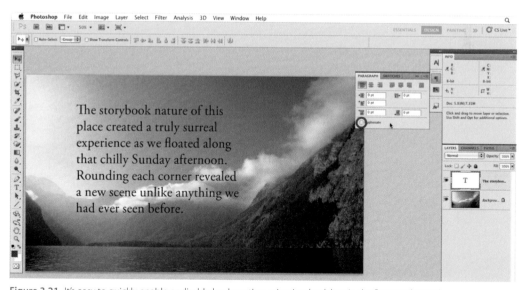

Figure 3.21 It's easy to quickly enable or disable hyphenation using its check box in the Paragraph panel.

Figure 3.22 You can specify where hyphens occur within a word and also where they can appear within the overall paragraph.

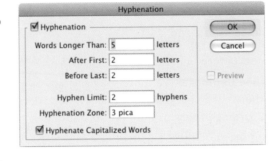

TIP

You can click directly on the icon for any of the paragraph spacing controls to set a value. Click+drag to the right to increase the value; click+drag to the left to decrease the value. This is a good way to interactively watch a preview of the adjustment as it's being applied.

There's a difference between pressing Return (Enter) to create a new line (aka line break) and pressing Shift+Return (Shift+Enter) to create a new line. When you press Shift+Return (Shift+Enter), you create a new line of type, but that new line will not be the start of a new paragraph. This is called performing a soft return.

▶ **Words Longer Than.** Sets the minimum number of characters in a word before a hyphen will be used.

▶ **After First.** The minimum number of characters at the beginning of the word before a break can be applied.

▶ **Before Last.** The minimum number of characters from the end of a word after a break.

▶ **Hyphen Limit.** The maximum number of consecutive lines a hyphen can be applied.

▶ **Hyphenation Zone.** Used with the Single-line Composer, the zone is a "buffer" from the right side of a paragraph that specifies where a hyphen cannot be applied.

More controls are available in the Paragraph panel that really help with the spacing of paragraphs. To create a new paragraph, you must press Return (Enter) to start the line for that paragraph. After you've gone through the area of type and specified each new paragraph with a hard return, you can then adjust all the paragraphs at once using three settings (**Figure 3.23**).

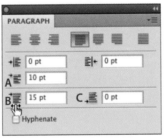

A Indent Spacing. Creates an indent at the start of each new paragraph (this value can also be negative to bump out the first line).

B Space Before Paragraph. Adjusts the amount of space before each paragraph.

C Space After Paragraph. Adjusts the amount of space after each paragraph.

Figure 3.23 Indent Spacing, Space Before Paragraph, and Space After Paragraph all help control the layout of area type.

Hanging Punctuation

You can place punctuation inside or outside the margins of your text with hanging punctuation. To activate this feature, select Roman Hanging Punctuation from the Paragraph panel menu (**Figure 3.24**).

"No iron can pierce the heart with such force as a period put just at the right place."

-Isaac Babel

"No iron can pierce the heart with such force as a period put just at the right place."

-Isaac Babel

Figure 3.24 In the frame on the left, Roman Hanging Punctuation is not selected; in the frame on the right, it is selected. Notice how the quotation marks are moved outside the margins.

Setting Type in Illustrator

For a motion designer, Illustrator is the tool of choice to create custom typographic designs. The ability to change text into outlines allows designers to then alter the text just like any other vector graphics. There are also more paragraph type options than are offered by Photoshop or After Effects, so it's easy to create layouts like two-column text or have text flow through different areas of the screen with threading, as in InDesign. Out of all the applications bundled in Adobe Creative Suite Production Premium, Illustrator gives you the most complete toolset for creating and manipulating custom type treatments.

Importing Type

To save time and reduce errors, don't retype anything that already exists in a digital file. In Illustrator, you can import both formatted and unformatted text. Whenever possible, if you want to retain the type formatting, save two different file formats for import. To import an external text file, choose File > Place and select the file to import (**Figure 3.25**). You can also just copy the text from its original document and paste it directly into Illustrator (**Figure 3.26**).

NOTES

If we receive a Word or Pages document, we'll usually also save it as an RTF (rich text format). This just helps cover the bases in case one file works better than the other.

Even though text is placed within Illustrator from an external file, there is no link back to the original file. The text is embedded within the Illustrator file.

Use the Direct Selection tool to change the size of the text area. Using the Free Transform tool will change the size of the text area as well as the size of the text.

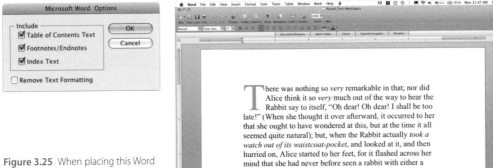

Figure 3.25 When placing this Word document, you have a few options, including the choice to strip out any formatting and just import the unformatted text.

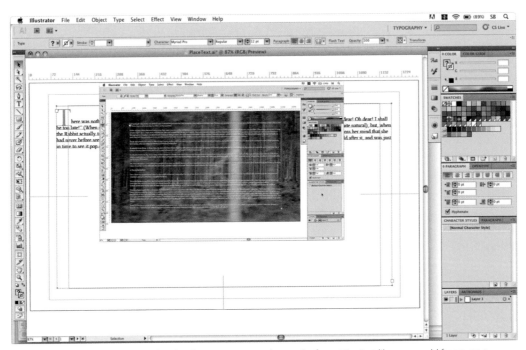

Figure 3.26 Once the text is placed within Illustrator, you can change the formatting just like you would for any text created directly within the document.

Point and Paragraph Additional Controls

Using the Type and Vertical Type tools in Illustrator to set point type is the same process we covered earlier in the chapter, so let's look at setting paragraph type. Paragraph type is known as area type in Illustrator, and it has some extra features that really set it apart from Photoshop:

TIP

In Illustrator you can switch type orientation between horizontal and vertical at any time. To convert type, choose Type > Type Orientation > Horizontal or Vertical.

▶ Text can flow across multiple areas within the document through a process called "threading" (**Figure 3.27**).

▶ Area type supports multicolumn layouts (**Figure 3.28**).

Figure 3.27 To specify areas to thread text between, click the plus (+) button in the lower-right corner of the area, and then click on the blank white box in the upper-left corner of the next area to choose where the text will flow next.

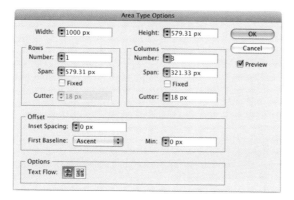

Figure 3.28 You can specify the number of columns by selecting the area type and opening the area type options. Choose Type > Area Type Options and specify both Rows and Columns.

Don't panic if you're setting type on a shape that has a fill or a stroke. Those settings will disappear. If you want to still see the original graphics, make a copy before you place type on a path.

Setting Type Along a Path

When you want your type to wrap around a specific object or be placed around a geometric shape, like a circle, you'll want to set type along a path.

You can set type along any path or shape, open or closed, in Illustrator. Two tools enable you to set type on a path: Type on a Path and Vertical Type on a Path. Click and hold on the Type tool to reveal these two tools. Several options are provided to control the placement of the type along a path. Before we get to those options, we need to actually place type along a path.

1. Select the Type on a Path tool and line up the cross bar in the cursor directly over the path (**Figure 3.29**).

2. With your cursor positioned, click the path where you want the type to start.

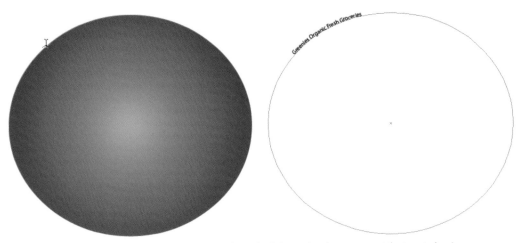

Figure 3.29 When you have the cursor lined up over the path, click exactly where you want the type to begin.

3. Type your text. If you want to change fonts or resize the type, be sure to select the type before you make any adjustments. In addition to changing the font size, you can use any of the other parameters in the Character or Paragraph panel to change the type along the path.

4. When you have the type sized properly, use the Direct Selection tool to manipulate the type around the circle. For type on an open path, you'll notice three brackets around the type—at the beginning, middle, and end. For a closed path, like a circle, the brackets don't appear quite so easily (**Figure 3.30**). In the circle example, the brackets slid around to the left of the text because the text was left aligned.

5. To place the text controls in their correct position around the type, click on the leftmost bracket and bring it around the bottom of the circle to the end of the text (**Figure 3.31**).

6. To center the type on the circle, click on the middle bracket and slide the text into position. Be careful not to slide the text below the path, or the type will flip its orientation (**Figure 3.32**).

TIP

You might find it easier to change the baseline and orientation of the type using the Type on a Path Options. These options really help when you can't quite get the type to orient properly along the path using the manual brackets. To open the options, choose Type > Type On A Path. You can apply a few interesting effects, but the area you'll probably want to change most often is the baseline or the flip setting.

Figure 3.30 On a closed path, the beginning and end brackets will be right next to each other; the middle bracket will be in the middle of the entire path, not just the text. The exact placement of the brackets will depend on the alignment settings.

Figure 3.31 Properly orienting the brackets around the type makes it easier to adjust the type placement later.

Figure 3.32 Dragging on the middle bracket will slide type as well as change its orientation.

To set additional type on the bottom of the circle, duplicate the current path type. Type on a path cannot have more than one orientation. For type to be placed on the bottom of the circle properly, it needs to be flipped to the inside of the circle. Once the type is at the bottom of the circle, choose Type > Type on a Path to open the options and change the Align to Path setting to Ascender (**Figure 3.33**). Now the ascenders of the type will align to the path instead of the bottom of the letters as usual.

Figure 3.33 Type on a Path Options.

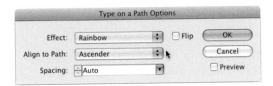

Creating Custom Type with Illustrator

Having the ability to create custom type is the number one reason a motion graphics designer would create title designs in Illustrator. It's easy to create a customized title starting with a basic typeface. You can then modify individual letters by manipulating the paths. This technique lets you create a totally unique type treatment, moving the title design from stock to custom (**Figure 3.34**).

Figure 3.34 Convert type to outlines to change it into a fully editable vector shape.

You'll first need to convert type to outlines. It's important to note that the type will no longer be editable after converting it to outlines, so save the file under a different filename or make an extra copy before converting the type. Convert the type layer into outlines by selecting the type and then choosing Type > Create Outlines or pressing Command+Shift+O (Ctrl+Shift+O).

When the type is converted, it is made up of paths just like any other shapes in Illustrator. Now you're free to use the full set of tools in Illustrator to push, pull, brush, effect—well, you get the idea. Mix it up and see what you can come up with. This is one area where experimentation is worth pursuing.

Setting Type in Photoshop

Setting type in Photoshop is efficient for motion designers because you can always convert type originally created in Photoshop into type that is native in After Effects. Layer styles also make animation easier because After Effects supports their import as editable (and in turn animation ready) effects. Type with Repoussé has taken Photoshop to new heights with 3D type and shiny new materials.

Paragraph and Area Type

When setting paragraph type in Photoshop, you can set type in a rectangular shape by selecting the Type tool and dragging to draw out the bounding box. This is a great way to keep text inside the title safe and action safe zones. Just drag your box inside the guides.

But what if you want to set type within a specific shape, just like Illustrator? Easy; in Photoshop, you don't even have to switch tools. With the Type tool selected, move your cursor directly over any vector shape in the project and wait for the two dotted brackets to appear around the text cursor (**Figure 3.35**). Once those brackets appear, click in the shape and type away.

TIP

To save time switching between tools in the Tools panel, use the Command (Ctrl) key to switch between tools on the fly.

Select the Convert Point tool from the Tools panel, and use it to change the Bézier handles and change the overall shape of the paths. When you just need to move anchor points, press Command (Ctrl) to switch to the Direct Selection tool. Use the Direct Selection tool to click and drag directly on anchor points to reposition them; use the Convert Point tool to adjust the vector tangent handles.

CLOSE-UP

Type Conversion in Photoshop

In Photoshop, you can switch your type between point text and area text or even change the orientation between horizontal and vertical at any time.

To convert type between point text and area text, the menu will contextually change between paragraph and point depending on what kind of type is selected at the time. To convert type, choose Layer > Type > Convert to Paragraph (Point) Text.

To change type orientation, choose Layer > Type > Horizontal or Vertical.

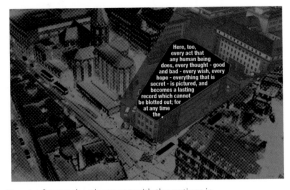

Figure 3.35 Placed type inside a custom vector shape in Photoshop. You can finesse the placement with the options in the Paragraph panel.

NOTES

Once you've created type along a path in Photoshop, the original path created is not directly linked to the text. You can delete the original path layer if it's not in use. To change the path the type layer is using, select the type layer and then select any of the vector tools like the Path/Direct Selection tools or the Convert Point tool to move the path handles.

Setting Type Along a Path

Type along a path works in a similar fashion to Illustrator. The main difference is how Photoshop automatically switches to the Type tool to recognize the edge of a path. Place your text on the path by placing the cursor directly over the path, or in the shape if the cursor is inside a specific vector shape (**Figure 3.36**).

TIP

If you are typesetting in a document that already contains other layers and graphics, sometimes those other elements may become distracting. To avoid this, you may want to solo the visibility of the text layer as you make the final kerning, tracking, and leading adjustments. Option-click (Alt-click) the layer eye icon to view that layer and turn off all other layers. You can then apply the adjustments to that layer; as long as you haven't changed the visibility of any of the other layers, just Option-click (Alt-click) the eye again to return all layers to their previous state of visibility. This works in Photoshop and Illustrator. You can solo layers in After Effects as well, but it has its own set of custom options. We'll cover those in the "Type in After Effects" section later in this chapter.

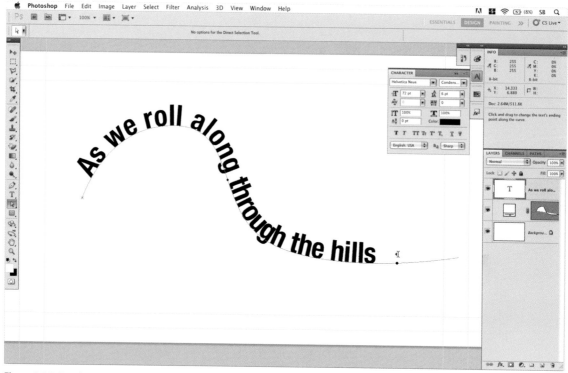

Figure 3.36 Use the Direct Selection or Path Selection tool to position type along a path in Photoshop.

Using the Direct Selection or Path Selection tool makes placing type along a path a truly interactive, visual experience. The functions are the same as in Illustrator; however, the brackets along the path in Photoshop are not visible until you hover your mouse over the three anchor points. The functions of each anchor point are the same as they are in Illustrator.

For animation, we recommend setting type on a path in Photoshop instead of Illustrator because the type and the path will import as fully editable objects within After Effects. Wondering why we just don't start creating path text directly in After Effects? It's just about time. It's faster to storyboard and create the effect in Photoshop. Plus, when it's approved, all the work from Photoshop will import directly into After Effects.

NOTES

To see the path and type in After Effects, import the Photoshop document as a composition. Open the composition, select the layer that should be type, and choose Layer > Convert to Editable Text.

Creating 3D with Repoussé

One of the best new features in Adobe Photoshop CS5 has to be Repoussé. Repoussé allows you to create actual 3D objects out of type with full control over the materials applied to the front, side, back, and different bevel faces (**Figure 3.37**). Before converting any type through Repoussé, make sure you've saved an extra copy should you need to go back and make any changes to the original type. Repoussé will rasterize any type into one solid object, so you'll no longer have individual character control.

If you want to find out more about Repoussé and all other things 3D, check out Chapter 8, "Designing and Working in 3D."

Figure 3.37 This "wood" type treatment was created in Repoussé. It has true 3D dimension, materials, and lighting.

Using Layer Styles with Type

Layer styles can add depth and dimension to your type with bevels, drop shadows, and glows. But, as I'm sure some of you may know, misuse of layer styles can cause flashbacks—

to 1998. So remember that more often than not less is more. We've found layer styles extremely useful in specific situations:

▶ If your type is competing with the background, try a subtle shadow or glow (**Figure 3.38**).

Figure 3.38 A soft outer glow of black can help create just enough separation from the background to make your type stand out.

▶ To add some dimension to your type, try using some layer styles (**Figure 3.39**).

Figure 3.39 To illustrate just how many layer styles will seamlessly import into After Effects, we've gone a little overboard to create this 3D look for the text.

One of the biggest reasons we like layer styles in Photoshop has to be their integration with After Effects. On import, you'll have the choice to merge the layer styles into the footage or leave them editable. By all means leave them editable (**Figure 3.40**). If you still can't see the editable layer styles in the Timeline panel, choose Layer > Layer Styles > Convert to Editable Styles (**Figure 3.41**). The layer styles will then appear in After Effects in the Timeline panel ready to animate.

Figure 3.40 After Effects supports the import of most layer styles from Photoshop, creating more sources for effects that can be keyframed and animated.

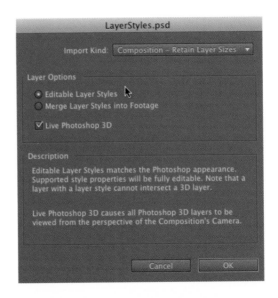

Figure 3.41 If you don't see editable layer styles appearing in the Timeline, convert them to editable styles in the Layer menu.

Type in After Effects

After Effects has a robust set of tools to set the type directly within the application. Although we set our fair share of type starting in After Effects, we usually prefer to create our initial type designs and layouts in Photoshop and then import those layouts into After Effects for animation.

Text Tool

Setting point type and paragraph type in After Effects is the same process as we covered in Photoshop. However, setting type along a path is a slightly different process. Once you're familiar with the text animators in After Effects, setting up text on a path is a breeze.

Text Animator Possibilities

The animation tools for text in After Effects are nothing short of amazing. You can layer different animations and moves onto the type to create some flexible and complex animations in a very short amount of time. To get familiar with the capabilities within After Effects, let's look at some of the preset animations. Choose Animation > Browse Presets and double-click on the Text folder in Bridge. Open any of the folders to browse through the different presets. Navigate through a few more folders to get the full effect of just how many different kinds of text animators and effects are possible in After Effects.

Creating a Text Animator

A text animator is almost identical to any other kind of animation possible in After Effects. With any layer in After Effects, there are properties that can be animated, positioned, scaled, rotated, and more. With text animators, you can apply those same animation properties directly to the text, as a kind of "subcategory." The process is very similar to parenting one layer to control another except this time it's all within the same layer.

To apply a text animator, twirl down the parameters for your text layer. In the column for switches, click the button next to Animate and select a parameter to animate. Using animators is a twofold process. First, make the change to the parameter. Second, animate the selectors that determine exactly which characters are affected by the parameter change.

To see a finished example, open the project YouNever-Know.aep. You can see that one animator has been applied to the type layer called *you never know* (Opacity). The only parameter that has keyframes is the offset. The values in the range selector determine how much of that text will be affected by the animator. Since the range starts at 0 and ends at 100, 100 percent of the type will be affected by the values in the animator. The Opacity value is set to 0, which means that any type that is currently selected will have an Opacity value set to 0. When the offset is animated, the length of the selected area will not change, it will just slide the selection, and any type that ends up falling outside of the selected area will be revealed (**Figure 3.42**).

Figure 3.42 Animating the offset is almost like sliding a stencil over a light to reveal different patterns and shapes based on the settings of the stencil.

Once an animator's range is applied and animated, click the Add button to continue to add more parameters to that animator. Because the settings are loaded into the same animator, the selected area and its offset will be the same for every parameter loaded into that animator. If you want to animate a different parameter with different timing, click the Animate button and add another animator. Every animator can have its own timings because every animator has its own Range Selector.

Creating Type on a Path

Since we just discussed how to create a text animator, you already know how to animate type on a path. It's just a question of tying the type to the path. You can do that in three steps:

1. Create a path.

2. Twirl open the layer properties and expand the Path Options.

3. Click the Path menu and choose Path 1 (or the name of any other path in the composition).

Now that the type is tied to the path, you can animate the type along the path just like you'd apply any other animation to an animation group using animators.

4

Logo Animation

A pessimist sees the difficulty in every opportunity;
an optimist sees the opportunity in every difficulty.

— Winston Churchill

Logo Animation

If you've been in motion graphics for any amount of time, most likely you've been asked to animate a logo. Often, this is a kind of "right of passage" for young motion graphics artists. Unfortunately, so is dealing with not receiving the most optimum file formats to work with. Even if the stars align and we somehow end up with the proper files in their preferred format, logos also come with rules. Usually supplied by the original logo designer, these rules specify how the logo is to appear to best represent its brand. In this chapter we'll examine various workflows to help you find those opportunities where others might find difficulty.

Preparing Your Files

Where do you start? Do you begin in Adobe Illustrator, Adobe Photoshop, or Adobe After Effects? Well, there is no right or wrong answer. Each application and file format has its own advantages and disadvantages. By the end of this chapter, you'll learn how to move seamlessly between these applications and begin to develop your own personal animation workflows, no matter where you start.

Logos Have Rules

Whether it's a large corporation or a small business, everything from the color to the placement of that logo says something about that business. With this knowledge, most companies will create a style guide to go along with their logo. The style guide is created to ensure that the logo will always be used and seen in the best possible light. It has a direct impact on what exactly can and can't be done when animating the logo. For example, some style guides will specify that the logo can only appear on a solid white background. Many guides will specify exact color values, specific fonts, text placement, and its respective point size. **Figure 4.1** shows an example of a style guide so you see what we mean.

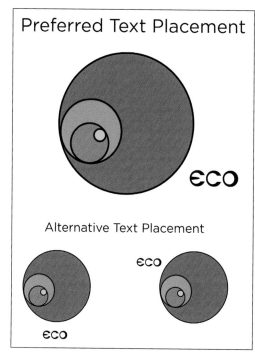

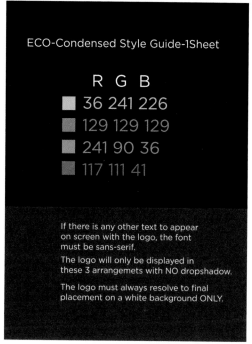

Figure 4.1 Some style guides are very detailed; others are short and to the point. This is an example of a "one sheet" style guide. Smaller guides like this are often found in digital form along with the logo.

Every logo should have a style guide to help define precisely how the logo is to be used. Sadly, we've found that most style guides only account for print or Web usage. If there are no specifications for video, Web specifications are often the best place to start for help. They both use RGB color space and have lower-resolution requirements.

Should you ever receive a logo without a style guide, the Web is a great place to go for guidance. Use the company website as a rough reference for placement and usage; that way you'll always have a fallback if questions arise.

TIP

If the logo you're using has a lot of rules and regulations about its appearance, it's always a safe bet to animate the background that will appear behind a logo rather than manipulating the actual logo. You can learn more about backgrounds in Chapter 7, "Designing Backgrounds."

TIP

If you can't get the client's logo as a vector file, there's a great website to check out. Brands of the World (www.BrandsoftheWorld.com) offers several well-known and even obscure logos. While you're there, be sure to check out its free font section as well.

NOTES

In Illustrator, sublayers will be flattened to their corresponding parent layer upon import into After Effects. Make sure any separate elements live on layers at the top of the layer hierarchy.

TIP

Even if a logo file isn't a native Illustrator file, it can easily be converted. Just choose File > Open and select a supported vector format (like EPS or SVG). You can then split the file into layers and save it as an Illustrator file.

Best Files for Animation

When you're getting ready to animate a logo, some file formats are more preferable than others. Unfortunately, all too often you'll end up with a "less-than-preferred" file format. When this happens, it's usually time to consider how much extra work will be required just to get the logo ready for animation. Don't accept your first dead end as being the end of the road. Make a right turn and keep looking and asking. Even if you sometimes end up re-creating the logo from scratch, we've found that double-checking with clients will often give them that extra push required to dig up a better solution.

We follow some general rules when it comes to file formats for animation. Vector files such as those created from Illustrator are always best because they allow you to scale your logo up to any size without losing quality (thanks to the After Effects Continuously Rasterize option).

Layered vector files are even better. If each element resides on its own layer in Illustrator, you can easily import the layered Illustrator file as a composition directly into After Effects for animation. Because layers are preserved on import, they are ready for animation. Even if the original logo doesn't have layers, it's often possible to split the file.

If you can only get a bitmap version of the logo, focus on the measurements for width and height, and make sure they are least twice the resolution of your final video format. For example, when working at a resolution of 1280x720, we would want a file that's at least 2560 pixels across or 1440 pixels high. This way there is some flexibility to scale up the logo in the animation. We often refer to this as the "200% rule" for preparing stills for video. Of course a layered file would be best, like a PSD or a TIFF for the same reasons we mentioned earlier.

Preparing Logos in Illustrator

With its vector tools and ability to customize type using OpenType, Illustrator has long been the preferred application for designers when creating a logo. It is quite common to receive logos as Illustrator files. Usually, preparing these files for animation is pretty painless, but here are a few gotchas to watch out for.

Color Space

Because most logos were originally created for use in print materials, the files will most likely be in CMYK. And because video is RGB, you'll want to convert any CMYK documents to RGB before animation. Converting a file from CMYK to RGB is not nearly as problematic as the other way around. This is because CMYK has a narrower range of colors, also called a gamut. You should see little to no shifting in colors when you convert from a CMYK to RGB color space. To convert your Illustrator document to RGB, choose File > Document Color Mode > RGB Color. To better understand how the two spaces overlap, take a look at the color gamut chart in **Figure 4.2**.

You might find it interesting that RGB and CMYK at their core are designed to function quite differently. RGB is an additive color model. RGB starts with black (no colors at all) as a base color, and as you add more colors, eventually you will get to white (a mix of all colors) (**Figure 4.3**). CMYK works through subtraction. An image starts with white as the background color. As colors are "added," they actually subtract from each other as they mix together. So, if you mix all colors in the spectrum together in a CMYK document, the result is black (**Figure 4.4**).

When changing color space in Illustrator, the colors loaded in the swatches palette are determined upon document creation and will not be converted with your document settings. To change color space, it is best to copy and paste your logo into a new document created with any of the Video and Film presets.

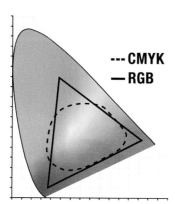

Figure 4.2 As you can see, RGB colors include more colors than CMYK except for some very small areas. It's really only when you have a color value that's outside the range of your desired color space that you end up with a color shift.

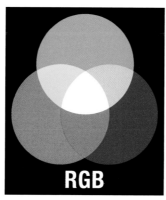

Figure 4.3 Red, green, and blue are added together to create white.

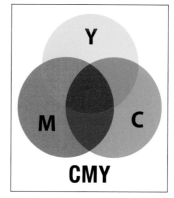

Figure 4.4 Cyan, magenta, and yellow are subtracted from each other to create black.

NOTES

We'll explore using artboards in greater depth in Chapter 10, "Designing with Vectors." You'll learn how and when to use multiple artboards in one Illustrator document.

Preparing the Artboard

If your document is CMYK, its artboard dimensions are most likely also set for print dimensions. Because Illustrator works with vectors, converting the artboard to different dimensions doesn't technically change any of the artwork within the document. However, when you start moving that file between applications, the artboard dimensions have an impact. For example, when importing a layered Illustrator file into After Effects as a composition, the dimensions of the composition will be determined by the size of the artboard. To change the size of an artboard, choose File > Document Setup and click the Edit Artboards button at the top of the dialog box (**Figure 4.5**). However, you'll find it faster to resize the artboard and convert color space by using the copy and paste technique we outlined in a previous note.

Figure 4.5 Changing artboards to the dimensions of their intended video format will help you preview the size of the logo in relation to the screen.

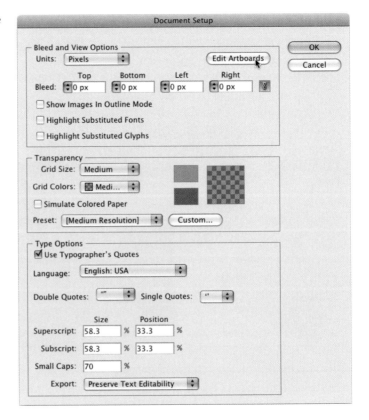

Release to Layers

If you're starting with a flattened file in Illustrator, the Release To Layers option is a quick way to have Illustrator create layers from the elements that make up the logo. You have two options when using Release To Layers (**Figure 4.6**):

▸ **Release to Layers (Sequence).** Places each object onto its own layer.

▸ **Release to Layers (Build).** Creates a sequential build with all the objects, starting with the bottommost object on the bottom layer and then duplicating each layer and adding objects until the topmost object is added to the top layer.

TIP

You can quickly create a storyboard from your sequential build. Export your Illustrator file to Photoshop, making sure to select Write Layers. Open the newly created Photoshop document and choose File > Scripts > Export Layers to Files. Choose a destination folder and click the Run button. With each frame of the build saved as an individual file, it's easy to place these frames into a storyboard template.

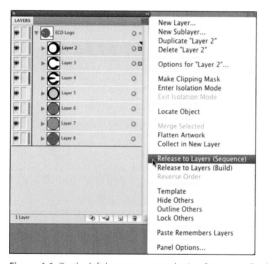 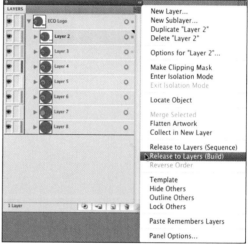

Figure 4.6 On the left, layers are created using Sequence. On the right, layers are created using Build.

Once you've released to layers, it's quite common to end up with too many layers. To fix this, you'll need to group layers together by selecting their corresponding targets in the Layers panel and pressing Command+G (Ctrl+G). Don't forget to name your layers as you group objects together. A random name like "Layer 56" won't be very helpful when animating in After Effects. In addition to the organizational benefits, the group command also helps make selecting objects in your canvas easier as well (**Figure 4.7**).

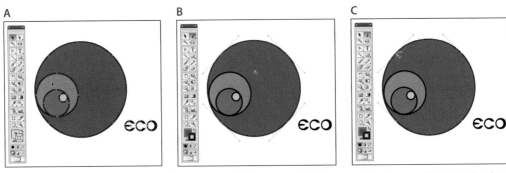

Figure 4.7 To quickly select a group in the canvas, use the Selection tool (A). If you want to select one element within that group, use the Group Selection tool (B). If you need to select the individual anchor points of an object, use the Direct Selection tool (C).

Working with Template Layers

You can manually trace over an image by changing its layer into a template layer. Usually, we use template layers in Illustrator to allow us to trace more artistic interpretations of an image directly overtop of the original image (**Figure 4.8**). Unlike painting in Photoshop, Illustrator creates brush strokes with fully editable vector paths. This is amazingly helpful when you need to go back and adjust a brush stroke that might just be a little off.

Figure 4.8 Fully editable brush strokes created with Artistic Watercolor brushes are traced directly over the template layer.

There are three ways to create a template layer in Illustrator (**Figure 4.9**):

▶ When placing an image, select the Template option in the pop-up window.

▶ Double-click a layer and select Template.

▶ Choose Template in the Layers menu.

Figure 4.9 It's always easy to spot a template layer because the layer will lock, the image will dim its opacity, and the eye icon in the Layers panel will change. Converting a layer to a template layer allows you to trace over the layer without worrying about accidentally moving the image as you work.

Using template layers in Illustrator is also a great way to create extra elements to use in the animation. As motion designers, we have the benefit of time (don't laugh). Even if the animation needs to end on the original logo, that doesn't mean we can't play with it along the way. In the Timeline for an animation, we can cut between treated versions of a logo or just use some of the elements to help highlight and add accents to different parts of the animation (**Figure 4.10**).

NOTES

Does painting look interesting? Don't worry; we cover Illustrator's extensive paint and drawing tools in Chapter 10. You'll learn how to create realistic brush strokes with the Bristle brush; create custom brushes; and use the Blob brush, Path tool, and erasers, to name just a few tools.

Figure 4.10 Creating multiple versions of a logo gives you flexibility when it comes time to animate. Just using a simple jump cut between the traced and untraced version can spice up the animation without having to use a single keyframe.

Live Trace

If you want to create some stylized versions of a bitmap image, Live Trace can save you loads of time tracing (**Figure 4.11**). It will automatically trace a bitmap image, creating a vector graphic. Several settings control the amount of detail as well as the colors used after tracing.

Figure 4.11 You can create multiple styles quickly by using the Live Trace Presets.

| Color 6 | Simple Trace | Grayscale |

1. To activate Live Trace, simply place or open a bitmap image in Illustrator. When placing an image in Illustrator, the adjustments will appear at the top of the screen in the Control panel.

2. Click the arrow button between the Trace button and the Mask button, and choose a preset from the list to apply your Live Trace.

Live Trace with Layers

Live Trace as a function is very powerful because of its presets and ability to quickly deliver some very accurate tracings, but sometimes you'll want more—more detail and more control over individual areas of an image. When it comes to selecting and isolating specific parts of an image, there's nothing better than Photoshop. So go ahead and use Photoshop to separate the different sections of the image onto their own layers.

TIP

You can have more control over Live Trace by selecting the Tracing Options at the bottom of the Preset list. Use Tracing Options to experiment with multiple settings with Preview selected.

NOTES

We'll explore the Live Trace command in greater depth in Chapter 5. You'll learn how to convert a footage clip into a vector animation.

When you're ready to use Live Trace in Illustrator, choose File > Open and select your new layered PSD document. Choose Convert Layers to Objects in the Options area (**Figure 4.12**). All the layers are imported just as they were in Photoshop.

Figure 4.12 Layered Photoshop files work well for import into Illustrator.

Preparing Logos in Photoshop

Because video is not vector based, we use Photoshop a lot when preparing files for animation. If you're starting with a flattened bitmap image file, Photoshop makes it easy to re-move the background or separate your logo into multiple layers for easy animation.

Color Space

As discussed earlier in the chapter, RGB color space is very important for maintaining color accuracy when creating and converting artwork for use in video. If your logo was delivered in CMYK, choose Image > Mode > RGB Color to convert your file.

Even if you're placing an external file into your Photoshop document, it's always wise to make sure that document is already converted to RGB before placement.

Resolution

As you learned earlier, follow the 200% rule for the best resolution results, and be sure to consider the overall pixel count determined by pixel height and width.

Pixel Aspect Ratio

There are so many different dimensions, frame rates, and codecs that remembering the exact settings, workflow, limitations, and or advantages can get confusing to say the least. When you add nonsquare pixels into the mix, there's yet another detail to consider. Using the Film and Video project presets found throughout the Creative Suite can help lend some organization to the specifics of each format. The Creative Suite offers many options that allow you to preview nonsquare pixel footage throughout many of its applications.

When we design for large projects, we've often found it easiest to actually convert any nonsquare pixel footage into a square pixel composition so there is one less detail to think about. Once everything is square pixel, we no longer have to worry about pixels being distorted, interpreted, or displayed improperly. Again, because large motion graphics projects have so many files moving between various applications, one less item to worry about really can make a difference.

Keep in mind that nonsquare pixel assets can be easily converted into a corresponding square pixel resolution. For example, if you had a project in an Adobe Photoshop Extended document that was created with the DVCPRO HD 1080p preset (1280x1080 nonsquare pixels), you could use one of three ways to convert that to the HDTV 1080p preset (1920x1080 square pixels) (**Figure 4.13**):

▶ Choose File > Place and place the DVCPRO HD 1280x1080 footage into a project with corresponding square pixel dimensions, in this case, HDTV 1920x1080.

▶ Copy and paste the layers between the two projects.

▶ Drag and drop the layers into the proper project.

NOTES

Changing the Pixel Aspect Ratio of a Photoshop document using the View menu does not actually change anything in the document. This setting only creates a preview of what the document will look like once the pixels are stretched.

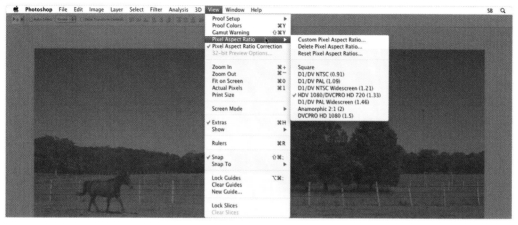

Figure 4.13 If you use any of the three conversion methods listed, Photoshop will automatically properly resize the footage to fit the square canvas settings. To preview a document with nonsquare pixels, choose View > Pixel Aspect Ratio and select the desired ratio. Photoshop will then distort the document to simulate its final dimensions.

Removing a Background Using Channels

Consider a typical "worst-case" scenario: Let's say we have clients with time constraints, and the only version of a logo they can get us quickly is embedded in a video clip. Before Photoshop Extended, we'd usually ask the video editor to quickly save out a still frame. Either way, as a still or video file, once our logo is open in Photoshop we can separate the logo from the background.

With newer tools like the Quick Selection tool and the Refine Edge command, separating an object from its background isn't nearly the challenge it used to be. However, sometimes it might just be faster to use an "old-school" technique using channels. Before many of the selection tools were created in Photoshop, channels were often the easiest and fastest way to select specific areas in an image. To view the channels of a Photoshop document, navigate to the Channels panel (**Figure 4.14**).

When you're using channels, look for the most contrast between the logo and the background (**Figure 4.15**). You want to create a selection using the luminance values from one of the channels. To have more options for animation, don't worry about keeping the drop shadow as a part of the logo. You can always add that back in later.

NOTES

When you're trying to view different channels in the Channels panel, don't click on the eye icons. Click directly on the name of the channel to view that channel. Be sure to activate all the channels again by selecting the RGB channel before you return to the Layers panel.

Figure 4.14 Each channel shows the luminance values for each color channel that makes up that image.

Figure 4.15 The Blue channel looks like a good starting point.

To create a selection from a channel, drag the desired channel down to the Layer button in the Channels panel to create a duplicate (**Figure 4.16**). This new copy is now an alpha channel. If you were to save this document right now, this new alpha channel would control the transparency for all the channels combined. To be honest, in this example it's hard to see one channel that works better than another. Since there is no clear winner, this is the perfect time to use more than one channel. Let's mix it up with Calculations!

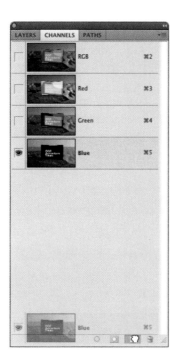

Figure 4.16 Duplicating a channel is a good start to making a clean mask.

Using Calculations to Create Layer Masks

The Calculations command controls how you blend together multiple channels. You can even blend together the same channel to get various results. Using Calculations can save you loads of time when you're trying to create quick selections. You'll clean up the mask later with the new Refine Mask function, so don't worry about any jagged edges or selecting all of the image. You just need to create a general selection that's close.

1. Convert the background layer into a regular layer by double-clicking it in the Layers panel, and then rename the layer **Logo**.

2. With the Logo layer selected, choose Image > Calculations (**Figure 4.17**).

   The key to success with Calculations is to try and try again. Play around with different settings to see where they take you. **Figure 4.18** shows some of the many settings within Calculations.

Figure 4.17 Although all the options may seem a bit overwhelming, it's these options that give Calculations its versatility.

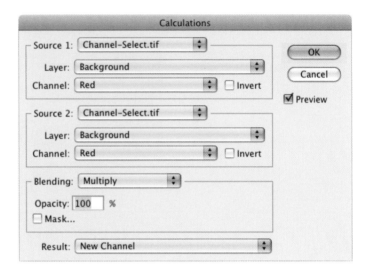

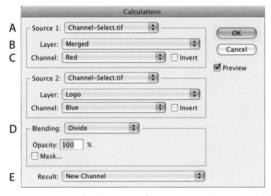

A **Source.** Gives you the ability to blend channels between more than one open document.

B **Layer.** Creates the ability to blend between individual layers as well as the entire document.

C **Channel.** Specifies exactly which channels to blend between.

D **Blending.** Controls the specific blending modes happening between the above layer and chosen channel settings.

E **Result.** Specifies what format or file to deliver when the Calculations command has been processed. You can save the blend as a new channel, in a brand-new document, or as a selection.

Figure 4.18 After changing a few options, you have a much better starting point for your mask.

Have fun and change a few settings in the Channel areas and the Blending mode options. If you're using the example file from the book, don't worry about specifying layer settings because there is one layer in this example.

3. When you get an outcome that might work, choose a setting for your result. For this example, we chose Selection.

4. Choose Window > Mask to open the new Masks panel, and click the Add Pixel Mask button to apply the selection as a mask to the layer (**Figure 4.19**).

Figure 4.19 The new Masks panel makes working with selections and masks a joy.

5. Since the mask is masking out the logo, not the background, click the Invert button in the Masks panel.

Although the result might be close to what you want to achieve, you still have some work to do. Let's clean up the mask manually.

1. To view the grayscale mask you created, Option-click (Alt-click) the layer mask thumbnail (**Figure 4.20**).

Figure 4.20 Viewing the mask is a fast way to see which areas need attention.

2. To flatten out the variable White and Black levels left in the mask, press Command+L (Ctrl+L) to apply a levels adjustment (**Figure 4.21**). Click the black eyedropper

tool and click on any gray pixel. Any pixel darker than the one you clicked will turn black. Repeat the same process using the white eyedropper tool. If you flatten out too many of the gray values, you'll end up with a very aliased image. Again, don't worry about that now; you'll fix it soon using the new Refine Mask command.

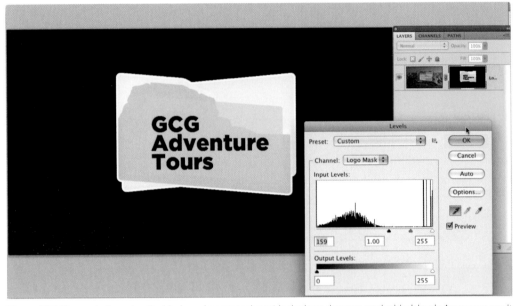

Figure 4.21 The mask after using the black eyedropper tool outside the logo shape to set the black levels. As you can see, it helped flatten out the background a lot.

NOTES

When applying Calculations between different documents, the pixel dimensions need to be the same. If the documents have two different color spaces, you can only calculate one channel from the source document to blend with the composite of the destination document. In other words, you cannot blend both composite channels between two documents that have two different color spaces.

3. Now that the center of the logo is masked out, just paint out any random extra pixels remaining outside the logo with the Paint tool.

CLOSE-UP

Changing Views With Layer Masks

When cleaning up a layer mask, place a solid flat color layer directly below the masked layer. Choose a color in direct contrast to the masked layer, and you will see any stray pixels that aren't 100 percent masked out. To view the grayscale mask, Option-click (Alt-click) the mask thumbnail. Repeat the key command or just click the layer eye icon to redisplay the layers. Shift-click the layer mask to turn it off and display the unmasked original layer. Repeat the same process to turn the mask back on.

Finalizing Masks with Refine Mask

Instead of using blur to fix the rough edges of the mask you've been working with, you'll use the new Refine Mask function. To activate Refine Mask, click the Mask Edge button in the Masks panel (**Figure 4.22**). If you've ever found pulling a clean mask to be a challenge, this new feature should make life much easier.

Refine Mask actively analyzes the contrasts around the defined edge of a mask to improve detail along the edges of a mask. The panel is divided into four distinct sections that contain several options (**Figure 4.23**).

Figure 4.22 Mask Edge does an amazing job of refining edges with little or no painting involved.

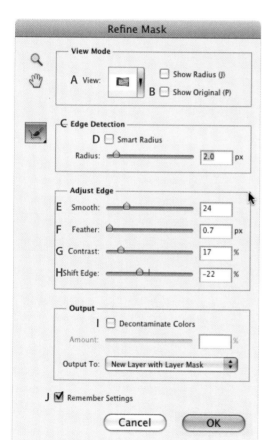

Figure 4.23 The mask will dynamically update as each slider is adjusted.

A **View button.** Displays the logo over different backgrounds or the original unmasked layer.

B **Show Original.** Toggles the visibility of the layer with the original mask applied.

C **Edge Detection.** Controls the width of the edge selection. Use a larger number for softer edges and a smaller number for more precise edges.

D **Radius.** Toggles the visibility of the edge selection being made by Refine Edge. **Smart Radius** automatically adjusts for sharp and soft edges within the selection.

E **Smooth.** Smoothes out any minor irregularities along the edge of the selection to remove any jagged edges.

F **Feather.** Softens the transition between the affected and unaffected pixels in the selection.

G **Contrast.** Sharpens any soft-edge transitions in the selected edge.

H **Shift Edge.** Moves the border of the mask in or out. This is similar to choking or expanding a matte when color keying.

I **Decontaminate Colors.** Removes any extraneous color fringing along the edge of the mask by changing the color of the edge to better match the contained source.

J **Output To.** Determines the format to apply the new refined mask.

TIP

If you have edges that are soft and sharp, select the Smart Radius option first.

Change the View mode to help clarify exactly how the various adjustments are affecting the mask. Although an edge may seem clean over black, it may show different results over white (**Figure 4.24**). In addition to the slider adjustments, there are four tools within the Refine Mask panel (**Figure 4.25**).

Figure 4.24 Use the key commands listed to the right of each name to quickly change between View modes.

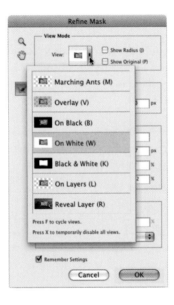

Figure 4.25 The Refine Radius and Remove Refine Mask tools help refine the selection of the edge being affected by the Refine Edge command.

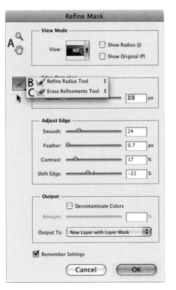

A **Zoom and Hand tools.** Function exactly like the corresponding tools in the Photoshop Tools panel, controlling magnification and navigation around the canvas.

B **Refine Radius tool.** Allows for precise control in defining edges through painting directly on the canvas.

C **Remove Refine Mask tool.** Provides paintable control for removing areas affected by the Refine Mask function.

Figure 4.26 shows how we fixed the aliasing on the original matte using Refine Mask. Consider the following tips when using this function:

Figure 4.26 After some trial and error, the Refine Mask command has really helped smooth out the mask.

▶ Only use Smart Radius if you have irregular edges that transition from smooth to sharp to smooth again.

▶ Wait to paint. Make sure all the sliders are first set to 0. Start by adjusting the Radius slider, and then move on to the other sliders.

▶ Use the Refine Radius and Remove Refine Mask tools to further refine the mask with more precise control. Be as accurate as possible with the placement of your brush as you paint. If you need to make a minor fix, start painting away from the area and slowly move the brush back toward the area to watch the adjustments.

▶ If you want to compare the original mask with the refined mask, choose one of the New Layer options in the Output To menu when you've finished your adjustments.

File Formats in Practice

When creating graphics for use in a film or broadcast, it's quite common to have to deliver graphic elements to an editor for final placement into the project. Most editing systems natively support layered Photoshop documents, but some may not. If the editor is working outside an Adobe workflow, two of the more popular and widely supported formats for still graphics are TIFF and TARGA. Because they are uncompressed by default and also support alpha channels for transparency, they are a good choice for graphics.

Manually Creating Alpha Channels

Saving a TIFF or TARGA file out of Photoshop is a straight-forward process. But if you want a graphic to have transparency, you need to save that transparency information as an alpha channel. Here's a quick shortcut: Command-click (Ctrl-click) on the thumbnail of a layer to load any painted pixels as a selection (**Figure 4.27**). If you want to add more than one layer's information, hold down Command+Shift (Ctrl+Shift) as you click on more thumbnails in the Layers panel.

NOTES

When using Command-click (Ctrl-click) to select transparent pixels, watch out for layer styles and Repoussé. Both need to be rasterized before their effects can be loaded as part of a transparency selection. Be sure to save another copy of the layer or document since these effects will no longer be editable. To rasterize layer styles or Repoussé, create a new blank layer, select both the new layer and the layer containing the layer styles (or Repoussé), and press Command+E (Ctrl+E) to merge the layers together. Then you can Command-click (Ctrl-click) on the thumbnail of the layer to load the transparency data.

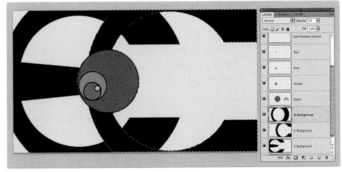

Figure 4.27 Once you're comfortable using Command-click (Ctrl-click) for quick selections, don't be surprised at just how often you'll use it.

To save the selection as an alpha channel, choose Select > Save Selection and click OK. With the transparency saved as an alpha channel, the document is ready to save as a flattened TIFF or TARGA file while still preserving the transparency.

Preparing for Animation

Layers are as essential to motion graphics as letters are to the written word. So, just like each letter has a purpose in composing a word, each layer should have a purpose in your compositions as well. When brainstorming about logo

TIP

To quickly and easily create a flattened file with an alpha channel, load the preset video actions in the Actions panel. The Alpha Channel from Transparency action will properly load all transparency, including any layer styles or Repoussé information, and create the proper alpha channel data.

animation, it's always a good idea to start with some solid basics. The animation of a logo can be just as much of a brand mark as the still logo. Always try to ensure that the animation stays true to the brand.

Importing Logos into After Effects

There are three main ways to import files into After Effects (**Figure 4.28**). Which one you choose really depends on the sources you have at hand:

Figure 4.28 Each of these three import options is designed to help speed up the animation process when importing layered Photoshop and Illustrator documents.

▶ **Project files.** If you've already animated a logo, you can import one After Effects project into another. This will bring all the compositions and sources into your current project. This workflow is best if you have some standard elements that you need to reuse from project to project.

▶ **Composition.** If your source is a layered Photoshop or Illustrator file, you're in luck. Someone worked hard to create all those layers, so preserve them. Layered files can and should be imported as compositions.

▶ **Footage.** If you're in a hurry or are dealing with flat-tened sources, your choices are pretty limited. Any graphic you import into After Effects can be imported as footage. This is the most common option if your logo is a flattened graphic or a prerendered movie file with an alpha channel.

Let's explore the options you have when working with compositions or footage import.

Compositions

When importing a layered document for animation, choose Composition – Retain Layer Size. This makes animation faster because each layer is individually sized, and its anchor point is placed at the center of each layer as opposed to the center of the composition. With the anchor point already set to the center of each layer, transform properties like scale, position, and rotate will function as expected, centered on each layer. Importing layered Photoshop and Illustrator files as compositions is a great time-saver and results in a smooth workflow.

Footage

Anytime you import graphics or video into After Effects you're creating footage. Even when you import a layered Photoshop or Illustrator file as a composition, each layer that was imported is considered to be footage. To look at the specific properties of any footage item in After Effects, just select the footage item in the Project panel and look at the text to the right of the preview thumbnail at the top of the panel. You can find out more information if you Option-click (Alt-click) directly on the footage item.

It's sometimes necessary to change how After Effects in-terprets footage, such as to specify how the alpha channel or frame rate should be handled. To access the Interpret Footage dialog box, select the footage and choose File > Interpret Footage > Main (**Figure 4.29**).

TIP

When modifying footage in the Interpret Footage dialog box, you may notice that some of the fields are grayed out. Don't panic; that just means that the selected foot-age didn't have those properties to change in the first place.

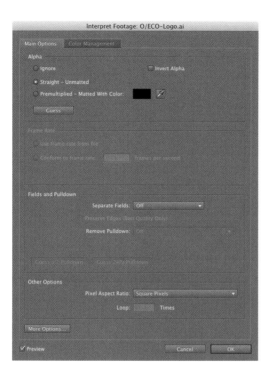

Figure 4.29 In the Main Options tab of the dialog box you can change the settings for the alpha channel, field order, frame rates, and pixel aspect ratio. If you're being plagued by strange render issues with certain shots, Interpret Footage is always a good place to start your troubleshooting process.

Since most motion graphics projects end up with a range of footage sources (to say the least), it's a good idea to be meticulous about organization. So if you haven't checked out Chapter 1, we covered several techniques for dealing with footage and keeping your projects organized while working in After Effects.

Interpreting Alpha Channels

Alpha channel information can be stored with color channels in two ways: straight and premultiplied. Whenever any footage with transparency is imported into After Effects, alpha channel data is being interpreted. For example, if you select any Photoshop footage in the Project panel, you'll see the words Millions of Colors + (Straight). The + denotes an alpha channel is present, and (Straight) means the footage has color channels that do not include information related to the alpha channel. Photoshop works with straight channels because they have the best color accuracy. Premultiplied channels are most common when dealing

TIP

If you're not quite sure what kind of channels you're dealing with, you can have After Effects guess for you as it analyzes the file on import. Just press the Guess button toward the top of the Interpret Footage dialog box.

with moving graphics. Adobe Premiere and After Effects support both kinds of channels.

If you ever notice a strange "halo" effect around your graphics, it's most likely due to how the alpha channel was interpreted. To fix this, just access the Interpret Footage dialog box and change the channel interpretation (**Figure 4.30**).

Figure 4.30 In addition to changing the interpretation, if you're getting a strange fringe color, you can use the eyedropper to sample the specific color and clean up that edge.

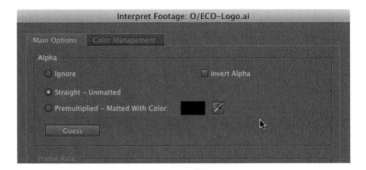

Converting Photoshop Text to Vector Type

One of our favorite integration features between Photoshop and After Effects is editable text. Any editable text in Photoshop that is imported into After Effects can actually be converted into editable text in After Effects. Although this doesn't happen by default, it's an amazingly helpful feature. In the Timeline, just select any layers that were text in Photoshop and choose Layer > Convert To Editable Text. Now the text is exactly the same as it would be if you created it directly in After Effects.

Why should you convert your text in After Effects? Well, it's worth it! You can scale the text infinitely. You can also take advantage of the text animation controls in After Effects. We explore text animation more in Chapter 3, "Typography for the Screen."

Using Continuously Rasterize

Continuous rasterization is applied when the Continuously Rasterize switch is selected on a vector graphic layer (**Figure 4.31**). This allows a vector graphic to scale without pixelation. Using continuous rasterization does increase render time because the graphic is continuously redrawn using the vector data. When you scale a vector logo over 100 percent and want to prevent the image from pixelating, using continuous rasterization is a must.

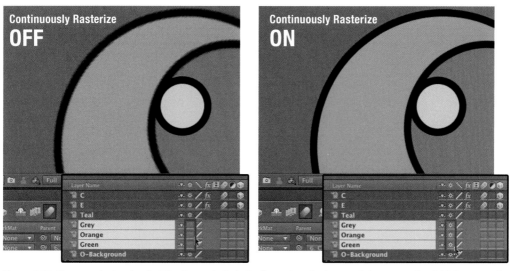

Figure 4.31 You can select or deselect Continuously Rasterize for each vector layer and choose exactly which layers need to remain sharp when scaling up to 100 percent.

Continuously Rasterize, Behind the Scenes

Toggling the Continuously Rasterize switch changes the render order of the composition. How the effects and masks are processed will occur in a different order depending on whether Continuously Rasterize is on or off.

If you're dealing with a standard layer or the Continuously Rasterize option is deselected, your composition will process as follows:

1. Masks
2. Effects
3. Transformations

If you select the Continuously Rasterize option, the render order changes to:

1. Transformations
2. Masks
3. Effects

The Continuously Rasterize option can be a little confusing in that it actually can perform two functions. If selected on a layer that is a nested composition, the option will collapse transformations.

Logo Animation Techniques

Now, let's explore some additional techniques that we use most when it comes to animating a logo. We provide some step-by-step instruction, but the information we offer is more of a broad overview of ideas meant to motivate you.

Even if you have perfectly prepped source files, animating logos can be a little complicated. Not only do you need to find inspiration, but you'll also need to determine just how much creative latitude you have to manipulate the logo. The more you find out at the beginning of a project, the less heartache at the end.

Because almost all art is created through inspiration, many of the techniques we discuss are based on finding insight through the unique properties of each logo. And because a logo is an iconic representation of a brand, it's important to consider that as well.

Using Audio for Inspiration

If you ever get stuck with a logo or graphic that just doesn't excite you, audio is always a great place to turn. Ask your client for any other collateral marketing materials. Even if the client doesn't have any audio or video materials, use what you know about the brand to find something on your own. Adding audio to even the smallest animation will go a *long* way when it comes time to present that animation. As you're listening to various tracks of music, visualize your animation playing out to the key points in the music track.

If you need to find the music on your own, Adobe Soundbooth is a great place to start. In Soundbooth you'll find a large amount of royalty-free audio to use in your projects. We cover Soundbooth more in depth in Chapter 9, "Designing with Audio." Let's return to the process of animation once you've found the right audio soundtrack.

To time key points of your animation with key points in the audio, you'll need to use markers. Markers will translate across applications in Creative Suite 5. When you add markers in Premiere or Soundbooth, they'll import into

After Effects either through import or Dynamic Link. Markers offer easy points to synchronize reveals for different pieces of a logo. After all, you'd like your logo to time out to the music or sound effects track whenever possible. We typically try to mark audio using applications like Soundbooth or Premiere Pro, but if you need to create markers directly within After Effects, there are several ways to do so.

To time an animation to audio, start with just the audio file first. To ensure that the audio is playing in realtime, load an audio only preview by pressing the . (decimal) key on your keypad instead of a RAM preview. As the audio preview is playing, you can add layer markers or composition markers into your projects. We recommend adding an adjustment or solid layer to hold just the markers or add them directly to the audio track.

To create a layer marker, select the layer you want to mark and press the * (multiply) key on your keypad (Ctrl+8 on a Mac if you don't have a keypad). The marker will be added to the selected layer wherever your current time indicator is in the Timeline. For best results, invoke an audio preview and literally "tap out" the beat you want. If you need to remove a marker, you can right-click and delete it. Check out the files in the Chapter_04_Media folder included on the DVD to see just how useful the audio and markers were to create the ECO logo animation.

Gaining Control with Hierarchy

When you have audio for your project, it's time to use the elements that make up the logo for further inspiration. Having a layered Illustrator file is essential, but once all those layers are imported into After Effects, you'll have to deal with a whole new set of challenges. Using the ECO logo animation as an example, as you spin one circle, you'll want the other circles to move interactively. To make animating all these layers effortless, you need to create a hierarchy among the circles (**Figure 4.32**).

TIP

If you're not getting enough of a preview, you do have options. You can change the duration of audio previews in Preferences. Open the After Effects Preferences window by choosing After Effects > Preferences > Previews (Edit > Preferences > Previews). Enter a longer duration into the Audio Preview field.

Figure 4.32 The intertwined circles in this logo are screaming for some kind of animation where they can spin around and "interact" with each other.

Parenting Layers

If you've ever experimented with character animation, you've probably heard of the term rigging. For example, if you rotated the arm on a rigged character, the chain of animation would make the forearm, hand, wrist, and fingers follow the position of the rotation. In After Effects, the primary steps for rigging are achieved through parenting the layers (**Figure 4.33**). You could also use Expressions for extra control between parameters, but for now let's stick to parenting.

Figure 4.33 Even though there are multiple levels of parenting, you can always clearly see the exact details by looking in the Parent column.

If the Parent column is not available along the top of your Timeline, right-click (Control-click) next to the word Source Name, select Columns, then select Parent from the list that appears (**Figure 4.34**) to show the Parent column. There are two ways to parent layers in After Effects:

Figure 4.34 In addition to activating the Parent column, you can activate a host of other columns via the same key command.

▶ Select the layer you want to be the parent layer and click the menu in the Parent section of the Timeline panel. Choose the layer you want to control. That layer is now known as the child of the parent layer (**Figure 4.35**).

Menu

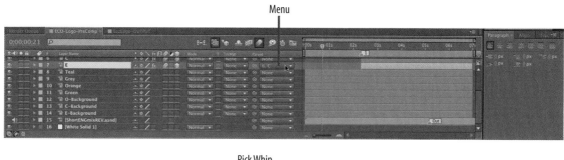

Pick Whip

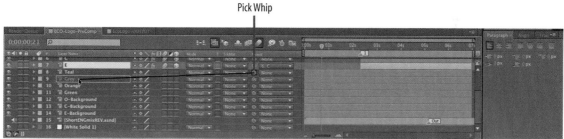

Figure 4.35 It's rather straightforward to assign the parent/child relationship using either the menu or the pick whip.

▶ Drag the pick whip for the parent layer to the layer name of the child layer. When the name is highlighted, let go of the pick whip. The child layer name should now appear in the parent layer, just like when you chose it from the list (Figure 4.35).

Null Objects

When you have to move a number of layers around a scene simultaneously, you can select all the layers and choose Layer > Pre-Compose. If you need to have access to all those individual elements, as well as every other layer in the composition, you'll want to create a null object. To create a null object, choose Layer > New > Null Object. With a null object, you can take all those layers you need to animate together and make them children of the null object.

Then you can apply your keyframes to the null object just like a pre-comp. Just remember that null objects do not control opacity. Anytime you think you might need a bit more control over the elements onscreen, a null object is always a good place to start.

Finishing Touches with Adjustment Layers

TIP

To only apply effects to certain areas, use a mask directly on the adjustment layer.

More often than not, logos end up looking a little flat. It's just the nature of optimizing an icon to look good on anything from print to an iPod to a king-size home theater system. Here is where adjustment layers come to the rescue. You can apply an effect directly to the adjustment layer, and that effect will treat any layer that is below the adjustment layer in the composition (**Figure 4.36**). However, when you're working with iconic logos that have sharp edges and clean lines, it's very important to get the animation pixel perfect. Then take some time to look at some different ways to treat the footage.

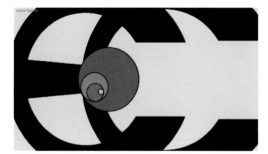 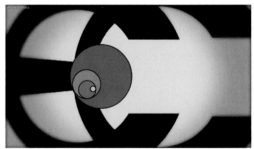

Figure 4.36 The filters applied to the adjustment layers add depth and style to the logo animation.

To create an adjustment layer, choose Layer > New > Adjustment Layer. In the ECO logo animation, we used adjustment layers to apply the finishing flares, blurs, and color corrections. To draw attention to the center of the screen, we applied a blur and vignette to the edges of the canvas, masking out the center of the adjustment layer. To add some pop to the open, we used the CC Light Burst 2.5 effect to create the flash/glow at the beginning of the animation.

You can even use adjustment layers with the Generate effects like Circle. Because the logo was so circular in animation, we wanted circular "rays of light" to fly out from behind the main part of the logo at key audio points. They were often pretty subtle, but it's those little things that can make or break an animation.

Check out the project files and QuickTime movie included on the accompanying DVD if you want a closer look at the ECO logo animation project.

5

Stylizing Footage

Fashion fades, only style remains the same.

—Coco Chanel

Stylizing Footage

We often find that the footage we're handed is a bit flat. That's not to say it's poorly shot, it's just usually lit and acquired in a way better suited to narrative storytelling. Rarely is the footage we're handed specifically shot with the motion graphics artist in mind.

So what can you do with that evenly lit, properly color balanced footage? That's easy; mix it up. We don't mean make mistakes; rather, dramatically alter the footage for stylistic purposes. Push the color, change the "film stock," and add some grit.

Photoshop and After Effects allow you to do lots of cool things to your footage. Both offer powerful image-editing capabilities. In this chapter we'll focus less on individual recipes and more on practical techniques. By learning some core tools and technology, you'll know how to create your own looks that match the mood and style of the project at hand.

Processing with Photoshop Extended

Chances are that you think of Photoshop as the most powerful image-editing application—for still photos. But the truth is that Photoshop is fully capable of working with motion footage as well.

Included with the Production Premium and Master Collection toolsets is Photoshop Extended. Besides its ability to work with 3D models, the ability to use video layers is essential to a motion graphics designer. You can now open a video file as easily as any still image, really; just choose File > Open, and then choose any QuickTime compatible movie file (**Figure 5.1**).

Figure 5.1 The Motion workspace in Photoshop CS5 gives you quick access to common tools you'll need to process video files.

Video Layer Considerations

To appreciate the flexibility of Photoshop Extended's video layers, you need to truly understand how they work. You can open a video file directly into a new Photoshop document with the Open command. This automatically sizes the document to match the video clip and adjusts the Timeline to match its duration.

If you already have a design, you can add a video clip to an open document. To import video as a video layer in an open document, choose Layer > Video Layers > New Video Layer From File. This adds the clip into the existing layers. However, the best option may be File > Place (**Figure 5.2**), which adds the video layer as a Smart Object (more on this technology in a moment).

TIP

To see a video layer in motion, you'll need to call up its Timeline. In Photoshop you can view video controls by choosing Window > Animation or use the Motion workspace.

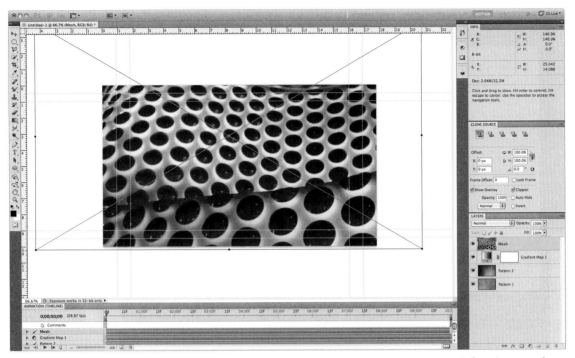

Figure 5.2 To constrain scaling the width and height when placing, hold down the Shift key as you drag. To scale from the center of an object, press Option (Alt). After you press Return (Enter), the video layer is sized.

Unlike other image formats, video layers are linked, not embedded. So you'll need to keep two details in mind. First, always keep the PSD file and the video asset in their initial location (or even in the same folder). If you move the video file to a new location or just copy the PSD file, you'll need to locate the video source file and reconnect. Second, you use up very little space when adding a video layer. Because the files are linked, the Photoshop document will only contain details about what is added to the shot.

With these facts in mind, you can see how technically easy it is to integrate video layers into your design workflow. Photoshop Extended supports several different movie and sequential image formats. Although there's a wide range of formats that work, it's best to avoid the more heavily compressed formats. **Table 5.1** contains the video and sequence formats supported by Photoshop Extended.

TABLE 5.1 Photoshop Extended Supported File Formats

QuickTime Video Formats	Image Sequence Formats
MPEG-1	BMP
MPEG-2	DICOM
MPEG-4	JPEG
MOV	OpenEXR
AVI	PNG
FLV (if Adobe Flash installed)	PSD
	Targa
	TIFF
	Cineon
	JPEG 2000

If you'd like greater control over a video layer, you can adjust how Photoshop interprets it (**Figure 5.3**). Select the video layer in the Layers panel and choose Layer > Video Layers > Interpret Footage. If the video layer was converted into a Smart Object, double-click the Smart Object icon at the corner of the image thumbnail in the Layers panel to open it.

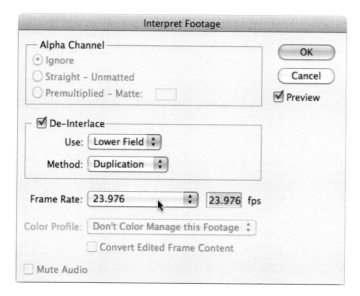

Figure 5.3 Photoshop lets you control properties like frame rate and interlacing.

Smart Filters

If you try to run filters on video clips in Photoshop, it can be a frustrating experience. The filters apply to the clip only one frame at a time, which doesn't do much when you're trying to get real results. But there's an easy way around this limitation.

Smart Filters allow filters in Photoshop to behave like effects in After Effects. That is to say, you get infinite flexibility and the ability to make changes at anytime during the design process. To use Smart Filters, you'll have to first convert a layer into a Smart Object.

There are a few ways to create a Smart Object:

▶ Choose File > Place and navigate to the video layer.

▶ Right-click on a video layer and choose Convert to Smart Object.

▶ Choose Filter > Convert for Smart Filters

Every filter in Photoshop (except for Liquify and Vanishing Point) can be used as a Smart Filter. Once applied, the names of the Smart Filters appear in the Layers panel directly below the Smart Object they've been applied to. Smart Filters can be adjusted, masked, or removed at anytime (even after a document has been closed and reopened).

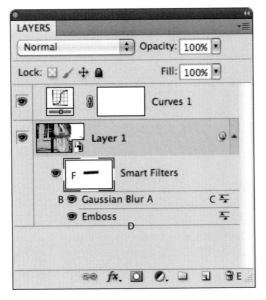

A Double-click the filter's name to modify the filter.

B Click the visibility icon to disable the filter.

C Double-click the double arrows to the right of the filter name to edit the blending options for the filter, including Mode and Opacity.

D Drag the filter up or down in the stack to change the order in which the filters are applied to the image.

E Drag a filter to the trash icon in the Layers panel to discard it.

F If you'd like to mask the filter's effect, you can paint with black on the layer mask that is attached to the filter.

Adjustment Layers

Besides Smart Filters, Photoshop offers another nondestructive workflow for manipulating images. Adjustment
layers are designed to be easy to use and edit. They're added as a layer above the actual image; they can be blended,
masked, or deleted at anytime. Most of these adjustments
can even translate to After Effects when you import a layered Photoshop file as a composition.

The Adjustments panel (**Figure 5.4**) contains 15 commands.
Each of these (or a close equivalent) is available in After
Effects. If there's such overlap, why would you choose to
work in Photoshop?

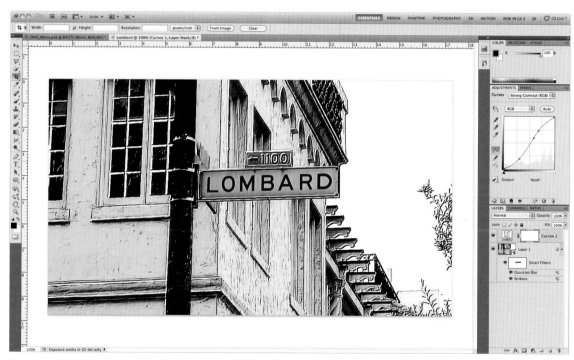

Figure 5.4 The Adjustments panel offers large and precise controls to simplify the adjustment process.

▶ The user interface is snappier in Photoshop for most
adjustments.

▶ You have advanced options like the On Image controls
for adjusting Curves, Black & White, and the Hue/
Saturation adjustment layers with interaction with the
source layer.

▶ Image quality does not dynamically adjust as you make changes to image adjustments. This allows you to make more accurate judgments for exposure and color.

▶ Several starting presets are provided, and new presets are easy to store.

▶ Photoshop supports additional color spaces, such as Lab, that allow for additional flexibility when adjusting color or exposure.

The easiest way to control adjustment layers in Photoshop is the Adjustments panel. With the Adjustments panel, you have easy access to all the tools needed to nondestructively adjust or enhance the color and tone of footage layers. You'll find the Adjustments panel directly above the Layers panel in the default workspace.

A Adjustment icons. Provide quick access to each type of adjustment layer.

B Adjustment presets. Lists of common settings, as well as custom settings, to use with adjustment layers.

C Return arrow. Returns to the Adjustment layer list so you can add another adjustment layer above the current one.

D Expanded view. Widens the panel to offer more room for the controls.

E Clip to Layer. Isolates an adjustment layer to only the layer directly below it.

F Toggle Layer Visibility button. Toggles the visibility of the adjustment.

G View Previous State button. Click and hold to show the previous appearance of the layer.

H Reset button. Resets the adjustment to its neutral starting point.

I Delete This Adjustment Layer button. Discards an adjustment layer.

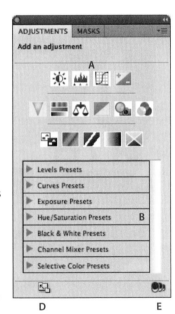

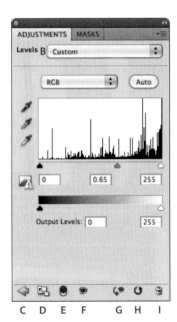

Using a PSD File with a Video Layer

A little-known technical secret is that the entire Photoshop engine is inside After Effects. This means that if a feature works in Photoshop, it should work in After Effects. Video layers are no different. Simply save your file as a layered Photoshop file.

When you import the Photoshop file, you can choose either the footage or the composition option (both work just fine). When you play the layer, the file is treated the same as any footage layer. If you used adjustment layers in Photoshop, those will import as well with the composition import option. If you want to return to Photoshop and make an edit, just highlight the layer and press Command+E (Ctrl+E) or choose Edit > Edit Original.

Rendering Video from Photoshop

If you're looking for a more permanent solution that creates an actual video clip, you can export a new video file from Photoshop. Unfortunately, the export process is not quite as easy as the After Effects render queue, but it is fairly straightforward.

Photoshop uses the standard QuickTime export engine to render. This will support most third-party codecs if they are loaded (including those from Avid, Apple, and Cineform). To start the process, choose File > Export > Render Video to generate a new QuickTime movie. You'll have to manually set export settings to write the correct file (**Figure 5.5**). The process is very similar to the render queue (except you can't save presets for future jobs).

TIP

If you want to deinterlace the video when you export it, click the Size button in the Movie Settings dialog box. Choose Deinterlace Source Video. This option combines the two fields in each interlaced video frame.

NOTES

If you want to use a batch process, you can bring your Photoshop documents with embedded videos into Adobe Media Encoder. This allows you to batch process and output several different file types as needed.

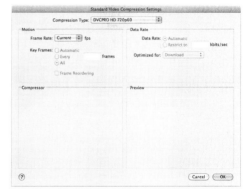

Figure 5.5 The Render Video dialog box contains most of the controls you'll need (left). Click the Settings button to open the Movie Settings dialog box (center) to control Video or Audio properties. You can click either Settings button in the Movie Settings dialog box to access advanced controls over video or audio codecs (right).

Color Grading

The process of color grading goes well beyond simple correction. The goal is not just to fix problems with color or exposure. Rather, it's to manipulate the color and tonal values for narrative purposes. There are no wrong answers here, merely opportunities to explore. Photoshop and After Effects provide some rich features that will open up new creative opportunities. Let's expand your toolbox.

Photo Filter

Both Photoshop and After Effects offer an adjustment called Photo Filter. The effect is designed to simulate colored glass filters that professional photographers often place in front of the camera lens.

These filters can be used to "cool" or "warm" a picture, or to add special effects (**Figure 5.6**). Photoshop offers 20 presets to choose from, and After Effects offers 18 (missing are one warming and one cooling preset). There is no major advantage to Photoshop or After Effects because this effect functions identically in both applications.

TIP

You'll often need to change time of day to maintain continuity in a scene. Photo Filters are a great help for color temperature.

Figure 5.6 The Photo Filter controls change the temperature of a shot. The before shot has been composited on top of the after shot so you can see the change. In this case, the apparent time of day is four hours later.

Here is an overview of the Photo Filter choices:

▶ **Warming Filter (85) and Cooling Filter (80).** These adjustment layers are meant to even out photos that were not properly white balanced. The Cooling Filter (80) makes images bluer to simulate cooler ambient light. The Warming Filter (85) makes images warmer to simulate hotter ambient light.

▶ **Warming Filter (81) and Cooling Filter (82).** These adjustment layers are similar to the previous filters but cast a more pronounced color. The Warming Filter (81) makes the photo yellower, and the Cooling Filter (82) makes the photo bluer.

▶ **Individual colors.** The Photo Filter also has 14 preset colors to choose from. These can be used for two primary purposes: to add a complementary color to a scene to remove color cast or for stylistic reasons.

▶ **Custom.** In addition to the built-in presets, you can also choose custom colors from the Photo Filter interface using the standard Color Picker.

Black and White Conversion

It may seem odd initially to discuss black and white conversion in the same context of color grading. But a true black and white image in film is heavily influenced by the colors present in the original image. Although some motion graphics artists choose to simply strip away color to make a grayscale image, there is a better way.

Black & White Effect

Both Photoshop and After Effects offer a Black & White adjustment. In Photoshop, it's easiest to use as an adjustment layer. In After Effects, you can apply the effect directly to a clip or an adjustment layer.

With the same effect in both places, how do you choose? Well, in our opinion this is where switching to Photoshop is worth the effort. The interactive controls and On Image tool make it much easier to create a custom black and white conversion.

NOTES

As you modify the Photo Filter adjustment layer or effect, be sure to select the Preserve Luminosity check box. This option ensures that the footage doesn't darken from the effect. You can then use the Density slider freely to increase the intensity of color without changing the brightness of the shot.

When you apply the Black & White effect or adjustment layer, Photoshop applies the default grayscale conversion. The power here lies in your ability to adjust the conversion using the color sliders (**Figure 5.7**). To jumpstart the effect, Photoshop offers an Auto button. Normally, we avoid Auto buttons, but in this case it works quite well. When applied, the effect creates a custom grayscale mix based on the image's color values and attempts to maximize the distribution of gray values.

Figure 5.7 The Auto mix often produces excellent results and can serve as the starting point for tweaking gray values using the color sliders.

On Image Tool

As you create a custom conversion, Photoshop provides an excellent tool. The On Image tool (**Figure 5.8**) lets you click inside an image and drag. In the Adjustments panel, select the On Image tool; then click the image to sample a target. The mouse pointer changes to an eyedropper if you move it over the image. Just click and hold on an image area to highlight the strongest color for that location.

Photoshop automatically selects the most influential color slider for that part of the image.

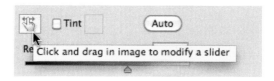

Duotones

In addition to creating a black and white image, you can create a duotone. The easiest method is located right inside the Black & White controls. For either Photoshop or After Effects, select the Tint check box and then specify a tint color.

If you'd like more control over the tint, there are several other methods you can use:

▶ **Add a solid color fill layer** in Photoshop or a solid in After Effects. You can then adjust the Opacity and Blend Mode to get more precise control over the tint.

▶ **Use a gradient map,** which assigns new colors based on a tonal range. In Photoshop, use the Gradient Map adjustment layer. In After Effects, add the Colorama effect to an adjustment layer. More on both methods in a moment.

▶ **Use a Hue/Saturation adjustment layer,** which offers precise numeric controls for the value and intensity of color. This layer can also be blended.

Stylizing Color with Gradient Maps

One of the least used adjustments for controlling color is a gradient map. What does a gradient map do? The name says it all: It takes a gradient and then maps it based on luminance values.

The effect is particularly useful for colorizing backgrounds and textures. It's most effective on footage, however, because it can create some dynamic looks. We find the effect most helpful for stylizing footage to use in show opens or title sequences because it provides a unifying effect that also simplifies the footage so it feels coherent.

If the gradient map is so valuable, why have you likely not added it to your repertoire? We suspect the lack of adoption is due to two factors: initially confusing interfaces and terrible default presets. But let's not allow such simple hurdles to block the path to great effects.

The key to using a gradient map is to always apply it as an adjustment layer. On their own, the gradient map command in Photoshop and the Colorama effect in After Effects are brutal. Colors quickly become posterized and unusable.

Using Gradient Maps in After Effects

Let's explore the Colorama effect, which is the more confusing option of the two. The Colorama effect has several controls, but you only need a few to get real results.

1. Add a new adjustment layer above your footage or design by pressing Command+Option+Y (Ctrl+Alt+Y).

2. Add the gradient map by choosing Effect > Color Correction > Colorama.

   The finalist in the world's worst preset is applied. Your composition probably looks like it lost a fight with a rainbow (**Figure 5.9**). Don't worry; things will get a lot better.

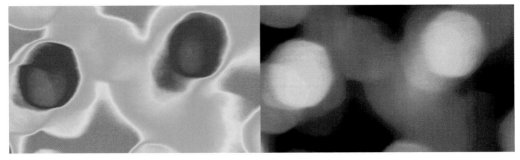

Figure 5.9 The Colorama effect is in the running for the worst preset effect ever (left). But don't let its initial ugliness scare you off. It offers many useful presets, such as Fire (right).

3. Let's explore which colors are being applied to the effect. Twirl open the Output Cycle parameter group.

   Items in the scene that were originally black are now mapped to the top of the color wheel, which is red by default. As the original tonal value gets lighter, they will be mapped to other colors on the Output Cycle wheel. In the case of the default preset, a rainbow is being applied.

4. Choose a different preset to see your options. For this exercise, click the Use Preset Palette menu and choose the Fire preset. New colors appear on the wheel and are applied to the image (**Figure 5.10**).

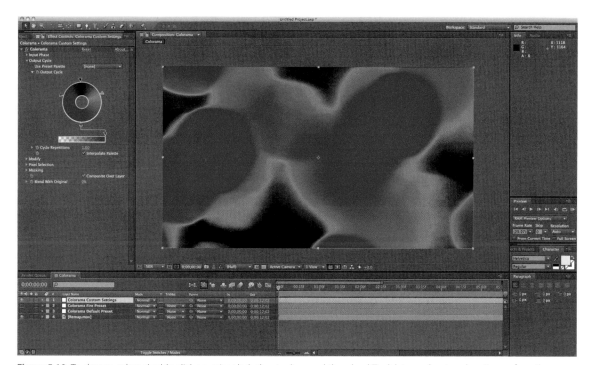

Figure 5.10 To change colors, double-click any triangle (color stop) around the wheel. To delete a color stop, drag it away from the wheel. To add a new color stop, click anywhere on the wheel where there isn't a color stop.

5. To apply the gradient more gently, utilize a blending mode. Try modes such as Overlay, Soft Light, Multiply, or Color for more pleasing results. You may want to desaturate the layer first to limit the colors.

The Colorama Effect offers several other advanced controls that are worth exploring. You won't need to use these in all cases, but it's good to know that precise controls exist:

▶ **Force Colors.** If you want the image to use only the specified colors (as opposed to a gradient), you can force the Colorama effect to posterize the image. In the Output Cycle parameter group, deselect the Interpolate Palette option.

▶ **Alpha Channel Control.** The Colorama effect affects all channels, even the alpha channel, by default. To prevent your alpha channel from being modified, twirl open the Modify parameter group and deselect Modify Alpha.

▶ **Isolating the Effect.** You can limit the range of the Colorama effect by using the Pixel Selection parameter group. You can use the eyedropper to select a target color, and then adjust Tolerance and Softness controls to refine the selection.

▶ **Blend with Opacity.** For the selected color stop, you can adjust its opacity. Drag the color stop above the checkerboard to the left to make the stop more transparent.

Using Gradient Maps in Photoshop

Wine glass image, Creative Commons Some Rights Reserved—Dave Photography

The Gradient Map command in Photoshop is a bit more straightforward. The easiest way to apply the effect is to click the Gradient Map button in the Adjustments panel. Click the menu next to the gradient thumbnail to choose from any loaded gradient presets. To modify the gradient, click the gradient's thumbnail. The Blu-ray menu in the figure uses a gradient map to unify the color of the background.

Photoshop offers two types of gradients, Solid and Noise. Solid gradients involve color and opacity stops (**Figure 5.11**) with gradual blends in between. Noise gradients (**Figure 5.12**) contain randomly distributed colors within a specified range. To switch between methods, click the Gradient Type menu. Let's explore the Solid gradient type and its options first:

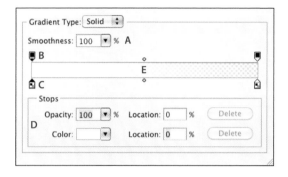

A Smoothness
B Opacity stops
C Color stops
D Stop Editor
E Midpoint

Figure 5.11 Solid Gradient Editor.

▶ **Smoothness.** This controls how quickly the gradient's colors blend together. You can set it to 100% for the most gradual blend or decrease its value for a sharper transition.

▶ **Opacity stops.** Most think of gradients as only containing color blends, but they can also have opacity values as well. Most default gradients have two stops (both set to 100% opacity). To add another stop, click in an empty area on the top of the gradient spectrum. To adjust a stop, click on it, and then modify the opacity field.

▶ **Color stops.** A basic gradient contains only two colors. You can choose to use several colors (or even repeat colors) to achieve a desired effect. Double-click a color stop to access the Adobe Color Picker.

▶ **Stop Editor.** If you'd prefer to adjust gradient controls numerically, you can edit the opacity, color, and location (0–100%, read left to right).

▶ **Midpoint.** To refine the blend between two stops, you can adjust the midpoint. By default, the midpoint is halfway between two stops. You can drag the point to influence the blend.

Figure 5.12 Noise Gradient Editor.

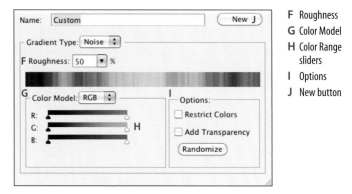

F Roughness
G Color Model
H Color Range
   sliders
I Options
J New button

The Noise gradient type and its options include:

▶ **Roughness.** Noise gradients use a roughness setting to determine how many different colors are used to create noise. A lower value uses fewer colors.

▶ **Color Model.** Photoshop's gradient controls offer three color models: Red-Green-Blue, Hue-Saturation-Brightness, or L*a*b. Most After Effects users will find RGB or HSB the most intuitive.

▶ **Color Range sliders.** Use the sliders to adjust the range of colors available to the gradient. To get a pleasing effect, limit the noise gradient to fewer colors.

▶ **Options.** You can restrict colors for Web-safe usage (which has no affect for broadcast-safe colors). You can also introduce random transparency. To create a new gradient, click the Randomize button. Every time you click, a new gradient will be generated (which is a great way to experiment).

▶ **New button.** To store a gradient as a preset, type a name into the Name field. Click the New button, and an icon will be added in the Presets window. This new gradient is not yet permanently saved, but instead is stored temporarily in the Preferences file. If this file is deleted or damaged, or if you change presets, the new gradient set will be lost. You must click the Save button and navigate to the desired folder. Be sure to append the filename with .grd to inform Photoshop that it is a gradient set.

The Power of Curves

The simple truth is that Curves is the most powerful image adjustment tool at your fingertips. The curved line lets you remap color and tone with multiple control points. The problem is that Curves is fairly unintuitive, at least in After Effects.

When you use Curves in Photoshop, you have a few tools at your disposal to make Curves easier:

▶ **Adjustment panel.** Photoshop's Adjustment panel displays extra histogram data while you're tweaking the Curves adjustment.

▶ **Eyedroppers.** Photoshop offers eyedroppers to sample and set black, white, and gray points.

▶ **On Image tool.** The On Image tool in Photoshop lets you click on the image to set a control point on the Curves adjustment.

How does using Curves in Photoshop help you in After Effects? Well, it's pretty easy to exchange data between Photoshop and After Effects. Simply export a still frame from After Effects or even open the footage file in Photoshop Extended. Make an adjustment using a Curves adjustment layer (you'll also find several useful presets in the Adjustments panel).

You can save your Curves adjustment as a preset. Click the Adjustment panel submenu (the triangle in the upper-right corner) and choose Save Curves Preset. Switch back to After Effects and apply the Curves effect. Click the Open button in the Effect Controls panel (it looks like a folder icon) and select the preset you created. After Effects will use the saved Curves from Photoshop.

Leave Color Effect

An effect that keeps popping up everywhere it seems is the Leave Color effect. You've seen the look in films such as *Pleasantville* and *Sin City* as well as a line of popular spots for Gatorade. Essentially, a color is targeted and all others are removed (**Figure 5.13**).

1. Add a new adjustment layer above your footage or design by pressing Command+Option+Y (Ctrl+Alt+Y).

TIP

You can create a still image by moving the current time indicator to the desired frame and choosing Composition > Save Frame As > File.

2. Choose Effect > Color Correction > Leave Color.

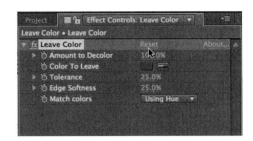

Figure 5.13 By default, nothing appears to happen when you apply the Leave Color effect. You'll need to adjust the parameters before the effect becomes apparent.

3. With the eyedropper, choose the color you want to leave.

4. Click the Match colors menu and choose the Hue model.

   The Hue method is much more limiting than the other match color models (which is generally what you'd want with the Limit Color effect).

5. Drag the Amount to Decolor slider toward 100%. A value less than 100% can create good emphasis (**Figure 5.14**).

Figure 5.14 The figure on the left has a Decolor amount of 100%. The figure on the right uses a lower value of 75% for a pleasant effect.

6. Refine the selection using the Tolerance and Edge Softness sliders.

Processed Looks

Every designer wants a bigger toolbox. For the rest of this chapter, we offer several techniques for processing your footage. These techniques often combine the applications within Creative Suite to create visually rich footage. Use these recipes to recharge your design process, and feel free to adapt or modify them as the situation requires.

Film-Look

Video sources often look a bit flat, lacking contrast and saturation. This is often on purpose because many shooters are instructed to provide lots of latitude for adjustment during postproduction. Fortunately, it's pretty easy to spice things up with just a little effort (**Figure 5.15**).

Figure 5.15 The original footage has been spiced up with a blur adjustment layer. Changing its blending mode creates a blooming effect that richens color and increases depth.

The easiest way to pull off a film-look effect is with an adjustment layer. Apply a heavy blur effect, typically with a radius value between 15 and 90 pixels. Depending on the speed of the machine and your budget for render time, you can use effects like Gaussian, Radial, or Fast Blur. For some blur effects, be sure to select the Repeat Edge Pixels option to avoid a gap.

Switch the blending mode of the adjustment layer. Try different blending modes such as Overlay, Soft Light, or Multiply. In fact you may want to try all of the different modes to see which one you like. The quickest way to cycle modes is to select a layer and press Shift + = to cycle forward or Shift + - to cycle backward. Depending on your source, you may need to use different modes.

When you generally like the boost in color and contrast, you can then adjust the opacity of the adjustment layer to taste. To make the clip easier to manage, you may choose to pre-compose the footage layer and its adjustment layer (Layer > Pre-compose).

TIP

If you're crunched for render time, be sure to check out the Box Blur effect. It renders very fast and should become part of your toolset.

If you're trying to simulate a true film look, be sure to add in some grain to simulate film stock. Add a new solid filled with 50% gray. Then use the Add Grain effect to complete the look. You'll find several actual film stocks in the Preset list. Adjust the blending mode and opacity to taste.

TIP

Do you need to get to the masks controls quickly? Just press MM (a double-tap) to get to the mask properties for a selected layer.

Power Window

A classic technique colorists use is to add vignettes or power windows to guide the viewer's eye. These can be truly effective, and they help create the right mood for a shot. Just don't make the mistake of thinking a darkened shadow should be pure black.

Start by adding a dark solid, usually an indigo, navy, maroon, or chocolate color. Apply an oval mask to the selected layer by double-clicking the Ellipse tool in the Tools panel. Change the mask's mode to Subtract and feather its edges. For best results, switch the blending mode of the layer. We find that Multiply or Color Burn with a reduced opacity tends to work best.

Sketched Footage

If you want to add a grit or sketch look to your footage, there's no need to pick up third-party effects for After Effects. Just take a short trip over to Photoshop Extended. Remember that you can open a video clip like any other image, and then choose Filter > Convert for Smart Filters to access a world of nondestructive options.

Included with Photoshop is the Gallery Effects package as well as the versatile Filter Gallery. Although their default looks may look a little "canned," you can quickly create some great effects by using combinations and blending modes.

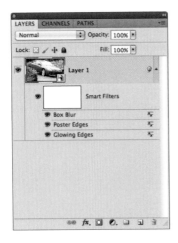

Look 1
Glowing Edges: Edge Width 5 | Edge Brightness 11 | Smoothness 8 | Screen Mode | 50% Opacity
Poster Edges: Edge Thickness 6 | Edge Intensity 4 | Posterization 3 | Overlay Mode | 100% Opacity
Box Blur: Radius 25 pixels | Soft Light Mode | 50% Opacity

Look 2
Dark Strokes: Balance 4 | Black Intensity 4 | White Intensity 3 | Multiply Mode | 75% Opacity
Surface Blur: Radius 25 | Threshold 30 | Normal Mode | 80% Opacity

Presets Make a Great Starting Point

It seems like most designers fall into two camps when it comes to preset effects. Some love them because they speed up the design process, whereas others hate them for homogenizing the design process.

Both camps have a point.

The presets included with After Effects are meant to serve as a great starting point. They offer a way to expose users to effects and combinations that might have been over-looked. But rarely should they be used "as is," or the design quality can be cheapened.

After Effects offers several great presets that can stylize your footage. There are three ways to access these effects:

► In the Effects & Presets panel, twirl down the Animation Presets folder. Inside you'll find two categories that should prove useful: Image – Creative and Image – Special Effects.

► In the same panel, you can type into the search window to search the presets. This is a quick way to locate a preset if you know the name of what you're looking for.

► If you'd like to see a visual preview of the effects, choose Animation > Browse Presets. This command launches Bridge and lets you see animated thumbnails for the preset effects. If you find one you like, just double-click to apply it.

▶ Download even more great presets at www.adobe.com/
go/learn_ae_cs3additionalanimationpresets. Plus
they're free!

Now that you know how to find the presets, you need to
learn the best way to use them. Here are a few tricks we
employ to get the most value: First, always apply the effect
to an adjustment layer. This way you can lower the opacity or change the layer's blending mode to quickly evolve
the effect. Second, to get quick access to any keyframes,
just press U for the selected layer. Third, you can press the
E key to see all the effects added to the layer so you can
quickly access controls.

The presets should serve as a launching point for your own
designs. If you create a look you'd like to save, you can always choose Animation > Save Animation Preset to store it.

Converting Footage to Vectors with Creative Suite

A hallmark of the Creative Suite is how multiple applications
can work together. Although there are several workflows for
"tooning" footage, including the excellent Cartoon effect in
After Effects, there are reasons to take the time for a truly
advanced workflow. Here, we'll harness After Effects, Illustrator, and Bridge to truly vectorize footage.

The process is all built around Illustrator's Live Trace
command. This option is usually used to turn raster images
into vector files. Through a few special steps and flaming
hoops of fire, it can be made to work on video clips as well.
The benefit of using the Live Trace command is that the
new footage is a vector file (**Figure 5.16**).

Figure 5.16 The original footage is converted to a vector file using Illustrator's Live Trace command. The process takes a
short while, but it produces excellent results that can be dramatically resized.

Not only does this offer a great "look," but it also results in some major technical advantages. Footage can be dramatically resized (such as for film output) because the new footage is truly vector based. The end files can also be output to Adobe Flash if further vector animation or interactivity is desired.

Preprocess Footage with After Effects

Before converting your footage to vectors, you'll need to preprocess it with After Effects. The goal is to get the best-looking footage. After Effects offers several options. Choose Effect > Color Correction to improve your footage. Consider the following to enhance your clips:

▶ To adjust midtones of an image (**Figure 5.17**), use Levels or Levels (Individual Controls).

A Few Words on Contrast

To create the cartoon look with Live Trace, you need to shoot video properly. For best results, get a high level of contrast between the subject and background. You'll need to have even lighting without a lot of shadows, and your subject should be clearly recognizable. If the footage isn't created this way, you can use Color Correction effects to preprocess the clip.

Figure 5.17 The footage contrast has been increased and color cast altered to improve the conversion.

▶ If your image has a color cast, use Color Balance.

▶ For footage with problems in the brightest and darkest areas, use the Shadow/Highlight adjustment.

▶ If your video is flickering with different color levels, use the Color Stabilizer effect.

▶ Use the Auto Levels effect with the temporal smoothing option to adjust a clip quickly.

▶ Try softening the footage slightly with a Bilateral or a Box Blur effect (**Figure 5.18**) to produce smoother vectors. Select the Colorize check box to restore the original image color.

Figure 5.18 The Box Blur effect is a quick way to simplify an image (left). Be sure to select the Colorize check box to restore the original image's colors (right).

Using Nonsquare Pixels? Better Resize!

The Output Module also contains an option to resize the rendered file. If you are using nonsquare pixels (which many video cameras do), be sure to convert to the closest square pixel equivalent. For example, DVCPRO HD may be 960x720 pixels natively, but you'll want to convert to 1280x720.

Once your footage is prepped and simplified, you'll need to convert it to an image sequence. This is easy to do with the After Effects render queue. Add your composition to the render queue and change the Output Module settings format to TIFF Sequence with Alpha. Use TIFF files, as opposed to other formats, because they won't add additional compression or noise to the footage. Be sure to click the Output To area in the Render Queue panel and target a new folder (call it **Live Trace Images**). You can then render an image sequence.

Process Footage with Adobe Illustrator

Adobe Illustrator offers powerful tools for creating and modifying vector objects. Normally, you'd use Illustrator to create original vector artwork for your motion graphics projects. In this case you can convert raster images to vector files with a great tool called Live Trace. The interface is a little daunting at first but is easy to master.

On its own, the tool doesn't offer batch processing, but we'll get around this. To start, you'll need to create your own conversion settings that work for the footage in hand. Launch Adobe Illustrator and then choose File > Open. Choose a representative still frame from the image sequence you created earlier.

1. Click with the Selection tool (V) to make your photo the only active object. For best results, make sure you're viewing the image at 100% magnification for the following steps.

2. With your photo active, choose Object > Live Trace > Tracing Options. A new dialog box opens where you can tweak the Live Trace settings (**Figure 5.19**):

Figure 5.19 The Live Trace dialog box offers several controls. Be sure to fully explore your options to create a custom look.

- ► Select the Preview check box to see your work.
- ► Change Mode to Color to create a colored vector file.
- ► Modify the Max Colors setting to taste. You can have up to 256 levels of color (which is very realistic but slow to create). Experiment with options between 20 and 256 colors depending on your needs. We typically stick to values between 50 and 150 colors.
- ► In the Tracing Options dialog box, use a slight blur (often values less than 3 will work best).

3. You can dramatically change the look by tweaking the Trace Settings:

- ► Path Fitting controls the tightness of the strokes.
- ► Increase the Minimum Area slider to simplify the image.
- ► Each tweak takes a moment to redraw, so be sure to wait for the screen to refresh.

4. When you're happy with a look, you'll need to store it. Click the Save Preset button, and in the dialog box that appears, give the Live Trace preset a name that's easy to remember.

5. Click Cancel and skip applying Live Trace for now. You can close the open document without saving it.

Custom Is King

Although you can reuse your custom presets from job to job, we don't. You'll get far better results by tweaking your settings for each project.

Process Footage with Adobe Bridge

Converting your images one at a time would be very slow. Fortunately, you can automate this process. Once you've taken the time to create your custom preset, you can process your image sequence using Adobe Bridge. This batch process allows you to open and apply the preset to several images with minimal work.

1. Launch Adobe Bridge and navigate to the folder where you stored your image sequence. Select the first image in the folder, and then press Command+A (Ctrl+A) to select all the images in the folder (**Figure 5.20**).

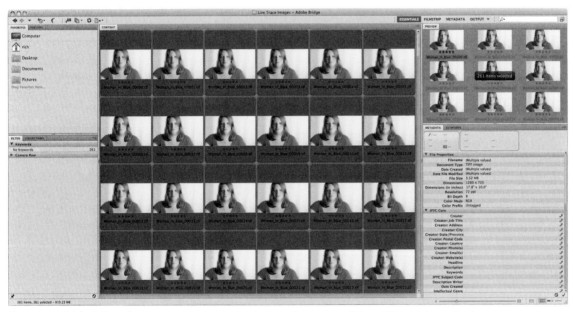

Figure 5.20 Adobe Bridge offers an easy way to access batch-processing commands for multiple Adobe applications.

2. Choose Tools > Illustrator > Live Trace to open a Live Trace dialog box (**Figure 5.21**), which you can use to batch process your files. From the Tracing Preset menu, choose the Tracing Preset that you created earlier.

3. In the Document Profile area, choose Video and Film. Enter a document size to match your original image sequence (such as 1280 px x 720 px).

4. Click the Choose button for a Destination. Create and choose a new folder named **Live Trace Results** (Figure 5.21).

Figure 5.21 Be sure to double-check your settings before you start the batch process. If you need to interrupt a batch, you can select just the unprocessed images and restart it.

5. When you're ready, click OK to start the conversion (and leave your computer for awhile because the process is somewhat time intensive).

Import Footage into After Effects

After Illustrator finishes processing all the still images into vector files, you can import them back to After Effects. Essentially, each animated frame will come back into After Effects and form a new movie clip. Once in After Effects, the clip can be re-synced with sound or scaled to a new, finished size.

Import the processed AI files into After Effects. Be sure to select the first file in the folder, choose to import as footage, and leave the Illustrator/PDF/EPS Sequence box selected. When you click Open, the clip is brought back into After Effects. You can then scale the clip as needed (be sure to use the Continuously Rasterize option).

The imported clip will not play at the same speed as the original footage without a little intervention (**Figure 5.22**). Simply select the original footage clip you based the Live Trace on and choose File > Interpret Footage > Remember Interpretation. You can then select the newly created vector clip and choose File > Interpret Footage > Apply Interpretation. If you have advanced options in use (like 3:2 pulldown for 24 fps material), just press Command+Option+G (Ctrl+Alt+G) with the new clip selected and change its frame rate to match the original.

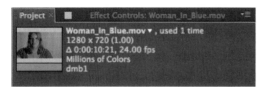 

Figure 5.22 The new clip doesn't match the original frame rate or duration. Be sure to adjust the new clip's interpretation to match the original footage.

After you've synced the clip, you can try blending the original image with the vector copy to get some edge detail.

6

Repairing and Retiming Footage

There is one advantage to having nothing,
it never needs repair.

—Frank Howard Clark

Repairing and Retiming Footage

Unfortunately, you are not always in complete control of a project from start to finish. As a motion graphics artist, you will often be excluded from the field production stage. Footage will be shot without you (and often without regard to your needs). We learned an important lesson early on: If you're at the end of the line (which is where video editors and motion graphics folks are in the process), you're responsible for everything that's wrong with the final product. Sadly, there's not much you can do to change this fact.

Except of course, you can "fix it in post."

Now, we hate this phrase as much as you. Fortunately, After Effects and Photoshop offer some great options for repairing footage. You can fix color and exposure problems, change the speed or duration of clips, and even remove unwanted objects (**Figure 6.1**).

In this chapter we'll explore how you can wrestle your footage to the ground and pound it into shape. When you combine the techniques in this chapter with those you learned in Chapter 4, you'll have a much better chance of getting the results you desire from footage sources.

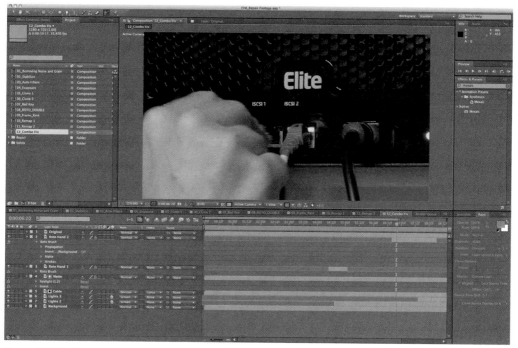

Figure 6.1 This shot required multiple techniques to repair it. The hand was isolated with the Roto Brush tool, and the cables were extracted with Keylight. New lights were added using the Screen blending mode as well. You'll learn all of these techniques in this chapter and can explore the shots on the accompanying DVD (footage courtesy Data Robotics, Inc.—www.drobo.com).

Repairing Footage

There are several reasons that footage might need repair. Archival sources (especially those that are tape-based) can wear with time or equipment failure. Rushed crews or poor preproduction can also impact the quality of a shot through inadequate lighting. Environmental conditions, such as a sunset or inconsistent cloud cover, can wreak havoc with footage as well.

Although the reasons may vary, you'll find a useful collection of tools in After Effects. The footage we'll show you is bad (in this case purposely so). We've exaggerated the problems so they're easier to see in the book. You can also open the project Ch6_Repair Footage.aep on the book's DVD to see the damage (and repairs) up close.

Removing Noise and Grain

An all-too-common problem with footage is noise or grain. Noise is typically caused by shooting in low light and can become very visible when camera gain or ISO is raised. Noise often results in unwanted "dancing pixels" and color aberrations in the shot. Both can be quite distracting (**Figure 6.2**).

Figure 6.2 The original footage shows a lot of color noise due to shooting in low light (focus is also impacted). The image on the right has been cleaned up significantly.

TIP

The Remove Grain effect is very processor intensive and takes a while to preview. To increase the speed of your workflow, be sure to adjust the Remove Grain controls in the order they are listed in the Effect Controls panel. You'll want to find effective degraining settings first, and then adjust the remaining controls.

Need to remove color cast? Switch to each channel's view in the Levels effect. Then move the white and black points to the edge of each channel's histogram. Finally, move the gray (or middle) slider to balance out the channel's histogram. When you're happy with the color and contrast, you can tackle the grain or noise.

Grain on the other hand can be caused by the actual film stock used. You may need to remove grain because it is distracting or because it is interfering with tasks like color keying.

The approach for both problems is virtually identical; you use the Remove Grain effect. The effect is very powerful and combines signal processing and statistical estimation techniques to repair footage. The Remove Grain effect attempts to isolate fine details and only process grain or noise. To further improve the quality of the effect, you can use temporal filtering, which analyzes the clip over time.

Before tackling the grain, we recommend setting the Levels properly. Often, adjusting the white and black points (as well as the gamma) can influence the grain or noise. Get the shot where you want it with a Levels adjustment. You can also adjust the Red, Green, and Blue channels separately to remove any color cast (**Figure 6.3**).

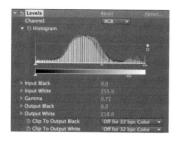 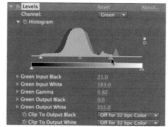

Figure 6.3 The Levels effect can restore contrast (using the Input parameters). You can also remove color cast by adjusting each channel.

Initial Cleanup of Grain

To clean up grain, start by choosing a layer in need of repair. To make the task easier, you'll want to view your composition or footage at 100% magnification so you can make accurate decisions. Apply the effect by choosing Effect > Noise & Grain > Remove Grain.

The primary controls are those in the Noise Reduction parameter group. Usually, the Noises Reduction settings are enough on their own, working in Multichannel mode. You can also isolate noise reduction to a single channel or to different amounts per channel with the Channel Noise controls.

Next, increase the Passes value to broaden the range of noise that is detected. Use a higher number of passes to reduce larger-sized noise. Note that more passes will increase render time. Once the ideal number is chosen, additional passes will have no added benefit.

The Fine Tuning control group can be used to refine the noise reduction. There are several properties to use for better image quality:

▶ **Chroma Suppression.** Use this option to suppress color in the noise (**Figure 6.4**). Just be careful not to go too high or you'll remove color from the image.

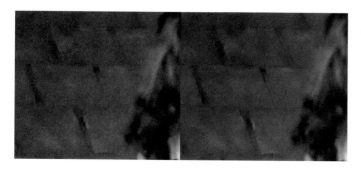

Figure 6.4 Color noise can be very distracting.

155

▶ **Texture.** This option preserves fine details. Lower values create a smoother, possibly artificial-looking result. Using a higher value may leave the final result difficult to distinguish from the original.

▶ **Noise Size Bias.** This control lets you favor smaller or larger noise. A value of 0 (zero) treats all noise equally. A negative value favors larger noise; a positive value preserves more of the smaller noise.

▶ **Clean Solid Areas.** This option can smooth out additional pixels. It works well if you have large areas of flat color. Be careful not to use too high of a value or the image may look artificial (**Figure 6.5**).

Figure 6.5 The original image (left) shows too much noise in the wall. The center image has some of the detail smoothed. The image on the right has too much cleaning applied and is overly smoothed.

As you make adjustments, you'll notice that the effect is initially previewed in a 200x200 pixel preview window. You can drag the preview window around the composition window as needed to change the preview area. If you want to control where the noise is sampled from, change the Viewing mode to Noise Samples and adjust the Sampling controls. When you want to see the entire frame, change the Viewing mode to Final. This mode takes longer to preview but should be invoked when you want to finalize the effect.

Smoothing Over Time

The Temporal Filtering controls can be used to reduce grain more subtly over time (reducing some of the chatter between frames). To enable Temporal Filtering, twirl down the Temporal Filtering controls and select the Enable check box.

Initially, set the Amount slider to 100% and create a short RAM preview at Full quality to see the results. If streaks or blurs occur around a fast-moving subject, reduce the Amount slider. Temporal filtering adds significantly to render times, so you may want to wait to apply it until after you're happy with all other settings.

Sharpen the Image

As you reduce noise, it's possible that the image may go soft. If your noise is caused by shooting in low light, your image might be soft to begin with. Fortunately, the Remove Grain effect has Unsharp Mask controls. Use these to increase contrast in the edges and restore image sharpness.

Use the Amount slider to increase the sharpening (be careful not to go too high or the image will looked sketched). You can then use Threshold and Radius to refine the details in the image.

Stabilizing Footage

A shaky shot can truly be distracting. Unfortunately, it seems like folks just don't have a love for tripods like they used to. Fortunately, After Effects can smooth out some of the shake and remove the jostle.

Stabilizing footage is identical to motion tracking; it's just what you do with the data that's different. Essentially, you need to identify elements in a scene that are in every frame, and then have After Effects track their position. For stabilization purposes, it's best to track objects that are supposed to be stationary. Once After Effects tracks these items, it can create keyframes to move the layer in the opposite direction (hence removing movement).

Stabilizing a shot typically requires two tracking points. You can choose to stabilize any two of the following: position, rotation, and scale. For example, if the camera was panning, you'd deselect Position and only affect Scale and Rotation. If the camera was zooming, you could use Position and Rotation only.

If you have other effects on a layer, you'll need to pre-compose first, and then apply the Remove Grain effect to the nested composition.

If an image is particularly bad, you can apply an instance of the Unsharp Mask effect to an adjustment layer.

If you're preparing video for the Web, removing camera shake will result in a cleaner compression and smaller file size due to the simplified image.

Here's how to tackle a shot:

1. Select the desired shot in the Timeline panel and choose Animation > Stabilize Motion. The selected layer should be set as the Motion Target in the Tracker panel.

2. Click the Stabilize Motion button in the Tracker panel, and then choose what to stabilize. For our sample shot, we used Position and Rotation (**Figure 6.6**).

Figure 6.6 If you don't see the Tracker panel, choose Window > Tracker.

3. Drag the current time indicator to the frame you want to start stabilizing. Typically, this will be the first frame of the clip.

4. With the Selection tool, adjust the track points. There are three primary elements to control:

   ▶ **Feature region.** This is the element that you want tracked. Adjust the smaller, inside box to surround the object (**Figure 6.7**). The feature should be distinct without other objects passing in front of it.

Figure 6.7 Adjust the bounding box to surround the tracked element.

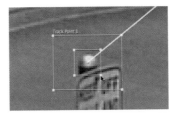

   ▶ **Search region.** This region identifies where After Effects will look for the object. A smaller region speeds up stabilization but may lose track of the

feature. Adjust the bounding box, but keep it relatively tight to the Feature region (**Figure 6.8**).

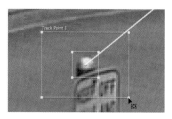

Figure 6.8 The larger the Search region, the longer the processing time.

▶ **Attach point.** The attach point is the small crosshair.
For stabilization, just place this on the center of the
feature you are tracking.

5. Repeat the adjustment for the second track point
(**Figure 6.9**).

Figure 6.9 If you're trying to stabilize rotation, be sure your two track points are a good distance apart.

6. Click the Analyze Forward button to begin tracking.
If the track loses accuracy, click Stop and make adjustments to your Search and Feature regions.

TIP

To improve the stabilization, you can click the Options button in the Tracker panel. The Process Before Match controls let you sharpen or blur the clip before tracking. This enhancement is only for the Tracker and doesn't affect final image quality.

7. When you're satisfied with the tracking, click the Apply button to convert the tracking data into keyframes. After Effects prompts you to choose a direction for the Apply Dimensions. You can use X and Y for most camera shake or only X or Y if there is a light vibration in the scene.

8. The Tracker likely produced too many keyframes, which can lead to unwanted bounce from overcompensation. Use the Smoother panel to reduce this. Click on an individual property (such as Anchor Point), and then click Apply. Use a higher value in the Smoother panel for greater reduction (**Figure 6.10**).

Figure 6.10 Experiment with different values in the Smoother panel to get fewer keyframes in the Timeline.

9. Switch back to the Composition panel. The shot likely drifts in the frame due to the stabilization. Scale the layer larger to avoid gaps at the edges (**Figure 6.11**).

Figure 6.11 Only scale as much as needed to hide the gaps; otherwise, your footage will soften.

Quick Fixes with Auto Effects

We're big fans of taking care to create handcrafted designs, but we're also realists. Chances are you've faced a few tough deadlines, and nothing's worse than missing your mark. Fortunately, the Auto effects options offer a quick and easy way to make up time and fix less-than-perfect footage.

All the Auto effects offer a Temporal Smoothing option. By using a range of surrounding frames, the effect will not flicker. This option is very useful and should be turned on for most clips. If your clip has several changes in it (or contains existing edits), be sure to combine the Scene Detect option with Temporal Smoothing for the best results.

NOTES

If the Auto effects are too strong, you can use the Blend with Original slider to back them off.

Choose one or more of the following options to save time repairing clips:

▶ **Auto Color.** The Auto Color effect adjusts the contrast and color of an image automatically. It works by analyzing the shadows, midtones, and highlights in the clip. It is best for fixing color issues (**Figure 6.12**).

Figure 6.12 The Auto Color effect correctly removed the color cast in the scene and restored some contrast. Footage courtesy of the American Diabetes Association—tour.diabetes.org.

▶ **Auto Contrast.** The Auto Contrast effect improves the overall contrast of the clip. Be sure to use the Black and White Clip sliders to further refine the footage (**Figure 6.13**).

Figure 6.13 The clip on the right has much better definition after the Auto Contrast effect was applied.

TIP

The Vibrancy adjustment is an excellent option to further refine color in a scene. It does a great job of boosting non-skin tone colors.

NOTES

Production folks often ask, is it best for a clip to be overexposed or underexposed? If we had our way, we'd say proper expose. But truth be told, it's a lot easier to fix a shot that's a little dark. Overexposed shots tend to blow out, and those areas lack any detail at all to work with. Unless you have the luxury of working with raw video files, favor an underexposed clip.

▶ **Auto Levels.** The Auto Levels effect maps the lightest and darkest areas of a clip to white and black. The intermediate values are also distributed to improve the exposure. When combined with Temporal Smoothing and Scene detection options, it works great on a long clip to remove flicker.

Controlling Exposure

We're often presented with clips that lack proper exposure, and we're sure you will be too. We understand that it can be difficult to achieve the required lighting in all circumstances. Crews are often pressured to "get the shot" and aren't given enough time or resources. Regardless of the cause, you'll have to fix it.

Although there are several ways to tackle an underexposed clip, we prefer one that's popular with those working in forensic video (yes, we mean law enforcement). By stacking multiple copies of a dark clip on top of each other and setting the copies to Screen mode, it's possible to blend the clips and add up details (**Figure 6.14**).

Figure 6.14 The original clip is quite dark. The middle image adds one copy in Screen mode, and the right image shows two copies.

The blended copies may show some unwanted artifacts, but a little touch-up is quite simple. By adding the Auto Contrast effect, it's easy to improve the details in the clip.

Even more useful is the Change to Color effect for cleaning up overly saturated skin tones. By selecting the unwanted color as the From well, you can then use the To well to target the desired skin tones (**Figure 6.15**). Once the colors are targeted, select the View Correction Matte check box to see which areas are being affected. Refine the matte with the Tolerance control group. Deselect the View

Correction Matte check box to see if your adjustment is working (**Figure 6.16**).

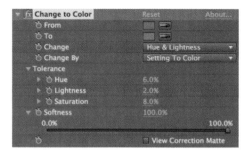

Figure 6.15 Be sure to zoom in on the image in the Composition panel to ensure a larger area for accurate sampling.

Figure 6.16 The image on the left shows the woman before the Change Color effect was applied. Using the View Correction Matte option (center), you can target an accurate adjustment (right). Notice that the red in the woman's cheeks is reduced.

Modifying Footage

As you work with video sources, you'll often wish that the images were a little different. Maybe you'll notice a distracting element or a detail in a shot that shouldn't be there. An image might be the result of a terrible key with the worst green screen you've seen in years. Or perhaps you'll be faced with the ultimate challenge, removing an object from a busy background.

Well, After Effects and Photoshop have you covered. You just need to learn a few new tools and how to force some old favorites to act differently.

Cloning an Object in After Effects

We've all seen it. The crew comes back from lunch; their bodies are more focused on digesting a big lunch than thinking about the complexities of the scene. As you review the clips, you see that a C-stand appears in the corner of the shot or maybe it's a boom mike that dips into the frame. Don't worry; you can fix these errors with a little selective duplication.

The Clone Stamp tool lets you copy pixels from one area (or even time) and place them into another. You can copy pixels and apply them to the same layer (**Figure 6.17**) or to a new layer entirely.

Figure 6.17 If you're dealing with a simple background, cloning is easy; just be certain to keep strokes parallel to the problem area to avoid subtle shifts in the background.

NOTES

If you need to clone to an empty layer, you'll have to use two viewers (one for each layer). Click inside the viewer to select it, press Command+Option+Shift+N (Ctrl+Alt+Shift+N) to split to two viewers, and then lock one of them to the current composition.

If you have a more complex background, you'll need to take a little more care to get an accurate clone. Like with all the painting tools, you'll need to open the footage in the Layer panel. Double-click in the Timeline panel to open the layer (**Figure 6.18**). Select the Clone Stamp tool in the Tools panel.

You'll use two panels to control the Clone Stamp tool. The first is the Brushes panel. Be sure to use a large enough brush to minimize the number of strokes you add. Each click creates a new stroke and can quickly make the effect more complex to manage. You also may want a soft-edged brush to blend the image better.

The second panel you'll use is the Timeline panel. You can open the Paint effect in the Timeline panel to see complete controls (**Figure 6.19**). The Aligned option is good for making multiple strokes to create a bigger paint effect. Deselect Aligned if you want to keep sampling from the same point with each new stroke.

Figure 6.18 To make more room for cloning, hover your pointer over the Layer panel, and then press the ` (accent) key to maximize it temporarily (it's the one next to the number 1 at the top of the keyboard). To switch back, just press the key again.

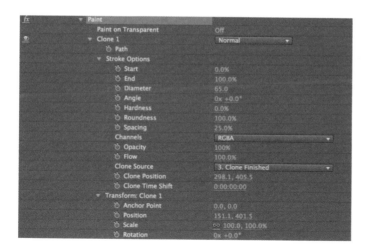

Figure 6.19 The Timeline panel offers precise controls for the Clone Stamp stroke.

You can also use the Lock Source Time option to offset the cloning across time. This can be useful to remove a moving element (such as a dipped boom microphone) or a temporary blemish (like video dropout).

When you're ready to clone, hold down the Option (Alt) key and click on a source point (**Figure 6.20**). Be sure to select an area with the texture or pixels you want to use. Hold down the Shift+Option (Shift+Alt) keys to get a preview of the cloning area (**Figure 6.21**).

Figure 6.20 Look for a clearly defined area that has the pattern you intend to use. Make sure it is free of unwanted pixels in the surrounding areas so you have room to clone.

Figure 6.21 Carefully align your brush so the new strokes are accurately placed. The overlay preview is a useful way to position your strokes.

Next, simply click and drag in the window to brush copied pixels (**Figure 6.22**). Remember that the Clone effect is applied from the position of the current time indicator forward. You can drag the handles for each stroke in the Timeline panel to adjust the duration of it.

Figure 6.22 The unwanted bulge in the brick wall was removed. To further guide the viewer's eye to the subject, a vignette was added (see Chapter 5, "Stylizing Footage," for details).

Advanced Cloning in Photoshop

You'll find a very similar Clone Stamp tool in Photoshop with most of the same abilities as its After Effects counterpart. You can offset strokes in time, preview strokes with onion skinning, and more.

So why turn to Photoshop? Well, there are three reasons:

▶ **Speed.** If you have a simple fix, Photoshop may be faster. You can clone to an empty layer above the video clip (just create an empty layer and then set the Clone Stamp tool to Sample All Layers). This individual layer can then be left floating above the shot. This works well for locked-off material.

▶ **Complexity.** If the shot is very complex, you may need to do more than just clone a few pixels. Photoshop offers several advanced painting tools that let you create a more detailed overlay (**Figure 6.23**).

Figure 6.23 A product shot needed to be modified to remove a branded product from the scene. A new faceplate was created in Photoshop using the video layer as reference. The shot was recomposited in After Effects, and the yellow cables were keyed out and composited on top. Footage courtesy Data Robotics, Inc.—www.drobo.com.

► **Advanced tools.** Photoshop offers additional tools that you can use to clone pixels. The Healing Brush, Spot Healing Brush, and Patch tools are useful to generate new pixels based on a selection. Instead of merely copying pixels, these tools can generate new pixels that match the tone and texture of their neighbors but avoid obvious patching (**Figure 6.24**).

Figure 6.24 The Spot Healing Brush quickly created a new pattern to remove the product logo. No sampling was needed because the tool created a new texture from the neighboring pixels.

Fixing Poorly Shot Keys

Green screen footage is a primary source of motion graphics design. Whether you need head shots for a show open or product shots for a commercial spot, the benefits of green screen are numerous—unless of course the footage was shot poorly (**Figure 6.25**). We've seen lots of bad keying footage, and the number one culprit is a poorly lit background.

Figure 6.25 This particular clip is so bad that we had to hide the subject. The crew forgot to turn on the light for the background. In the end, the client opted for a reshoot, but we still decided to play with the footage.

What do you do when keying won't work? Well, you try to pull mattes. You'll find this particular shot on the book's DVD, so you can explore this approach. The important thing to remember is that you need to change your mind-set. There are several ways to tackle bad chroma key. Here are two to try the next time you're faced with a poor clip.

The approach we use most often is a matte key. It is usually possible to push a clip far enough to create a good transparency. Unfortunately, you might destroy the quality of the subject. So, the solution is to use two copies of the footage.

Leave the original shot on the bottom layer. You can use Auto Contrast and Auto Color effects to attempt to get a better-looking subject. Simply color correct this layer so the person or product looks good (don't worry about the backdrop).

On the top copy, you need to create a matte. Mattes are typically black and white (with gray areas signifying partial transparency). Creating a matte can be performed in two ways:

▶ **Calculations.** You can try the Calculations effect to combine color channels into a grayscale image. Be sure to use two channels and create a high-contrast gray layer. You can then tweak the shot with a Levels effect (**Figure 6.26**).

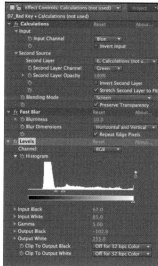

Figure 6.26 The Calculations technique works well with some footage but not all. Here the man's suit is getting a bit lost due to some unwanted transparency.

▶ **Hijacking Keylight.** Normally, the Keylight effect is used for creating a straight chroma key effect. It does offer a matte view, however, and this is the key to success.

Creating a Matte from Color

With adequate color information, you can successfully pull a clean matte. The black and white image can be used to cut a hole in the underlying video layer. Here is the process simplified. You may need to tweak it slightly depending on the footage you're using. In this case, our clip lacks much color and exposure details (**Figure 6.27**).

Figure 6.27 The crew left the lights for the background turned off.

1. Force a balanced image with the Equalize effect. We find the RGB method works best for footage that's meant to be keyed. Tweak the Amount slider until you have a good green to work with (**Figure 6.28**).

Figure 6.28 The Equalize effect attempts to redistribute the color and luminance values evenly.

2. Use a Levels adjustment to increase the brightness of the clip. It's okay for the subject to blow out, so focus on the background (**Figure 6.29**).

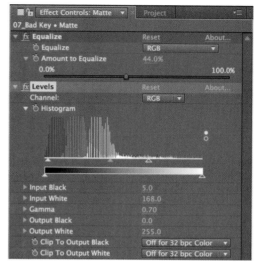

Figure 6.29 Adjusting the Levels sliders individually for each channel helps brighten and balance the image.

3. Use a Channel Blur effect to slightly blur the background. Only blur to the green channel for green screen (**Figure 6.30**) and the blue channel for blue screen.

Figure 6.30 You'll find an easy preset for channel blurring by typing the word keying into the Effects & Presets search field.

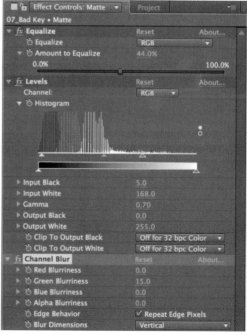

4. Use the Keylight effect to pull a chroma key. Instead of viewing the Final Result, leave the effect set to Screen Matte (**Figure 6.31**). Normally, this view is used internally by the effect to create the transparency, but you can hijack it as a matte layer.

Figure 6.31 Be sure to use the Screen Matte controls to refine your matte. You'll want proper contrast between the background and foreground, and you'll want to limit the presence of gray.

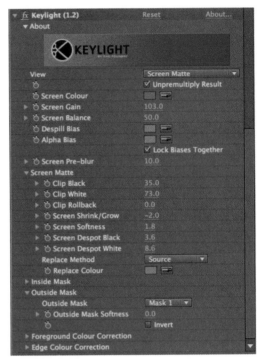

5. With the matte layer placed above the fill layer in the Timeline, you are ready to create transparency. Set the track matte for the fill layer to Luma (**Figure 6.32**).

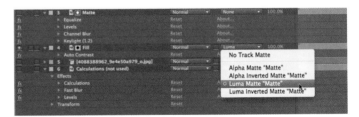

Figure 6.32 Renaming your layers in the Timeline makes it easier to track their function.

6. Finish out the key with any additional tweaks (such as vignettes or color correction) (**Figure 6.33**).

Figure 6.33 Despite challenging source material, a suitable key was achieved. Background image by Bryan Ochalla. Creative Commons.

Rotoscoping with the Roto Brush

The task of separating a foreground object from the background is traditionally quite challenging. The process, referred to as rotoscoping, can be time-consuming, involving masks and brush strokes with lots of work by hand. Of course, After Effects CS5 changes all that with the addition of the Roto Brush.

The Roto Brush requires only a few strokes, and then the tool can calculate transparency. You merely need to indicate to After Effects what a foreground is and what a background is. After Effects can then intelligently propagate your strokes throughout the entire clip.

The Initial Effect

The Roto Brush is a very useful tool with several options. Here are a few suggestions for an efficient workflow:

▶ **Find a good frame.** Double-click a clip to open it in the Layer panel. Drag the current time indicator so you can see that the desired subject is fully in the frame. Try to minimize overlap (**Figure 6.34**). This frame is called the base frame.

Figure 6.34 A reflector was accidently left in the shot behind this actor (look over the man's shoulder for the white and gray object). Footage courtesy the National Foundation for Credit Counseling—www.DebtAdvice.org.

Your layers must be in Full Quality mode for After Effects to make accurate strokes.

▶ **Add your first stroke.** Activate the Roto Brush tool by pressing Option+W (Alt+W). Drag down the center of the object to create the first stroke (**Figure 6.35**). When you release, After Effects takes a moment to update the first stroke. A magenta outline appears to signify the foreground object (**Figure 6.36**).

Figure 6.35 Use a large brush to quickly paint the initial stroke.

Figure 6.36 The Roto Brush typically produces a fairly accurate edge on the first try.

▶ **Add a background stroke.** Define the background to let After Effects know what information to discard. You can Option+drag (Alt+drag) to create a background stroke (**Figure 6.37**).

Figure 6.37 Red strokes define the area to be subtracted.

▶ **Add more strokes.** Keep drawing foreground and background strokes until an accurate selection is made. Try to make the segmentation on the base frame as accurate as possible. It serves as a guide for all the other frames, so getting it right is important (**Figure 6.38**).

Figure 6.38 Take the time to get a good edge. You'll further refine it with the Refine Matte properties in a moment.

▶ **Fix more frames.** Press the Page Down key to move forward a frame. After Effects will keep building the Roto Brush effect using motion tracking, optical flow, and other techniques to propagate the information between frames. As needed, use more strokes to refine the matte as you move through time.

▶ **Define the range.** The Roto Brush effect is only applied for part of the clip (20 frames forward and 20 frame backward). This is indicated by small arrows that appear in the span bar. As you add more corrective strokes, the effect's duration expands. You can also drag the range in the span bar to increase it (**Figure 6.39**).

Figure 6.39 By default, the Roto Brush effect only lasts for 40 frames. Be sure to define the proper range for your shot. You may need to create new spans for parts of the clip that are significantly different from each other.

TIP

The Reduce Chatter option can minimize erratic changes from frame to frame. A higher value includes more frames in the calculation of edges.

▶ **Refine the matte.** The Roto Brush effect offers a Refine Matte option (**Figure 6.40**). You can have After Effects compensate for motion blur (for faster-moving objects) as well as decontaminate colors at the edges. Press Option+5 (Alt+5) to toggle the alpha boundary and view your results.

Figure 6.40 Adjusting properties like Smooth, Feather, and Refine Matte can clean up your edges.

Complete the Shot

Once you've extracted the object, there are several things you can do with the rotoscoped clip. You can place the clip over a new background or into a graphic sequence. You might also want to modify the original background by desaturating or blurring it to give more precedence to the subject (**Figure 6.41**).

Figure 6.41 The reflector target over the actor's shoulder was removed using the Clone Stamp tool. Because the actor was recomposited on top of the painted background, we did not need to be very accurate with our cloning to hide the unintended clutter.

What about a complex scene? If you have multiple subjects, use multiple clips. It's easier to let the Roto Brush track a single subject; just duplicate your clip and use another Roto Brush effect for a second subject. The Roto Brush effect can also be combined with traditional techniques like brush strokes and masks (**Figure 6.42**).

Figure 6.42 The second actor's head is a dark silhouette on a dark background. Although the Roto Brush worked well here, we favored a simple mask drawn with the Pen tool and then keyframed its position.

Retiming Footage

Getting a shot to time out can be quite tricky. Sure, if your clients would pick the music and storyboard everything ahead of time, timing would be effortless. But that just never seems to happen. Even with good planning, there's always the human element, difference in performance, or even just gravity that seems to interfere. After Effects offers several ways to affect the timing and speed of clips. Knowing which one to choose goes a long way toward your success.

Frame Rate Conversion

The need to convert frame rates is quickly emerging as a top technical challenge. Gone are the simple days of Standard Definition video workflows. In their place are multiformat cameras and the many frame rates of High Definition (HD) video.

Conforming a Clip

An easy way to change the rate of a clip is to conform it. This can be done by changing how After Effects interprets the clip. Conforming changes the rate at which the frames are played back. The clip will be slowed down or sped up depending on the rate you choose. No frames are discarded with this method, nor are new ones created.

1. Select the footage item in the Project panel and choose File > Interpret Footage > Main.

2. Select the Conform To Frame Rate and enter a new frame rate for Frames Per Second (**Figure 6.43**). Double-check the rest of the settings. When you're satisfied, click OK.

NOTES

If you conform a clip, you can throw the audio out of sync with the video (or hear a change in speed). You may want to stretch audio and video layers with the Time-stretch property.

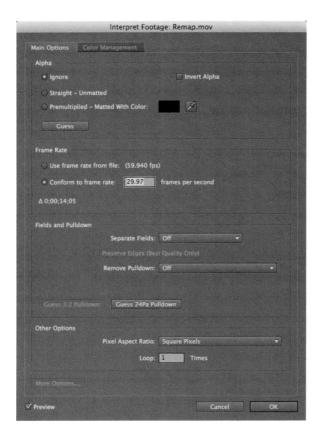

Figure 6.43 The source footage has a frame rate of 23.976, whereas the intended frame rate is 29.97. This mismatch in footage versus composition frame rate can be resolved in several ways.

Resampling Footage

If you place a clip into a composition and their frame rates differ, After Effects will convert the footage to match. This means that the composition frame rate specifies how many times per second the original source clip is sampled. The difference between the source footage frame rate and the composition frame rate can affect how smoothly footage plays back.

A very common scenario is the need to convert 24p material to a different frame rate. For example, many people shoot 24p for the "film look." This rate is fine if you're outputting to the Web, DVD, Blu-ray, and of course film, but it doesn't work for broadcast. For television, you'll likely need to convert to 29.97 for NTSC or 25 for PAL.

Retiming is fairly straightforward. You can import individual clips, a self-contained movie of the finished edit, or a Premiere Pro sequence and place it into an After Effects composition. Set the composition frame rate to match your desired output (**Figure 6.44**).

Figure 6.44 You should try all three resampling methods to see the different effects on your clip. The method you choose may vary depending on the source material. Footage courtesy the National Foundation for Consumer Credit Counseling— www.DebtAdvice.org.

Once you have the footage placed into a composition, you can choose three different ways to process the speed change. These methods are listed from lowest to highest quality (as well as fastest to slowest render times). Click the Frame Blending switch in the Timeline to change methods (**Figure 6.45**):

Figure 6.45 The three frame blending methods are accessed with the Frame Blending switch.

▶ **No Frame Blending.** If you leave the Frame Blending switch deselected, After Effects will simply repeat frames to pad out the clip (**Figure 6.46**).

Figure 6.46 Frames are duplicated to pad out the shot. Every fifth frame is repeated in a 24 to 29.97 frame rate conversion.

▶ **Frame Mix.** The Frame Mix mode takes less time to render and produces results by mixing two frames together. The frames are overlaid on top of each other, and this creates a ghosted image but avoids the jerkiness caused by the No Frame Blending option (**Figure 6.47**).

NOTES

Be sure to select the Enable Frame Blending switch at the top of the Timeline panel to allow frame blending in the composition.

Figure 6.47 You can see the two frames overlaid onto each other to create a new frame.

▶ **Pixel Motion.** The Pixel Motion mode provides the best results. New frames are created by comparing surrounding frames and generating a new frame that essentially morphs in between (**Figure 6.48**).

NOTES

The Quality setting for a layer also affects frame blending. For the highest image quality, be sure the layer is set to Best mode.

Figure 6.48 Pixel Motion takes the longest, but the quality is worth it. Thanks to motion estimation, the new frames produced are very crisp.

Time Remapping

One of the most useful (and least used) commands in After Effects is Time Remapping. The command offers total control over playback speed—rewind, freeze, speed-up, and more. Time Remapping is very useful in motion graphics design because it lets you fluidly control the timing of elements so they can sync up to music or time-based cue points.

Many find Time Remapping difficult, so here's a simplified explanation. Imagine that you have a clip that is 10 seconds long. When you turn on Time Remapping for a layer, two keyframes are added. The first key frame has a value of 0;00;00;00 and the last is 0;00;09;29. If you were to drag the second keyframe closer to the first, the footage would play back quicker. If you stretched the two keyframes apart, it would play slower. Easy enough?

Here is where it gets a little tricky: You can add as many keyframes as you want. Those frames can have any value assigned to them that relates to a frame in the original clip. You can then create a variety of time-based effects.

Controlling Direction

With Time Remapping, you can use keyframes to create complex motion. With each keyframe you can move forward or backward through time (you can even repeat the value across two adjacent frames to create a freeze frame). The controls become fairly intuitive after you've spent about five minutes with them. The easiest way to understand how keyframes work is to drag left to right to scrub their values (**Figure 6.49**). Once the keyframes are set, experiment with expanding or contracting them to change speed.

NOTES

When you use Time Remapping on a layer, the audio changes with it. You can create all sorts of audio effects this way, including pitch changes or reversing audio. Think of the fun you can have.

TIP

If you want to drift to a slow stop or get a gentle start, you can use Keyframe Assistants (such as Ease Out or Ease In) to add transitions related to keyframes.

Figure 6.49 Scrubbing the keyframe value makes it easy to choose the desired frame.

Let's give Time Remapping a try:

1. Select a layer in the Timeline panel that you want to remap, and then choose Layer > Time > Enable Time Remapping.

   Two keyframes are added by default at the beginning of the layer and one at the end.

2. Drag one of the existing frames to change the speed of a clip or add new keyframes and adjust to taste.

3. To smooth out motion, enable frame blending for the composition, and then turn on Frame Mix or Pixel Motion for the layer.

4. If needed, drag the layer's end point to extend (or trim) the layer. You can use the shortcut Option+] (Alt+]) to trim the Out point to the current time indicator.

Refining with the Graph Editor

Another way to work with Time Remapping is to use the Graph Editor. Add your keyframes in the standard Timeline view first, and then click the Graph Editor button to switch views (**Figure 6.50**).

TIP

You can use the J and K keys to move through the Time Remap keyframes in the Timeline.

If you want to create a smooth transition between speeds, change keyframes from linear to Bezier or Auto Bezier.

Figure 6.50 The Graph Editor makes it easy to understand speed changes.

When you make adjustments in the Graph Editor, the change is represented in the steepness of the line. The steeper the incline, the faster the speed. If you reverse time, the graph will slope downhill. As you drag a keyframe, you'll see the Preview window and the time in the tool tip update.

Here are some general tips when working with the Graph Editor:

▶ Dragging a keyframe down slows a layer's playback. (If the footage is reversed, drag up.)

▶ Dragging a keyframe up speeds up the playback. (If the footage is reversed, drag down.)

▶ To reverse playback, drag a keyframe lower than the previous keyframe.

▶ To freeze playback, you can copy and paste a keyframe so it repeats. You can also choose Animation > Toggle Hold Keyframe.

▶ To expand or contract keyframes, select all the time re-mapped keyframes in the Timeline. Hold down the Option (Alt) key and drag the last frame. The keyframes will expand or contract like an accordion.

Putting It All Together

Want to know a secret? The most complex techniques are really just a bunch of basic techniques strung together. The advanced pros know how to identify problems and then map the right skill to solve those problems. In this chapter you learned several real-world techniques; now let's explore how they can be combined.

On a recent project, we were producing a product trailer for a client. In one shot, we had an instance where cables were being plugged into a piece of computer hardware (**Figure 6.51**). What we didn't know was that lights were supposed to blink (if the other end of the cables were plugged into Ethernet ports). A reshoot would take too long, so we had to get creative.

Figure 6.51 The lights on the unit are supposed to blink. What's a designer to do in the eleventh hour?

The first issue was to get the needed lights. Instead of worrying about matching the angle and size while shooting, we simply shot the lights square on (**Figure 6.52**). By shooting the lights in the dark, only the lights showed up; the rest of the shot fell off to black.

Figure 6.52 Thanks to affordable HD cameras (like HDSLR and AVCHD models), it's getting easier for motion graphics artists to keep a camera around.

The lights were then sized in a composition and rotated in 3D space to align them to the hardware. Placing the layers into Screen mode dropped out the darkest areas, leaving only the lights on top (**Figure 6.53**).

Figure 6.53 Promoting the layers to 3D space made it easier to align them to the source footage.

Once the lights were in place, it quickly became apparent that the cables needed to be extracted and laid back on top of the light layers. In this case, we used Keylight to extract the layers and then used the earlier trick we showed you of leaving Keylight set to the View Screen Matte option (**Figure 6.54**).

Figure 6.54 Keylight can be used to create a matte for the blue wires (left). Once you have the data, you can use a Luma or Luma Inverted track matte (center). The final results can then be assembled in the Timeline.

To complete this shot, the hand needed to be isolated and composited back on top. The Roto Brush was well suited to extract the hand from the footage so it could be composited back into the scene (**Figure 6.55**).

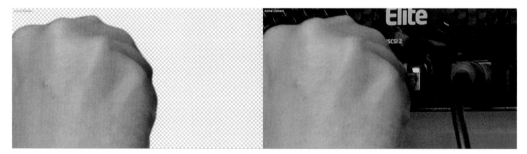

Figure 6.55 The Roto Brush made quick work of extracting the hand to its own layer.

Learning how to spot problems and quickly identify solutions comes with practice. But in this case, a complex fix ended up being less than 30 minutes of labor.

7

Designing Backgrounds

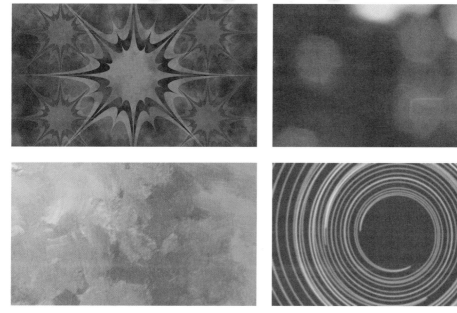

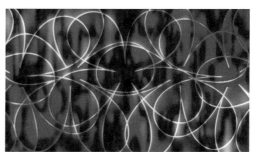

I hardly ever stretch the canvas before painting.

—Jackson Pollock

Designing Backgrounds

As a motion graphics designer, you often have to work harder than other types of designers. Unlike those in the print world who can usually get by with a white background for the printed page, you must put more thought into your projects.

Motion backgrounds have become a staple of broadcast and motion graphics design. In fact, entire companies exist just to create and sell backdrops. The use of backgrounds (whether static or dynamic) is essential to good motion graphics design. Fortunately, certain features in After Effects and Photoshop can be combined to create some fantastic "wallpaper."

Approaching Background Design

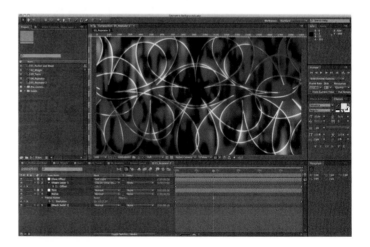

When creating backgrounds for a motion graphics project, you might be surprised at how much thought can go into the process. It's important to realize that you are creating the foundation for the completed project. Just as you can't build an architectural masterpiece on a swamp, you'll need to find a solid base for the rest of the animated layers to come.

Role of Backgrounds

The greatest challenge when it comes to creating and using backgrounds is that you need to show proper restraint. A background is just that—a background. Would you expect to see a gaudy patterned print at an art museum? You need to find the proper balance between an interesting background and preserving the visual hierarchy of information.

We understand why the challenge exists. As the stock animation industry has grown, competition has led to more and more companies trying to "stand out." This means that designs have become busier, louder, and generally obnoxious.

In contrast, let's look at the print industry. Sure, a designer might use a patterned paper or a colored backdrop but never in a way that negatively impacts the readability of text or diminishes the value of a photograph. Creating a background is truly an invisible art. The goal is to make something that adds to the overall design but does not stand out.

Gathering Sources

Creating backgrounds is a varied process. We find that the best backgrounds use source ingredients (as opposed to just combining effects). We recommend you consider the following options when designing them:

TIP

Need an instant background? Just take a video clip and apply a very heavy blur to it. If you need to unify it a little, try using the CC Tint or Colorama effect.

▶ **Footage plates.** Footage is one of the easiest sources to use, because it's already moving. Often, abstract or soft-focused footage works best (**Figure 7.1**).

▶ **Patterns and textures.** The use of patterns or textures is an easy way to create complex blending (**Figure 7.2**). These can include photos of natural items, scanned images, or generated textures.

▶ **Vector shapes.** Many backgrounds are created with repeating geometric patterns (**Figure 7.3**). These can be made using Adobe Illustrator, but you'll find the Shape Layer feature in After Effects to be robust as well.

▶ **Photos.** A well-composed photo can also serve as a background (**Figure 7.4**). If you're shooting your own photos, be sure to think of balancing negative space with the subject of the photo.

Figure 7.1 We'll explore footage creation strategies in Chapter 13, "DVD and Blu-ray Design."

Figure 7.2 You'll find an assortment of pattern layers in the Chapter_07_Media folder and can experiment with creating more in Photoshop.

Figure 7.3 Shape layers are easy to use and very versatile. You can create complex geometric shapes in just a few minutes.

Figure 7.4 A well-composed photo creates a natural frame. Here a skyline photo blends with a background texture and some color to create a pleasing background.

Importance of Looping

When creating an animated background, it's considered necessary that motion repeat seamlessly (called a loop). Looping ensures that a background can repeat infinitely, which can be highly desirable because it gives you design flexibility. Some uses for looping backgrounds include the following:

▶ DVD and Blu-ray Discs typically use motion menus. These often feature animated backgrounds. A seamless loop ensures a pleasant viewing experience.

▶ Digital signage (such as signs at airports or retail stores) is designed to be viewed in passing. The viewer often joins an animation "in progress." Ensuring that the animation repeats smoothly creates a less jarring moment for the audience.

▶ Broadcast and live events often depend on backgrounds. Unfortunately, the required duration may be unknown. Having a background loop means that it won't run out on you when it's playing back live. Animations can be repeated many times over to create any duration (or even an infinite one).

Using Generate and Noise Effects

One of the easiest ways to create seamless backgrounds is to use effects within After Effects. Although After Effects includes several effects, we've handpicked our four favorite that are flexible and easy to use: 4-Color Gradient, Cell Pattern, Radio Waves, and Fractal Noise.

4-Color Gradient

The 4-Color Gradient effect (Effect > Generate > 4-Color Gradient) is an easy way to generate gradients within After Effects (**Figure 7.5**). The gradient is created using four control points. You can assign a color to each point and specify its position. In fact, both color and position can be keyframed to create an animation. After Effects uses four solid-color circles blended together for the effect.

1. For best results, apply the 4-Color Gradient effect to an adjustment layer. You can use it in an 8-bpc or 16-bpc color project.

2. Assign the desired colors to the Color 1–Color 4 wells.

3. Increase the Blend Value to create a more gradual transition between colors. To reduce any further banding, increase the Jitter setting.

TIP

Backgrounds can also be enhanced with a bloom effect or vignette. Use the techniques you learned in Chapter 5,"Stylizing Footage."

Figure 7.5 Try combining an organic texture with the 4-Color Gradient effect. A great source for free texture layers is www.TextureKing.com.

4. Adjust the Opacity and Blending Mode of the effect. Although you'll find sliders for both in the effect, you'll have better control blending and fading the adjustment layer instead.

Cell Pattern

The Cell Pattern effect generates a loopable pattern based on cellular noise algorithms. With 12 patterns to choose from and several controls for size, contrast, and speed, you'll find the effect very versatile.

1. Choose a method from the Cell Pattern menu. Some patterns are sharp and angular, whereas others are more organic. Experiment to your heart's content, because you can change methods at any time (**Figure 7.6**).

2. Adjust the contrast of the effect to create the desired pattern. You can use the Invert check box to swap values of luminance. The Contrast/Sharpness slider modifies the overall detail level of the cells.

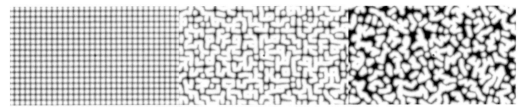

Figure 7.6 Here are three of the 12 cell patterns. From left to right, Plates, Pillow, and Tubular.

Figure 7.7 Different Disperse values were used to modify the Cell Pattern. A value of 0 creates a uniform shape. Increasing the value to 0.50 adds more randomness. A greater value of 1.50 starts to create very irregular shapes.

3. Modify the randomness of the cells with the Disperse slider. The lower the number, the more uniform the pattern (**Figure 7.7**). If you increase Disperse above 1.0, be sure to set the layer to Best Quality.

4. Adjust the size and position with the Size and Disperse sliders.

   The key to making an animated background is the Evolution option. As you animate evolution, the pattern will change over time. By default, revolutions are progressive, which means each cycle is an entirely unique value. However, there is a way to create a seamless loop point.

5. Under Evolution Options, select the Cycle Evolution check box to ensure that a revolution for the Evolution slider makes the pattern repeat.

6. Add a keyframe near the start of the composition for Evolution for 0x and one at the end for a full number (such as 2x). By using full rotations, you'll create a loopable pattern (**Figure 7.8**).

TIP

You can produce a different pattern by changing the Random Seed slider. Do not keyframe this value; rather, drag to choose a different starting pattern. You can also adjust the Size or Offset settings.

Figure 7.8 Using full rotations with the Cycle Evolution option enabled creates a loopable pattern.

7. To create a richly layered background, blend multiple layers with the Cell Pattern effect applied. You can stylize the background with the Colorama effect and a vignette as well (**Figure 7.9**).

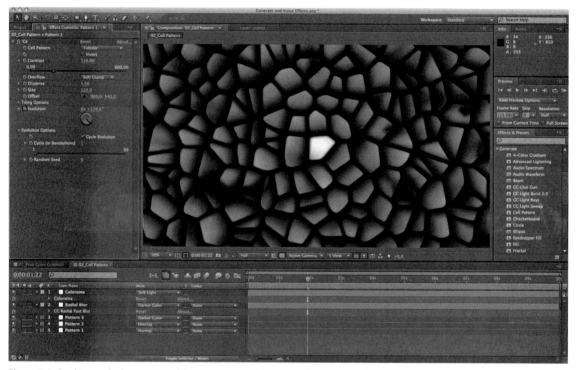

Figure 7.9 Stacking multiple instances of the Cell Pattern effect can create depth and visual interest.

Radio Waves

The Radio Waves effect creates a radiating wave pattern from an effect control point. The effect is quite versatile and can make a variety of wave shapes. You can also bounce the waves back from the edges of the composition with the Reflection control (**Figure 7.10**).

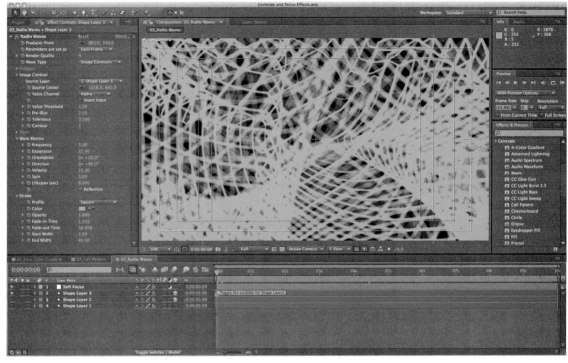

Figure 7.10 Reflected waves bounce back from the composition edges to create a fuller pattern.

The effect offers several controls and just screams to be played with. Here are a few of the most relevant controls that will give you immediate results:

▶ **Wave Type.** You can use a polygon, the edge of an image, or a mask. A cool effect can be had by using a shape layer and then animating that shape while using the edge method.

▶ **Frequency.** Experiment with high frequency settings to create several waves. Be sure to use smooth contours to create a gentle stroke.

▶ **Image Contour.** You can trace the edges of an object (even a moving object). Try using a stroke on a keyed object or an animated graphic.

▶ **Parameters Are Set At.** If you'd like the wave to evolve over time, choose the Each Frame option. This option is best if you've animated the object creating the Image Contours for the wave.

TIP

If you'd like to create a seamless wave, be sure to set the Lifespan of your waves to match the duration of your composition. This trick works if your Producer Point and Source Layer match at the start and end of the composition as well.

▶ **Wave Motion.** The Frequency option offers great controls over how frequently waves are generated. The greater the frequency, the more waves. You can also have additional movement with Expansion, Orientation, Velocity, and Spin. The Lifespan of a wave can be adjusted. The longer the life span, the more strokes onscreen at once.

▶ **Stroke.** Use the Fade-in Time and Fade-out Time to create smooth transitions between the stroke's entrance and exit.

Fractal Noise

The Fractal Noise effect creates results using Perlin noise. It can be used to create organic-looking backgrounds and textures (as well as to simulate natural effects like fog, water, fire, and lava). The effect is quite useful because it works even in 32-bpc color.

This effect is possibly the most flexible effect you'll find for generating patterns (**Figure 7.11**). It's literally a one-stop-shop and can save you time and money. On the surface it looks like a simple cloud generator, but dig a little deeper and you'll find much more.

NOTES

If you'd like the pattern to be up and running on the first frame of your composition, set the In point for the layer to −5:00. This pre-roll will ensure that the stroke has sufficiently built up.

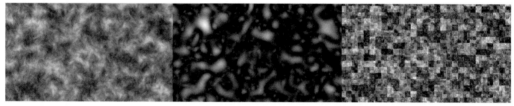

Figure 7.11 These three patterns were all created with the Fractal Noise effect. Different Fractal Type and Noise Type settings were used.

CLOSE-UP

The Origins of Perlin Noise

Perlin noise is named for Ken Perlin, a visual effects creator who worked on the film *Tron* as the synthavision technologist. The effect creates noise that is based on a procedural texture primitive. It appears random but in fact uses multiple copies of the same particle scaled to different sizes.

Here are a few of the most significant controls:

▶ **Fractal Type.** Choose different effects from the Fractal Type menu. Each type generates different random values.

▶ **Noise Type.** There are four different types of interpolation to use between the random values in the noise grid. These methods further modify the fractal type and can produce dramatically different results. Together, Fractal Type and Noise Type create 68 different possible combinations.

- **Transform.** Twirl open the Transform properties to find a collection of controls that dramatically affect shapes. Be sure to try the Perspective Offset option, which simulates different depths for the noise.

- **Complexity.** This slider determines the number of noise layers that are used to create the fractal noise. Increasing the number adds more depth, but also increases render time. You can also experiment with the Size and Contrast sliders to get various results as well.

- **Evolution.** The Evolution controls are where the animation is easiest to control. As you learned earlier, be sure to select the Cycle Evolution option. You can then keyframe full rotations of the Evolution property to create a seamless looping background.

Be sure to colorize the grayscale textures using one of the many colorizing effects at your disposal. CC Toner (**Figure 7.12**) and Colorama both work well to remap the grayscale values to a vibrant color. Also, experiment with edges; both blurs and emboss effects work well.

TIP

In the Transform controls, you can deselect Uniform Scaling. This is a great way to create water or wood-like textures.

NOTES

Although the Turbulent Noise effect provides several advanced controls, it lacks the Cycle Evolution option needed for a looping texture. If you just need to make an animated texture that renders quickly, give it a shot. But if you want that texture to loop, stick with Fractal Noise.

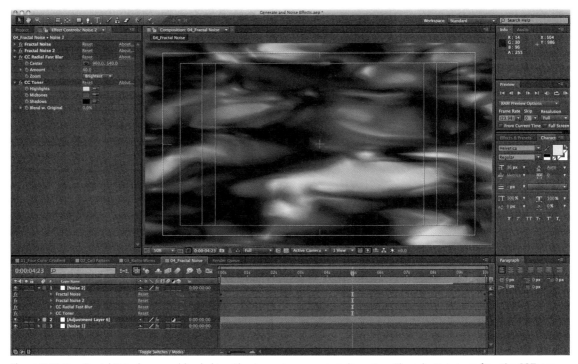

Figure 7.12 Two Fractal Noise layers are blended together to create a more complex pattern. The color tint comes from the CC Toner effect, which uses three colors to tint the image based on tonal values.

Browsing Backgrounds with Adobe Bridge

After Effects comes with several animation presets. A preset contains a combination of effects and keyframe values to create an animation. Presets can be easily accessed by choosing Animation > Browse Presets (**Figure 7.13**). By default, you'll find 13 categories to choose from, including Behaviors, Transitions, and Sound Effects. You'll also find Backgrounds tucked in a few places:

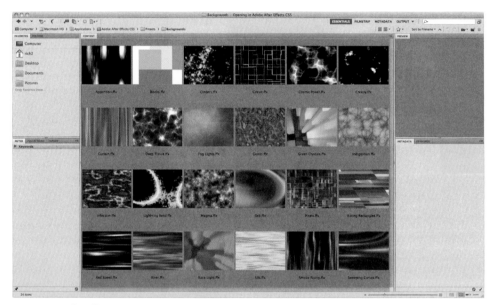

Figure 7.13 After Effects includes 24 built-in backgrounds that showcase the many options available through effects.

▶ **Backgrounds.** Contains 24 different backgrounds to choose from.
▶ **Shapes > Backgrounds.** Five backgrounds created using the After Effects Shape Layer feature.
▶ **Synthetics.** Eleven textures and background elements generated by effects.

Adobe also offers a secret set of additional presets. How secret? Well, they're made by Adobe, but they don't ship with the program. You'll find them on the Adobe Exchange community site, which offers additional downloads and resources for Adobe applications (www.Adobe.com/exchange). A direct link to download them is http://tinyurl.com/aepresets:

▶ **Backgrounds 2.** Seven additional background textures.
▶ **Elements 2.** A series of textures and shapes that can be layered or modified to work as backgrounds.

To apply a preset, simply double-click it in Adobe Bridge.

Animating Graphic Textures

You've already learned how to create looping backgrounds using After Effects; however, things are going to get better with a little teamwork. By combining the power of Photoshop and After Effects, you can create even more customized looping backgrounds. Because Photoshop is a rich graphics tool, much more variety can be had in the final result.

Let's explore two very different techniques that both produce excellent results:

▶ **Seamless patterns.** By using seamless patterns and the Offset command, looping backgrounds are a snap.

▶ **Gentle fade.** Knowing how to bury a transition can make looping a texture easy.

The Offset Technique

You'll first use seamless patterns and the Offset command to create a background. This underused technique wraps an image around your document. In other words, pixels push from one side and reappear on the opposite side. Depending on the desired movement of your background, you can offset horizontally, vertically, or both.

The technique is fairly straightforward and is easy to use. To begin, let's create two seamless patterns in Photoshop.

Building the First Pattern

The use of seamless patterns is a great way to make a repeating texture. There are many ways to go about creating a specialized texture; we prefer the simplest route. It is best to offset several simple layers than one complex layer. This will introduce more motion into the animated background.

1. Launch Photoshop and create a new document sized for video. For this example, choose the Film & Video > HDV/HDTV 720p preset (**Figure 7.14**).

NOTES

When designing seamless patterns, be sure to size the canvas to be an even width and height. When you use the Offset command, you'll want to move the image an even value to create the smoothest motion.

Figure 7.14 Stick with the Photoshop document presets to ensure properly sized video files.

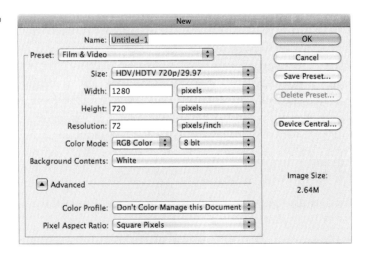

2. Load the Default colors of black and white by pressing the D key, and then run the Clouds filter (Filter > Render > Clouds).

   Now the cloud pattern needs to be offset. This filter pushes an image off the screen and rewraps the pixel data to the other side of the image.

3. Offset the image 600 pixels horizontally (Filter > Other > Offset). Be sure to specify that you want the pixels to wrap around the edge. If you want to move the background vertically, you must offset vertically. If you want to move the background diagonally, offset horizontally and vertically.

4. If visible, blend away the seams. Use the Spot Healing Brush (J) with soft edges. If needed, you can follow up with the Clone Stamp tool.

5. Repeat the Offset filter by pressing Command+F (Ctrl+F) to check for seams. Clone or heal as needed. Repeat until the seams are invisible (**Figure 7.15**).

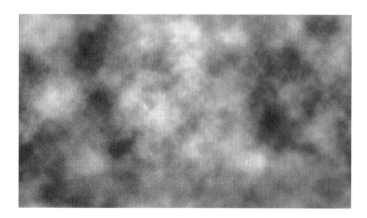

6. Save the layer as a TIFF file that After Effects will recognize.

Building the Second Pattern

To create a sense of movement, two textures must be moved across each other. You now have a simple background that can be looped. To complement this simple element, you can build additional textures or objects. Here is one additional recipe for another layer:

1. Create another new document sized with the Film & Video > HDV/HDTV 720p preset.

2. Make a radial gradient fill layer from black to white (**Figure 7.16**) or draw a radial gradient (flatten the image if necessary).

Figure 7.16 Be sure the gradient stays centered on the screen (an easy way to do this is to use the Gradient fill layer).

3. Run the following filters (in this order).

   ▶ Run the Twirl filter set to 400 pixels eight times (Filter > Distort > Twirl).

   ▶ Run the Motion Blur (Filter > Blur > Motion Blur) at a –90˚ angle and a distance of approximately 350 pixels.

   ▶ Run the Maximum filter set to 30 pixels to smooth out the texture (Filter > Other > Maximum) (**Figure 7.17**).

Figure 7.17 This pattern is designed to be offset horizontally because both edges fade to black.

4. Save the layer as a TIFF file that After Effects will recognize.

Animating in After Effects

Once the textures are built, you can animate them in After Effects. By employing a few simple technologies (blending modes, scaling, the Offset filter, and color mapping) natural, organic motion can be achieved.

To start, create a new project and import the two graphics you just created. Drag both graphics on the new composition icon located at the bottom of the Project panel. A dialog box appears asking you for specifics on the new comp. Choose to create a Single Composition and use a duration between 15:00 and 30:00. Set the composition size to match your source graphics (in this case you'll use HDTV 720p and a frame rate of 24p).

1. Select both layers in the Timeline and press Command+D (Ctrl+D) to duplicate them. Working with multiple copies

NOTES

The animating in After Effects technique in this section can be used for simple backgrounds, or you can combine several independent layers moving at different speeds for more elaborate backgrounds.

of the same layer will create the illusion of depth (similar to the Perlin noise you read about earlier).

2. Rearrange your Timeline so you have a 1/2/1/2 stack (**Figure 7.18**). Then turn off the visibility icon for the top three layers.

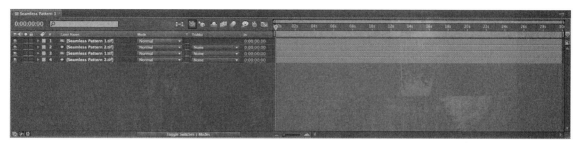

Figure 7.18 Using multiple copies creates the illusion of depth without a big increase in render time.

3. Select the bottom layer and apply the Offset effect (Effect > Distort > Offset).

The Offset effect is very simple to use once you understand it. You choose to keyframe how much the center of a layer is offset (using the Shift Center To property). Add a keyframe at the start of the layer for the default position; you can leave this keyframe unmodified.

4. Go to the end of the layer and add a second keyframe for the Shift Center To property.

Double-click on the keyframe to adjust its value. Change its measurement Units to % of composition. The keyframe currently reads 50% for both the X- and Y-axis. By adding a full 100%, the image will complete one full offset cycle. For this example, enter a value of 250% in the X-axis field to move two full cycles (**Figure 7.19**). Activate RAM preview to see your results. You should now have two full rotations.

Figure 7.19 By choosing the % of composition method, you can avoid doing math in your head. Just add a whole number for each rotation. In other words, 50% + 1 rotation = 150%; 2 rotations = 250%.

5. Activate Layer #3 and repeat the offset technique described in steps 3 and 4. Add a keyframe at the start of the layer for the default position and then at the end of the layer for three reverse rotations (−350%, 50%).

6. Adjust the blending mode and/or opacity of Layer #3 to achieve a soft look. In the example project, we used Overlay mode.

7. Activate Layer #2 and scale to 200% (it's okay in this case to scale up, because we just have a soft texture.)

8. Select Layer #4 and press U to see all the keyframes.

    Move your playhead to the start of the composition, and then click the word Offset for Layer #4. Copy the keyframes by pressing Command+C (Ctrl+C). Select Layer #2 and paste the offset keyframes.

9. Adjust the blending mode and/or opacity of Layer #2 to achieve a soft look. In the example project, we used Multiply mode.

10. Activate Layer #1 and scale to 200%.

11. Select Layer #3 and press U to see all the keyframes.

    Move your playhead to the start of the composition, and then click the word Offset for Layer #3. Copy the keyframes by pressing Command+C (Ctrl+C). Select Layer #1 and paste the offset keyframes.

12. Adjust the blending mode and/or opacity of Layer #1 (remember Shift++ and Shift+- also work in After Effects to cycle blending/transfer modes). In the example project, we used Soft Light mode at 70% opacity.

13. Add an adjustment layer at the top of your stack (Layer > New > Adjustment Layer).

    Apply a colorization effect, such as Colorama, CC Toner, or Tint. In the example, we chose Colorama with the Output Cycle set to the Ramp Red preset (**Figure 7.20**). You can also experiment with other effects on the adjustment layer, such as glows, blurs, or third-party effects.

Figure 7.20 You can use a Levels effect to clamp the Output Black or White points to keep the backdrop from becoming too bright.

14. Make sure all your quality switches are set to Best Quality, and render at the proper settings for your nonlinear editing or motion graphics application.

The Stitch in Time Technique

The second animating technique we'll show you is deceptively simple but produces great results. By using blending modes and a well-placed dissolve, it's possible to create a looping background. This technique is very versatile and will work with virtually any source layers. For this technique, you'll take three or more gradients made in Photoshop and blend them together using After Effects. These gradients can be grayscale photos, filtered layers, or preexisting files.

Preparing Textures with Photoshop

For this technique to work, you'll want to use a group of oversized grayscale textures (**Figure 7.21**). You could scale and filter in After Effects, but that is the slower method. Instead of scaling up and manipulating color and tone across time, you can process the images once they are in Photoshop and speed up rendering times.

Figure 7.21 Build up your own texture library so you can experiment with creating different animated patterns. These and additional textures are available from www.thepluginsite.com.

Here's a few ways to put Photoshop to use:

▶ Take advantage of Photoshop's excellent scaling abilities. By enlarging the gradients in Photoshop, you'll only need to scale down in After Effects.

▶ Use Photoshop's Nearest Neighbor scaling method to resize your images. You can access it in the Image Size dialog box (Image > Image Size) from the Resample Image menu.

▶ Soften any artifacts using the Median filter (Filter > Noise > Median). A low value of 5–10 pixels should be sufficient.

▶ Defocus textures with the Lens Blur filter (Filter > Blur > Lens Blur). Adjust the filter to taste, but favor an out-of-focus image. Click OK when you're satisfied.

▶ Remove any color from the texture using a Black & White adjustment layer. Be sure to flatten your final results.

Creating Motion with After Effects

Now that your assets are ready, you can animate the layers in After Effects to create movement. The process is very easy; you'll just use basic Transform properties like Anchor Point, Scale, and Rotation. The technique demonstrated can be used to create simple or complex flowing grayscale images. The goal is to combine multiple images in one composition and then map color to them to achieve a finished background.

Building the Composition

Start by creating a new project or adding the newly created textures to an existing project. Drag three or four graphics on the new composition icon located at the bottom of the Composition panel. A dialog box appears asking you for specifics on the new composition. Choose to create a Single Composition and a duration between 18:00 and 33:00. Set the composition size to match your source graphics (in this case you'll use HDTV 720p and a frame rate of 24p). The extra 3:00 will be used to create the overlap zone, so be sure to pad your initial duration.

Disable the visibility for all but the bottom layer. Select the bottom layer and press S for scale. Then hold down the Shift key and press R for Rotation and A for Anchor Point. By using Anchor Point instead of Position you'll get better results (especially when rotation is involved). Turn on the stopwatch icons for all three properties. Choose random values for the start keyframes. Move the current time indicator to the end of the composition and set different values. All you're trying to accomplish is movement (just be sure that the image always fills the entire screen with no visible gaps at the edges) (**Figure 7.22**). The goal is to create varied motion with keyframes and then blend the layers together. Be sure to keep experimenting as you design.

Invoke a RAM preview to see your results. The image looks pretty simple so far; it's just a sliding and scaling gray texture. But add a few more of these textures and motion will really start to take shape.

Activate the next layer and repeat the animation technique. Try to achieve a different motion path (thus creating "visual interference"). Try moving the texture in a different direction and at a different speed than the first layer. When you're satisfied, adjust the blending mode and/or opacity of the second layer to achieve a soft look. We favor modes like Overlay, Multiply, Soft Light, and Add.

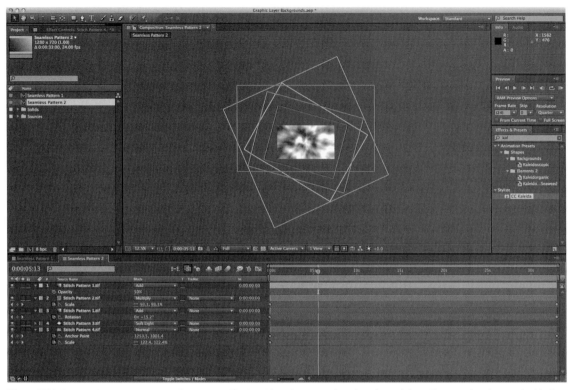

Figure 7.22 By zooming your canvas to a lower magnification, it's easier to see the edges for each layer. You can also change the label colors to make it easier to see each layer.

Continue to animate your remaining layers:

▶ Keep the movement speed relatively slow. Most back-grounds should appear soft and flowing.

▶ Feel free to duplicate an existing layer and apply slightly different keyframe values. This often creates a natural drift.

▶ You can reverse the keyframes on a layer by using the reverse keyframe assistant (Animation > Keyframe Assistant > Time-Reverse Keyframes).

▶ Be sure to try different blending modes. You can select a layer and use the shortcut Shift+= to cycle through modes. Try out several options because different layers blend to produce dramatic variations.

▶ Use your RAM preview to see your results as you build the composition.

▶ Do not add color or blur effects yet.

Creating the Loop

Once you have a flowing background, its time to make it loop. To do this, you'll need to create a split and a fade. Highlight all your layers and create a precomposition by choosing Layer > Pre-compose and name it **Pattern Pre-comp** (**Figure 7.23**). This nests all the layers into an intermediate composition.

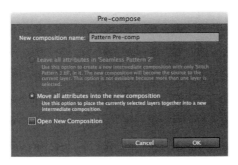

Figure 7.23 The Pre-compose command nests multiple layers into a new composition. This makes them easier to work with as a group.

Next, you need to shorten the main composition by 3:00 (the overlap you created earlier). Access your composition settings by pressing Command+K (Ctrl+K) and shorten the composition by 3:00. In other words, change the duration from 33:00 to 30:00.

Drag to the center duration of the composition. There's no need to be precise; just move about halfway down the Timeline. You can now split the layer in half, thus creating a loop point.

1. Select the layer and press Shift+Command+D (Shift+Ctrl+D) to split the layer (**Figure 7.24**).

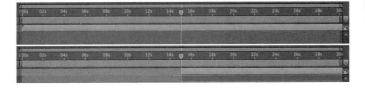

Figure 7.24 Splitting a layer allows for overlapping (which creates the loop).

2. Now you must overlap the layers. With Layer #1 active, jump to the start of the composition by pressing the Home key. Press the left bracket key ([) to move the layer's In point.

TIP

You can press the corresponding number key on the numeric keypad to select a layer (such as 2 for Layer 2).

To finish the background, try blending a grayscale photo. A simple image works best and can add subtle details, especially if the background is designed for a specific subject or project.

NOTES

We'll explore the process of shooting background plates and creating looping backgrounds in Chapter 13.

Figure 7.26 Stylize the background to add color and de-focus.

3. Select Layer #2, and then press the End key. Press the right bracket key (]) to move the layer's In point.

4. Activate Layer #1 and press O to jump to the layer's Out point. Press T for opacity, activate the stopwatch, and set a keyframe for 0% opacity.

5. Drag backwards three seconds and set a key frame for 100% opacity. This creates a gentle dissolve at the overlap point (**Figure 7.25**).

Figure 7.25 Carefully place your opacity keyframes to create a fade between the two layers.

RAM preview the composition to see the seamless animation. Now that you have a loop, you can further stylize it. We recommend the use of adjustment layers and any of the techniques you've learned so far. We usually start with a blur effect (such as Fast Blur or CC Radial Fast Blur). We then apply a colorization effect, such as Colorama, Tint, or CC Toner (**Figure 7.26**). Once you've stylized the composition, you can render it at the proper settings for your nonlinear editing, multimedia, or motion graphics application.

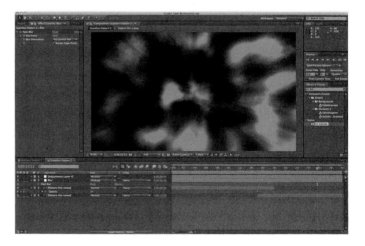

Designing with Brainstorm

Background design is often an art of subtle experimentation. Although you can certainly leave this task up to your own brain, After Effects contains an artificial intelligence solution called Brainstorm, which can create multiple temporary variants of your composition. These choices are presented to you and can be applied or selected for further modification.

The whole process relies on genetic algorithms that mutate selected properties. Simply make the properties you want to modify visible in the Timeline panel. You can select multiple items by holding down the Command (Ctrl) key and clicking. Brainstorm works on keyframes, numeric values, or options in a menu. Brainstorm can quickly modify multiple properties to create all new animations.

1. Set the work area and region of interest for the area you'd like to preview. Use a shorter area to speed up the process.

2. Select one or more properties or property groups you want to randomize in the Timeline panel. Then click the Brainstorm button at the top of the Timeline panel (**Figure 7.27**).

Figure 7.27 Although it's often overlooked, Brainstorm is a quick way to jumpstart the creative process.

3. Brainstorm creates multiple variant compositions, which play inside the Brainstorm dialog box simultaneously. You can control playback with the buttons at the bottom of the Brainstorm dialog box (play, pause, or rewind).

4. Move your mouse pointer over each preview to see controls for each variant (**Figure 7.28**):

A Maximize Tile
B Save As New Composition
C Apply To Composition
D Include In Next Brainstorm

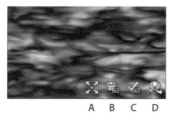

A B C D

Figure 7.28

213

▶ Click a variant's Maximize Tile button to see a larger size. Click the Restore Tile Size button to return to the grid.

▶ If you want to save a variant as a possibility, click the Save As New Composition button for that variant (the disk icon).

▶ To apply a variant, click the Apply to Composition button (the check mark icon).

▶ To include a variant in the next Brainstorm operation, click the Include In Next Brainstorm button for that variant (the thought bubble icon).

The beauty of Brainstorm is that you can continue to evolve your options. At the bottom of the window is a Brainstorm button. Click it to generate even more options. Any variants marked with the Include In Next Brainstorm button will carry forward and new ones will join them. If you'd like to increase the amount of randomness with each iteration, increase the Randomness or Spread slider. You can also move backward or forward through your variations by clicking the arrow buttons on either side of the Brainstorm button at the bottom of the Brainstorm dialog box.

Keep in mind that you have three choices with Brainstorm. You can save multiple variants as compositions (click the Save As New Composition button). You can apply a single variant to the selected composition (click the Apply to Composition button). Or, you can exit Brainstorm without applying changes (press the Esc key).

Animating Shape Layers

After Effects offers a deceptively robust system for creating shapes with Shape Layer. Each layer can hold one or more shapes, and the shape can be heavily modified with custom operations. By animating and layering shapes, you can create geometric motion backgrounds.

Creating Shapes

There are several ways to create shapes in After Effects. The methods vary to offer you the most choices as you design. There is no right or wrong here; just use the method that suits you best:

▶ You can create a new shape layer by choosing Layer > New > Shape Layer. Then click the Add button in the toolbar. You can add a Rectangle, an Ellipse, or a Polystar.

▶ If you choose a shape tool from the toolbar, you can also create a shape by hand. You can draw on a shape layer (just make sure the Tool Creates Shape option is marked in the toolbar). Be sure to hold down the Option (Alt) key if you want to create a path-based shape.

▶ If no layer is highlighted in the Timeline, just pick the shape you want from the toolbar. Double-click its icon, and a new shape is added to the window.

▶ You can also copy and paste shapes from Adobe Illustrator as paths into After Effects. See the article at http://tinyurl.com/aepaths for more details.

Modifying Shapes

On the surface, shapes seem pretty simple, but the Polystar is very flexible. The shape can either be a polygon or a star (depending on whether it is concave or convex). You can assign as many sides or points as you want.

When you're happy with the shape, remember that you have precise control over fill and stroke. By default, a shape has a fill and a stroke, but you can choose to use one or both. If you're designing shapes to use as a background, we recommend removing or reducing the stroke and setting the fill to a lower opacity. Multiple shapes can then be better blended.

To further modify a shape layer, you can apply multiple path operations. These can be used individually or combined. The multiple path operations options will be fully explored in Chapter 10, "Designing with Vectors."

TIP

Do you have a shape you like? You can store any shape as an animation preset (Animation > Save Animation Preset). This can speed up future uses by putting your shapes within quick reach. These presets can also be moved from machine to machine. If you'd like to see some samples, look in the Effects & Presets panel and locate the Shapes folder (it's inside the Animation Presets folder).

For purposes of creating a background, three of the path operations stand out:

▶ **Pucker & Bloat.** This option pulls the vertices of a path inward or outward (**Figure 7.29**). It can be used to create dramatically varied shapes from your stars or polygons shapes.

▶ **Wiggle.** You can add organic wiggle to the edges of a shape(**Figure 7.30**). Be sure to adjust the Wiggles/ Second property to slow down the effect so it's not too distracting.

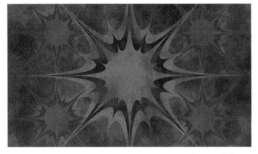

Figure 7.29 The Pucker & Bloat operator works on all shape types to create dramatically different variations.

Figure 7.30 To create natural, organic motion, use the Wiggle operator.

NOTES

Shape layers are purely created by After Effects and are not based on footage. This type of layer is called synthetic, and it does have limitations. You cannot open a shape layer in the Layers panel. You also cannot open a shape layer in another application like Illustrator for further editing. Synthetic layers exist only in After Effects.

▶ **Twist.** This operator rotates a path sharply around the center of an object (**Figure 7.31**).

Figure 7.31 The Twist operator creates rough patterns.

Repeating Shapes

The Repeater operation seems to have been made for animation. With it, you can easily create multiple copies of a shape and even apply a transformation to each copy. Better yet, those transformations can be keyframed for animation or offset to create cycling copies.

As you work with a repeater, you'll quickly see that it is very efficient. You can create hundreds of copies of an object in your composition yet only one in the Timeline. This speeds up rendering and certainly gives you a leg up on project organization.

1. Apply the Repeater operator to a shape layer. By default three copies are added.

2. Twirl down the Repeater and Transform Repeater controls in the Timeline.

3. Adjust the Scale and Position values to create a cascade effect. Each change you make is applied to each copy. For example, an 80% scale is applied to the first copy and the second copy is 80% the size of the last. In this manner the operations compound with one another.

   Try adding multiple copies and experimenting with options like Blend Modes and Rotation when creating backgrounds (**Figure 7.32**).

NOTES

You can use multiple instances of a repeater. For example, you could apply the first repeater to create a horizontal row. You could then apply a second repeater to expand the row vertically or along the Z-axis. The Repeater operator makes building grids and columns a snap.

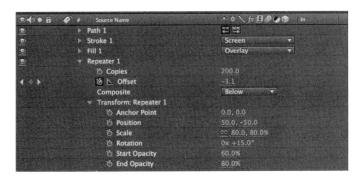

Figure 7.32 The Repeater operator contains several controls. Be sure to test them out to see the results you can generate. The Repeater provides intuitive feedback and is a control worth exploring.

4. Use the Composite option to control the stacking order. If you're making objects larger, we recommend the Above option; for smaller objects, choose Behind.

The Repeater action can be added at any point within the property group. If you place it below the fill and stroke, each copy is filled and stroked independently before repeated. On the other hand, if you move the repeater up, shapes will compound and be filled and stroked uniformly.

TIP

Working with the Shape Layers feature is a very organic experience. You'll definitely want to try out different values, especially when using blending modes and stylizing filters. Remember to also give Brainstorm a try if you'd like to mix things up a bit.

5. Keyframe the Offset value to slide the repeated objects along their path (**Figure 7.33**). This creates an animation that is very simple and elegant. This is a great way to create a repeating pattern.

Figure 7.33 Multiple instances of the Pi symbol are blended into a geometric pattern. By reducing the opacity of the shape and adjusting blending modes, an overlap occurs.

Be sure to experiment with effects as well. The CC Kaleida effect (**Figure 7.34**) can create elaborate patterns. Other effects like Blurs and Glows (**Figure 7.35**) also can liven up your patterned background.

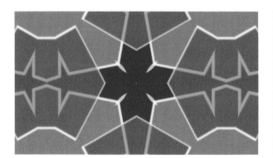

Figure 7.34 Multiple shapes animate past each other to create the initial pattern. Then two instances of the CC Kaleida are used to create a kaleidoscope effect.

Figure 7.35 The Offset operator pushes a five-petaled flower through the scene. The shape is combined with a looping background created with the Fractal Noise effect. The background is finished with the CC Radial Fast blur on a blended adjustment layer and a 4-Color Gradient effect for color.

8

Designing and Working in 3D

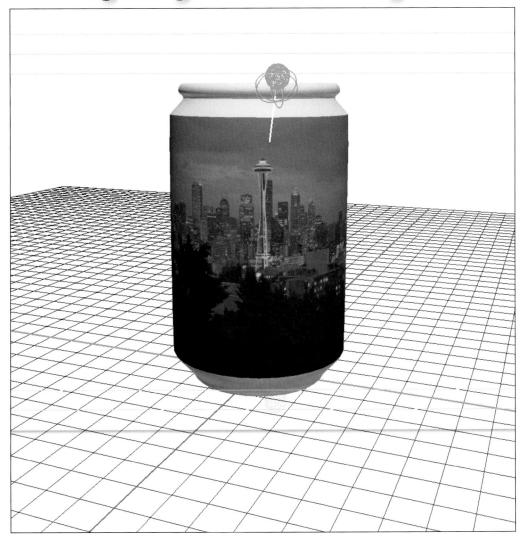

There is a fifth dimension, beyond that which is known to man. It is a dimension as vast as space and as timeless as infinity. It is the middle ground between light and shadow, between science and superstition.

—Rod Serling

Designing and Working in 3D

The use of three-dimensional artwork is increasing dramatically. Although it's not the right choice for every project, it is a flexible option that can significantly extend your design palette. More choices mean more ways to bring an idea to life.

Adobe offers many different ways to design and work in 3D, which you're about to explore. You'll find tools for creating three-dimensional design elements in both Adobe Illustrator and Adobe Photoshop. You'll also find 3D cameras and lights in both Photoshop and After Effects (with differences between them). It's important to explore all the tools at your disposal, as well as learn in which situations they work best.

Courtesy National Foundation for Credit Counseling

At the end of this chapter you'll also find additional tips to help you get quicker results with 3D cameras in After Effects. Working in three dimensions is a big leap for many designers, but the flexibility you'll gain and the results generated are worth the extra effort.

Understanding Perspective

Before we explore design techniques, let's take a moment to review the three dimensions you'll be working with. Things can get a little tricky because you have many options. For example, you can create artwork in Adobe Illustrator that looks three dimensional, but your view is locked. If you were to move the camera, you'd quickly see that the object is flat and lacks depth.

On the other hand, you can create true 3D models in Photoshop, and then import them into After Effects. Once there you can treat them as stationary objects or rotate your 3D camera for a new view. Of course, After Effects also lets you promote 2D (flat layers) and revolve them in 3D space as well (**Figure 8.1**).

Why so many options? Different situations have distinct needs and various tools have specific features.

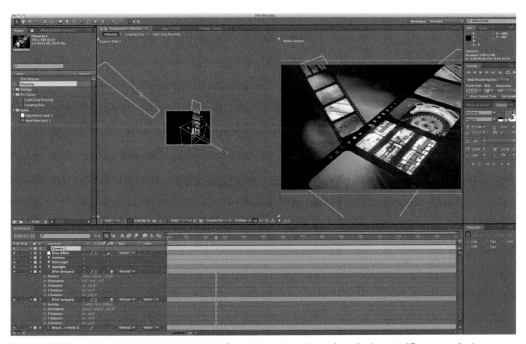

Figure 8.1 This scene was quickly built using only a few static graphics. By stacking the layers in 3D space and using advanced options like Depth of Field and Casts Shadows, you can enhance the perspective effects.

Working in 2D

When designing in two dimensions, objects have width and height. We realize that pretty much describes every graphic, and that's our point. Whether you're working in After Effects, Photoshop, or Illustrator, 2D is very easy to understand. If you want something to appear in front of another object, drag its layer above the other in the Timeline or Layers panel.

You'll also find that working in two dimensions is much faster than any other method. Typically, any effects you apply will render quicker than those in 3D space. We usually try to block out our elements and get timings right (or sync to music) while working in two dimensions (**Figure 8.2**) before we add the complexity of the z-axis.

Figure 8.2 Changing the stacking order of the layers changes their appearance. In this case the differences are influenced by stacking order and use of blending modes.

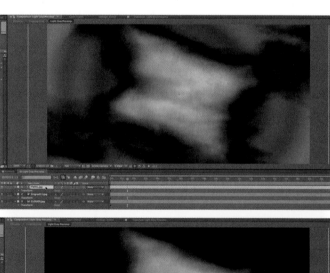

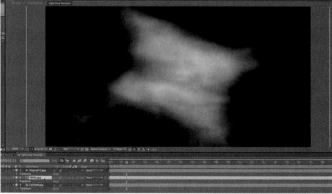

Working in 2.5D

The most common workflow you'll encounter in After Effects is what many refer to as 2.5D or pseudo-3D. Working this way normally involves using flat objects that can be revolved around the x-, y-, or z-axes. Another way of thinking of this concept is as "postcards in space" (a term popularized by Trish and Chris Meyer).

To convert an object to 3D, you just click the 3D switch in the Timeline panel. This will add a third value to the Anchor Point, Position, and Rotation properties as well as introduce a new property called Orientation (which is used for posing an object in 3D space, not animating) (**Figure 8.3**).

TIP

If you lose track of your surroundings when working in 3D, After Effects can help get you oriented. You can reset your custom view or camera by choosing View > Look at All Layers or View > Look at Selected Layers. You can also choose Layer > Transform > Center In View to move an imported object into viewable space.

Figure 8.3 The Orientation property helped position the sky layer correctly to create a perspective effect. Once angled, the Anchor Point property was keyframed to simulate the effect of clouds rushing by the scene.

Many designers working in 2.5D can get by without ever adding an actual 3D camera to their scene and instead work only with the composition default view. Although this is certainly possible, the use of cameras offers *much* greater control (even if it's just for framing and depth of field).

Working in 3D

When it comes to 3D content in After Effects, you face two real choices. The one you choose will be determined by your specific needs as well as the tools you have access to.

One option is to create or import 3D content into Photoshop and then bring that content into After Effects using the Live Photoshop 3D option. Photoshop has quite a few capabilities when you're working with 3D layers. Each 3D layer acts as a container for all the properties associated with the model on that layer. This means the lights, textures, and model are all on a single layer. This workflow allows you to import only static models (no bending, walking, running, etc.), but you can rotate a 3D camera around them in After Effects (**Figure 8.4**).

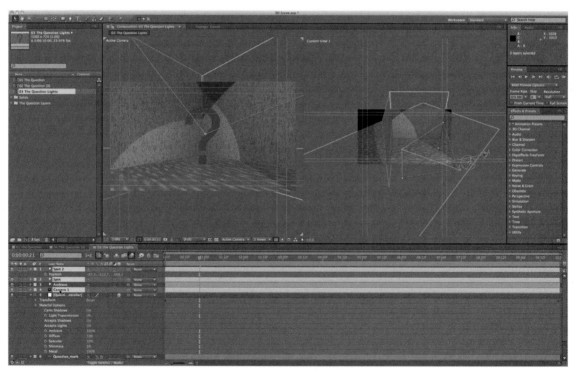

Figure 8.4 This simple scene was built using a 3D model and creating three surfaces in Photoshop. Once imported into After Effects, the Orientation and Position properties were used to pose the objects in 3D space.

If you are creating complex 3D models or animating those models, chances are you're working with a dedicated 3D application. After Effects can import advanced channel information for most 3D rendered formats. You can also import baked camera data in many formats.

Rendering 3D Content in Other Applications

After Effects can import useful data from the most popular 3D modeling and animation programs. However, you need to specify that you want to export that data in the first place.

In the 3D application, you can export your scene as a PIC, RLA, RPF, OpenEXR, or an EI image sequence. Make sure you select the option to include additional pixel information (such as z-space information), cameras, and IDs. If included, After Effects can interpret this data to make effects, cameras, and lights more useful (**Figure 8.5**).

> **NOTES**
>
> For more information on importing and using 3D files from other applications, see the online help article at http://tinyurl.com/aeother3d.
>
> When you import 3D files from a 3D application, you can access additional information. Just apply any of the 3D Channel effects, and then open the Info panel (Window > Info). You'll see important information displayed to help you navigate and work with the files.

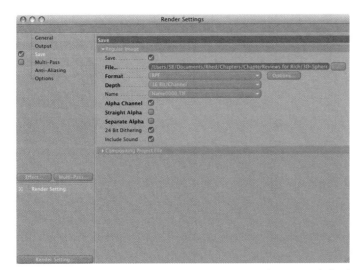
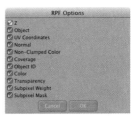
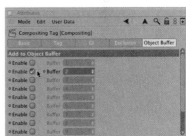

Figure 8.5 When rendering in your 3D application, you can choose to include advanced data with the files. Here, Cinema 4D includes information that can translate to After Effects through the RPF file format.

Depending on the format you use, this extra data will be stored with the files or as a sidecar data file. The Softimage PIC format will include a ZPIC file. The Electric Image format uses EIZ files. You won't import these sidecar files, but make sure they are in the same folder as their associated image sequences so After Effects can connect the data.

Isolating Effects for 3D Content with ID Mattes

Thanks to the additional 3D data that can be included with 3D rendered files, After Effects can isolate prerendered 3D objects in your scene to apply the effects. This can be a useful way to isolate color or tonal corrections, or to stylize elements with glows or noise.

The key to isolating objects is the use of the ID Matte effect (Effects > 3D Channel > ID Matte).

1. Apply the ID Matte effect to the desired layer, and then disable the effect. Leave the effect selected in the Effect Controls panel.

2. Select the actual item you want so the mouse cursor is over the desired subject. With the mouse pointer, click on the object in the Composition panel (**Figure 8.6**).

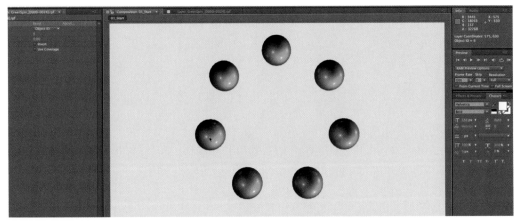

Figure 8.6 Make sure the ID matte is disabled initially. You can use it to identify the ID number for each object.

3. Look in the Info panel to determine the object's ID number.

4. Change the ID Selection parameter (in the ID Matte effect) to match the ID number in the Info panel.

5. Apply any desired effects to the matted layer.

6. Place a copy of the original layer below and remove the ID Matte effect as well as any unwanted effects. The two layers should composite together cleanly. You can also use multiple copies of the footage layer and the ID Matte effect to isolate each object with an ID (**Figure 8.7**).

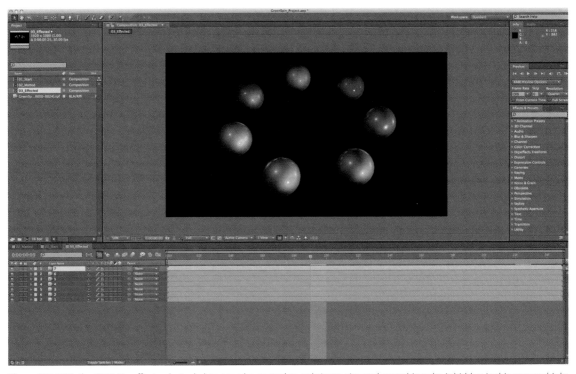

Figure 8.7 With the ID Matte effect, a desired object can be matted so only it remains and everything else is hidden. In this case multiple copies were used, and color was adjusted on each layer.

Stacking Order Matters

Designing can get tricky when you start to layer 2D and 3D layers in the same composition. As a designer, you need to understand how After Effects interprets layers so you can build your compositions correctly. Here are a few guidelines:

▶ When working in 2D, the highest layer in the Timeline panel is in front of all the other layers. The lowest layer is behind them.

▶ 3D layers are stacked based on their z-position value (assuming the camera is pointing at their fronts). This means that the object closest to the active camera is in front of the other layers. This is true even if the layer is at the bottom of the layer stacking order in the Timeline panel.

▶ Track mattes must always be immediately on top of the layer they are matting. This is true for both 2D and 3D layers.

TIP

If you want to keep a logo bug or other element on top of your 3D layers at all times, it's easy. Just place the element on the topmost layer in After Effects and don't enable the 3D switch. You can also do the same for a background layer that you want behind all your 3D layers. Just put a standard 2D layer at the very bottom of the layer stack in the Timeline panel.

▶ Layer blending modes still follow the stacking order in the Timeline panel.

▶ 2D layers mixed with 3D layers are ordered by their spot in the layer stack in the Timeline panel. Mixing 2D layers in between 3D layers prevents layers on either side from interacting with each other.

▶ If two or more 3D layers have overlapping z-position values, After Effects uses their layer stacking order in the Timeline panel to determine the top position (**Figure 8.8**).

Figure 8.8 These three layers are in 3D space with the same z-position. In this situation, stacking order takes over to assign visual precedence.

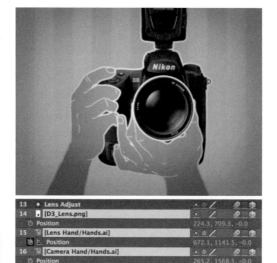

NOTES

Extrude & Bevel and Revolve are both useful for After Effects designers. The Rotate command should be avoided because it adds no functionality that can't be gained by promoting a vector object to 3D in After Effects and using the Orientation property.

You can copy and paste a vector shape from Illustrator to Photoshop. You can also export an Illustrator file as a layered Photoshop file. Either method allows you to convert your vector file into a true 3D object with the Photoshop Repoussé command that we'll explore later in the chapter.

Adding Depth in Illustrator

If you're working with vector artwork in Illustrator, you have three Illustrator effects that you can use to add depth. These effects are live, meaning that you can continue to refine the shape, stroke, or fill of the object as you design. You can also use the After Effects Edit Original command by pressing Command+E (Ctrl+E) to update Illustrator files seamlessly in an After Effects composition. The three Illustrator effects include:

▶ **Extrude & Bevel.** Creates beveled edges and 3D depth.

▶ **Revolve.** Acts like a lathe and sweeps the object in an arc to make a 3D shape.

▶ **Rotate.** Rotates the object in 3D space.

Extrude & Bevel Command

The Extrude & Bevel command in Illustrator is really two complementary effects that can be used together or independently. Extruding an object adds depth by extending the object along its z-axis. For example, extruding a square becomes a cube.

While you're extruding an object, you can also decide to apply a beveled edge. The edge can have a thickness that adds or subtracts from the depth of extrusion.

Here's how to extrude an object:

1. Select an object in Illustrator (**Figure 8.9**).

2. Choose Effect > 3D > Extrude & Bevel. Select the Preview check box so you can see the effect update as you make changes.

3. Use the Position controls to pose the object in 3D space. Dragging the cube is the easiest way to move the object. You can also choose from several preset views using the Position Preset menu.

4. Use the Extrude & Bevel settings to control the object's depth and bevel (**Figure 8.10**):

Figure 8.9 This star was created with the Star tool in Illustrator. The shapes are very customizable.

Figure 8.10 Illustrator offers multiple bevel presets as well as precise control to adjust the Extrude & Bevel effect.

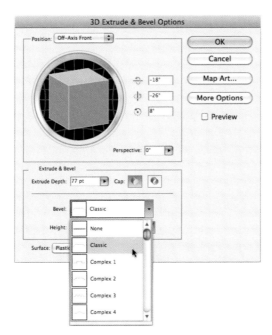

229

▶ **Extrude Depth.** Use the Extrude Depth control to set the depth of the object (up to 2,000 pixels).

▶ **Cap.** Use the Cap setting to determine if the extruded object appears hollow or solid.

▶ **Bevel.** Choose a Bevel preset to change the shape of the bevel.

▶ **Height.** Set a Height for the bevel between 1 and 100. If you go with a bevel that is too high, you may see intersection errors (they look like unwanted spikes).

▶ **Bevel Extent.** Set the Bevel Extent to In or Out. In carves the bevel into the original shape; Out adds the bevel to the outside of the original shape (**Figure 8.11**).

To update a 3D effect after it's been applied, select the object first. Then open the Appearance panel and double-click the effect you'd like to modify.

Figure 8.11 Different bevel effects were created using the Bevel Extent and the Cap settings.

5. Use the Surface preset list to control how the surface is shaded to simulate lighting. If you'd like greater control, click the More Options button.

6. Click OK to apply the effect.

Revolve Command

The Revolve command can take a vector line and sweep its path around in an arc. This can be used to create a 3D object. For best results, draw your line so its curve is pointing to the right (the lines are anchored on the left edge). Once the object is created, you can reposition it with the same Position controls found in the Extrude & Bevel effect. Follow these steps to use the Revolve command:

1. Select an object or line in Illustrator (**Figure 8.12**).

2. Choose Effect > 3D > Revolve. Select the Preview check box so you can see the effect update as you make changes (**Figure 8.13**).

By default, Illustrator revolves objects around the left edge. You can change this to the right edge using the From menu.

You can use the Offset slider to expand the path to create a ring-shaped object.

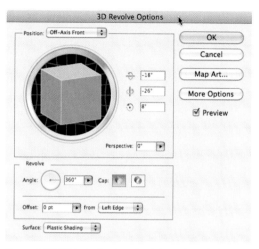

Figure 8.12 A line or a shape is all you need to create a 3D object. By default, the extrusion will rotate around the left edge, so position the vector object accordingly.

Figure 8.13 With the Preview check box selected, changes will update so you can experiment more easily. For complex objects, the screen may take a moment to redraw.

3. If your object has a fill, you can use the Cap option to make it appear solid or hollow.

4. Use the Angle property to set the number of degrees to revolve the path. Although you can use any number between 0 and 360, we typically start with 360 degrees (**Figure 8.14**).

Fun Effects with Revolve

If you experiment with the Revolve command, some pretty cool options are possible. Try using a dashed line and creating an irregular path. In this case a basket shape is possible, and you can create abstract 3D objects for motion graphics work. Technique adapted from RC Concepcion.

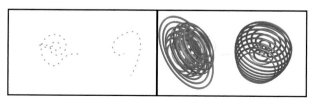

Figure 8.14 This 3D shape was quick to create with the Revolve command.

To make 3D tasks easier in Photoshop, choose Window > Workspace > 3D. This rearranges panels so that all the 3D tools are easy to access.

NOTES

Photoshop 3D objects can be quite resource intensive. Start simple and only work with one or two 3D objects (otherwise instability can occur). The most important device to have is a solid video card because the GPU is critical to smooth performance. Start small until you figure out what your system can handle.

Using 3D Objects in Photoshop

The Photoshop 3D engine is very flexible. It allows you to transform layers three dimensionally. More important, it lets you create new 3D elements, including primitive shapes (such as cones or spheres). Complex elements can be created using grayscale meshes or by using the Repoussé command for text or selections.

You can even import models from most 3D applications. The use of 3D objects can greatly expand your design alternatives, because models can be sized and rotated freely. If the model contains textures, those can come in as well and are fully editable.

The best part of Photoshop 3D? That's easy—how well it works with After Effects. We'll explore the complete workflow in this section and the next.

Creating 3D Layers

Photoshop offers four categories of tools that allow you to create 3D primitives or shapes. These objects can be positioned, lit, and surfaced. The tools include:

▶ **3D Postcards.** These layers are virtually identical to promoting a layer to 3D in After Effects.

▶ **3D Shapes.** Photoshop provides access to 12 shapes, including several useful primitives that can be stretched or modified.

▶ **Grayscale Meshes.** This tool allows you to create very elaborate, custom 3D models from grayscale textures.

▶ **Repoussé.** The Repoussé command lets you extrude text or selected elements into 3D models.

3D Postcard

Any layer in Photoshop can be converted into a 3D Postcard (**Figure 8.15**) by selecting a layer and choosing 3D > New 3D Postcard From Layer. A 3D Postcard works well when you add a floor or wall to catch reflections or shadows. Typically, however, we choose to perform this task in After Effects with a new solid.

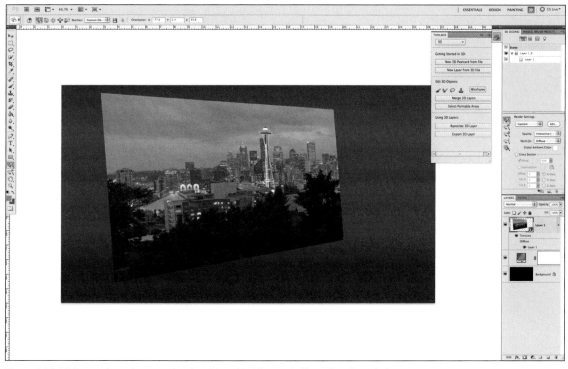

Figure 8.15 3D Postcards can be rotated and positioned in 3D space in Photoshop Extended.

What we find more useful is the ability to gain After Effects–style transformation controls when using 3D Postcards in Photoshop (Figure 8.15). When we are storyboarding animations, these controls are much more flexible than trying to fake transformations using the Free Transform and Perspective commands.

3D Shapes

If you want to create basic 3D objects, Photoshop has a flexible 3D engine with preset shapes. There are 12 shapes to choose from, including single-mesh objects like a Donut or Sphere, as well as multiple mesh objects such as a Cone, Cube, Cylinder, Soda Can (**Figure 8.16**), or Wine Bottle.

NOTES

Some of the shape presets, like Soda Can and Wine Bottle, are for graphic designers who are trying to produce product advertisements. This of course does not explain the Cowboy Hat preset.

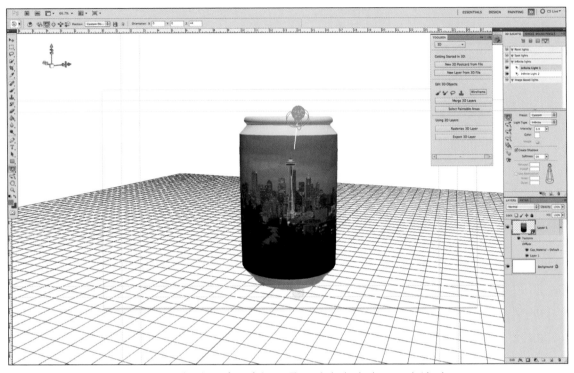

Figure 8.16 New textures can be wrapped to the surface of objects. This includes both photos and video layers.

To create a new 3D object, select the texture, photo, or video layer you want to use and choose 3D > New Shape From Layer. Then select a shape from the menu. Several of the 3D models contain multiple meshes (such as the Cube). You can decide to open a model's surfaces independently by double-clicking a mesh in the 3D panel. Once open, you can assign new textures to your model.

Grayscale Meshes

An interesting way to create custom 3D models is to use grayscale meshes (**Figure 8.17**). By starting with a layer filled with 50% gray (**Figure 8.18**), you can define what happens to the model. Using darker colors will create a recessed area. Using brighter colors will create higher areas. The command is invoked by selecting a grayscale layer and choosing 3D > New Mesh from Grayscale.

TIP

You can add your own custom shapes to the Shape menu. Each shape is merely a Collada (.dae) 3D model file. To add more shapes, place the Collada model file in the Presets\Meshes folder in the Photoshop application folder.

Figure 8.17 Using darker or lighter shades will influence the direction of the extrusion.

Figure 8.18 A quick way to access 50% gray is to press Shift+Delete to open the Fill dialog box.

This mesh can then be applied to a shape in Photoshop (**Figure 8.19**):

Figure 8.19 Photoshop offers four different 3D shapes based on meshes.

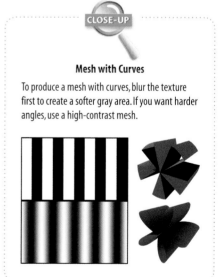

CLOSE-UP

Mesh with Curves

To produce a mesh with curves, blur the texture first to create a softer gray area. If you want harder angles, use a high-contrast mesh.

▶ **Plane.** Applies the depth map data to a planar surface.

▶ **Two-Sided Plane.** Creates two planes mirrored along a central axis. The depth map data applies to both planes.

▶ **Cylinder.** Applies depth map data outward from the center of a vertical axis.

▶ **Sphere.** Applies depth map data radially outward from a center point.

Paint Directly on Your Models

Whether you're working with a model you created or an imported 3D model, you can paint directly on it without having to unwrap its texture. This can be useful because it helps you understand how the paint strokes will affect the texture map of a particular model. This is also a great way to use dark tones to add shading. Use the 3D Rotate tool (K) and change your angle of view using the Position menu to make it easier to paint each side.

Do you need to kern quickly? You can easily adjust the space between pairs of letters right from the keyboard. With an active text layer, place the I-beam cursor between two letters. You can then hold down the Option (Alt) key and use the left and right arrows to tighten or loosen kerning. You may want to track the overall text looser to leave room for the beveled edge.

Repoussé

A new addition to Photoshop CS5 Extended is the Repoussé command. The command can be used to create a 3D model from a 2D object (like shape layers or text). Making a selection first can also isolate the effect. The target pixels can be extruded, inflated, and repositioned in 3D space. The resulting 3D model can be easily imported into After Effects for animation or compositing.

Creating 3D Text

One way to use the Repoussé effect is on a text layer. The command will convert the text from vector to pixels. However, you will no longer be able to edit the text. Be sure to adjust font properties such as kerning and color before running the command. We recommend avoiding white or black because it's difficult to see the properties of the effect. To use the Repoussé command, select a text layer and choose 3D > Repoussé > Text Layer. A dialog box opens prompting you to rasterize the text layer; click Yes.

The Repoussé window opens, offering several controls. The point of the Repoussé effect is to add to the perception of depth. To do this, perspective and edges are applied to the flat text (**Figure 8.20**).

You can use several controls to adjust the appearance of the 3D model. As you adjust each, the model needs to redraw. Depending on your graphics card, this process may take a few moments. Be sure to let the screen redraw before you adjust the next property. You can then better judge the modification (**Figure 8.21**).

Figure 8.20 The Repoussé window offers several controls. We recommend starting with the left column and working top to bottom as you make adjustments.

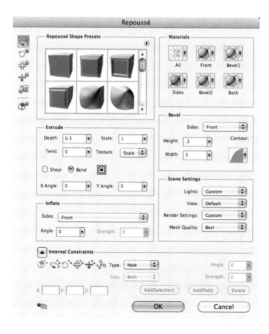

Figure 8.21 To make extrusion easier, Photoshop offers several preset starting points. Experiment with each to find a good starting point, but then customize them to avoid a "canned" look.

TIP

Photoshop offers additional controls for 3D viewing. In the bottom-left corner of the Repoussé window is an icon that provides access to options like 3D Ground Plane or 3D Lights. This is the easiest way to control shadows and reflections.

NOTES

The Internal Constraints controls let you adjust the resolution of the mesh. The controls enable you to specify settings for particular areas such as inflation or curves. These controls can be a little tricky, but experimentation is the best way to learn. Using the Internal Constraints controls is the most efficient way to refine a model and remove "spikes" or unwanted detail.

Although you can't edit the materials directly in the Repoussé interface, you can after applying the effect. In the 3D panel you can see the meshes and depth maps used. You can also double-click these items in the Layers panel to edit them.

The Extrude controls extend the shape into 3D space:

▶ **Depth.** Controls the length of the extrusion; the bigger the numbers, the greater the depth.

▶ **Scale.** Controls the width of the extrusion. Higher numbers equal greater width.

▶ **Twist.** Can turn the extrusion (like a corkscrew).

▶ **Bend or Shear.** Choose Bend for a curved extrusion or Shear for a straight one.

▶ **X and Y Angle.** Controls the horizontal and vertical tilt.

▶ **Change the Bend or Shear.** Modify the Bend or Shear origin by clicking a point on the reference icon.

The Inflate controls expand or collapse the text:

▶ **Angle.** Use a positive Angle setting to expand the object or a negative setting to collapse the object.

▶ **Strength.** Controls the level of inflation for the object.

The Scene Settings offer several controls over lights and camera views:

▶ **Lights.** Offers several presets for how the model is lit.

▶ **View.** Offers preset camera angles. These are useful to reset your view to a default angle.

▶ **Render Settings.** Control how object surfaces look and at what quality they render.

▶ **Mesh Quality Settings.** Increase the density of the mesh, which can dramatically improve appearance. However, the quality can increase the processing time of the effect. A good video card can improve performance.

The Materials controls let you assign color and texture to the sides of the model. You can apply a global texture to all faces or assign unique textures to the front, sides, back, and beveled edges (**Figure 8.22**).

When you're satisfied, click OK to apply the Repoussé effect (**Figure 8.23**). If you ever need to, you can return to the Repoussé window by selecting the object and choosing 3D > Repoussé > Edit In Repoussé.

Figure 8.22 Be sure to visit Photoshop.com for a wide range of free 3D materials for use with the Repoussé command.

Figure 8.23 The generated model has true depth that can interact with the After Effects camera system.

Extruding a Selection

In addition to text layers, you can use the Repoussé command on a selected area. Create a layered file or export a layered file from Illustrator as a Photoshop document (File > Export). To load a selection, hold down the Command (Ctrl) key, click the thumbnail icon in the Layers panel, and then choose 3D > Repoussé > Current Selection (**Figure 8.24**).

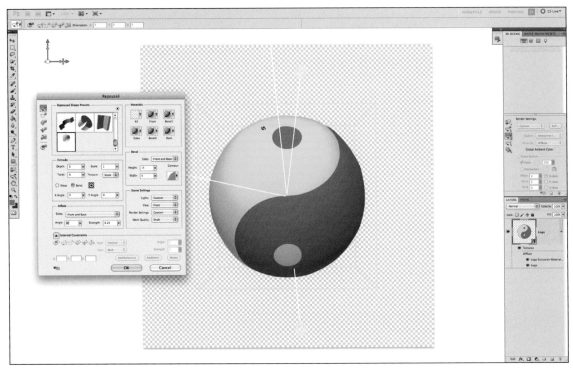

Figure 8.24 Using an active selection, any object can be beveled or extruded.

The Repoussé window opens displaying the controls we explored earlier. A useful option as you adjust objects is to use the View menu to choose a camera angle. Use properties like Inflate and Bevel to create a new effect. When you're satisfied, you can click the menu next to the preset controls to make your own presets.

3D File Formats

Photoshop Extended is an essential part of the pipeline to move 3D models into an After Effects project. Photoshop recognizes a wide range of file types and provides broad support for most manufacturers.

Photoshop supports several common 3D formats, including:

▶ 3DS (3D Studio)

▶ DAE (Digital Asset Exchange, COLLADA)

▶ KMZ (Google Earth)

▶ OBJ (common 3D object format)

▶ U3D (Universal 3D)

Importing 3D Models

Most 3D applications can save to one of the supported file formats that Photoshop recognizes. Even if you aren't proficient in 3D, you can easily find high-quality models to use. To add a model to an existing Photoshop document, choose 3D > New 3D Layer from File (**Figure 8.25**). Keep in mind that not all models you find online will be perfectly built, so if a model doesn't behave as expected, simply try another or edit it in a 3D modeling application.

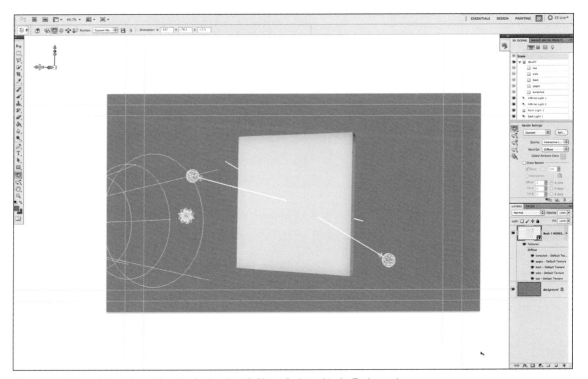

Figure 8.25 3D models can be easily resized using the 3D Object Scale tool in the Tools panel.

Once you've imported a model, you can adjust the textures on its surface. Simply double-click any of the textures listed in the Layers panel. A Photoshop file opens that represents the texture layer (**Figure 8.26**). Add the desired texture or video layer by choosing File > Place. Close and save the texture document, and the 3D model will update (**Figure 8.27**).

Figure 8.26 The benefit of the Place command is that the new texture is added as a Smart Object. This gives you additional flexibility to scale or transform the texture.

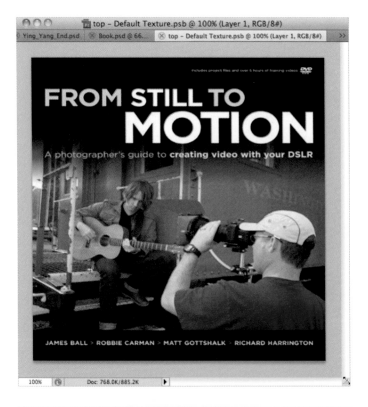

Figure 8.27 To complete the model, you'll need to adjust its position and lighting. We'll explore both in the "Adjusting 3D Elements" and "Adjusting Photoshop Lighting" sections.

The Hunt for Models

You can find usable 3D models for Photoshop in several places. Here are a few suggestions:

- ▶ You'll find a collection of models at www.photoshop.com/products/photoshop/3d/.
- ▶ On the Photoshop Extended install disc or disk image, you'll find a folder called 3D models inside the Extras folder.
- ▶ For several free 3D models, look at www.artist-3d.com.
- ▶ Google offers a 3D Warehouse in support of SketchUp and Google Earth (sketchup.google.com/3dwarehouse). The Google Earth formats often work well in Photoshop Extended too.
- ▶ Look at Archive 3D for an extensive collection of free models (www.archive3d.net).
- ▶ A great website for both free and for-sale 3D models is TurboSquid (www.turbosquid.com).

Adjusting 3D Elements

When you're working with 3D models, you have an important choice to make. You can choose to import them as is and rely on After Effects for its camera system. We choose this method when we're happy with how the model looks on first import and want to move quickly to animation.

Often, however, we need to create preview panels or storyboards using Photoshop. In this case we turn to the Photoshop camera system to pose the model as desired. This effort transfers to After Effects because you can choose to use the Photoshop or After Effects camera in your composition. Photoshop offers several tools that are accessible through the Tools panel and Options bar (**Figures 8.28**, **8.29**, and **8.30**).

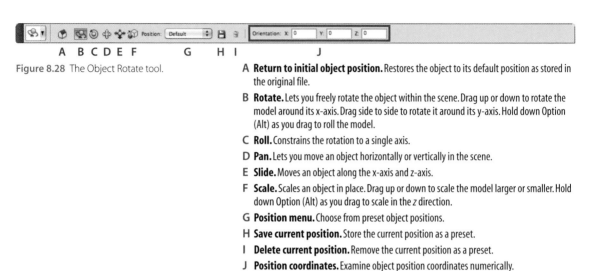

A B C D E F   G   H I   J

Figure 8.28 The Object Rotate tool.

A Return to initial object position. Restores the object to its default position as stored in the original file.

B Rotate. Lets you freely rotate the object within the scene. Drag up or down to rotate the model around its x-axis. Drag side to side to rotate it around its y-axis. Hold down Option (Alt) as you drag to roll the model.

C Roll. Constrains the rotation to a single axis.

D Pan. Lets you move an object horizontally or vertically in the scene.

E Slide. Moves an object along the x-axis and z-axis.

F Scale. Scales an object in place. Drag up or down to scale the model larger or smaller. Hold down Option (Alt) as you drag to scale in the *z* direction.

G Position menu. Choose from preset object positions.

H Save current position. Store the current position as a preset.

I Delete current position. Remove the current position as a preset.

J Position coordinates. Examine object position coordinates numerically.

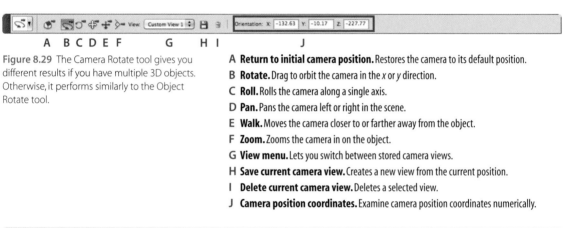

A   B C D E F   G   H I   J

Figure 8.29 The Camera Rotate tool gives you different results if you have multiple 3D objects. Otherwise, it performs similarly to the Object Rotate tool.

A Return to initial camera position. Restores the camera to its default position.

B Rotate. Drag to orbit the camera in the *x* or *y* direction.

C Roll. Rolls the camera along a single axis.

D Pan. Pans the camera left or right in the scene.

E Walk. Moves the camera closer to or farther away from the object.

F Zoom. Zooms the camera in on the object.

G View menu. Lets you switch between stored camera views.

H Save current camera view. Creates a new view from the current position.

I Delete current camera view. Deletes a selected view.

J Camera position coordinates. Examine camera position coordinates numerically.

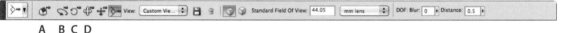

A B C D

Figure 8.30 The Zoom controls.

A Perspective Camera. Shows the camera as parallel lines, which converge to vanishing points.

B Orthographic Camera. Shows the camera as parallel lines without convergence. It also displays the 3D model in accurate scale without any perspective distortion.

C Standard Field of View. You can drag to change the field of view of the 3D camera (the Maximum field of view is 180).

D DOF. Lets you set the depth of field. Distance determines how far a plane exists for what's in focus from the camera. Elements that fall outside of the plane will begin to blur.

Boost Your Memory

Working with 3D objects, cameras, and lights can become very memory intensive. You'll find that both RAM and CPU can get maxed if your system is a little lean.

To help you properly distribute system resources, Photoshop offers 3D preferences. You can assign how much VRAM is dedicated to Photoshop's 3D engine (which can boost performance for complex projects).

You can also set limits with the 3D preferences in regard to the Ray Tracing engine. Raising the threshold will produce higher-quality renders (but will also boost render times). If you're working on a tough deadline, you can temporarily lower quality to speed up the design process as well.

Adjusting Photoshop Lighting

When you create a 3D model, Photoshop will light the scene using two infinite lights. These illuminate the scene evenly from one direction with equal brightness. This style of lighting is flat and simple, which is a great starting point. If you import a 3D model, it can bring its own lights along with it.

In both cases, you'll likely want to tweak the lights. At the bottom of the 3D panel, click the Toggle Misc 3D Extras button and choose Show All. Make sure that you're using the Application frame (Window > Application Frame). This makes it much easier to see the actual lights (**Figure 8.31**).

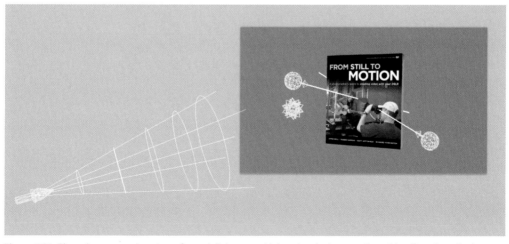

Figure 8.31 Photoshop uses unique icons for each light type, which makes the icons easier to identify and manipulate.

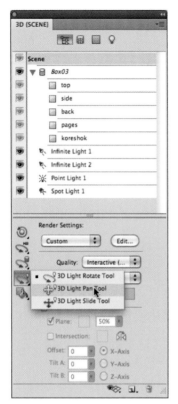

You can select any of the lights in the 3D panel and use the Light Type menu to change its type. Additionally, you can add new lights as needed to enhance the scene. Controls in the 3D window are contextual and will change based on the style of light you've chosen. Adjust the lights with the lighting controls so you are happy with them (**Figures 8.32** and **8.33**).

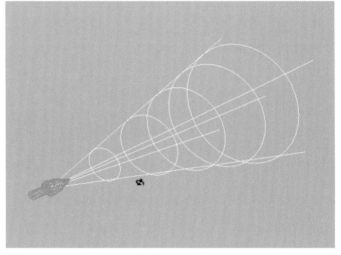

Figure 8.32 You can click the select tools to adjust lights from the 3D panel. There are three tools for adjusting rotation, panning, and position.

Figure 8.33 A selected light changes color to make it easier to see.

Importing 3D Objects into After Effects

Importing 3D content into After Effects uses Photoshop as a portal. Once you've placed the 3D object as a 3D layer or created a new 3D layer with a shape or mesh, the groundwork is set. Simply adjust the lighting and textures, and then save your file.

When you're ready to import, switch to After Effects, choose File > Import, select the layered PSD file, and click OK. A new window opens asking you to confirm how to load the PSD file. Choose one of the two As Composition methods. Be sure to select the check box next to Live Photoshop 3D (**Figure 8.34**). Click OK to complete the import.

NOTES

For future changes, we recommend storing your 3D model files in the same folder as your layered Photoshop document. This will make updates much easier when you need to jump back and forth between Photoshop and After Effects.

If you forget to import with the Live Photoshop 3D option, you can convert the layer later. Select the layer and choose Layer > Convert To Live Photoshop 3D.

When the import is complete, you can open the precomposition for the 3D object. Inside you'll find an After Effects 3D camera as well as the 3D object and a control layer that contains an instance of the Live Photoshop 3D effect.

The live Photoshop 3D layer in After Effects uses several expressions to control the file. These are attached to a null layer, which is used to control the live Photoshop 3D layer. **Use this null layer rather than directly manipulating the live Photoshop 3D layer's Transform properties.**

The Live Photoshop 3D effect recognizes any animation of the composition camera in After Effects. You can also force After Effects to use the animation of the 3D object or camera from the PSD file (although we find the cameras in After Effects to be more robust). Choose Use Photoshop Transform or Use Photoshop Camera in the effect properties in the Effect Controls panel for the Live Photoshop 3D effect if you want to override After Effects. It is generally better to animate the After Effects camera, but the object may be slightly repositioned within the frame.

It's important to understand how lights are processed between Photoshop and After Effects. By default, the lights you add to Photoshop are essentially baked into the file.

NOTES

If you want to modify the texture or lights for a 3D object, you must return to Photoshop. Select the 3D object and then choose Edit > Edit Original. If you want to change the model itself, you'll need to use a 3D authoring program, not Photoshop or After Effects.

Initially, After Effects lights won't work on a Photoshop 3D object. If you adjust properties for Photoshop, they will update in After Effects.

Once in After Effects, you can promote the imported Photoshop file to a 3D layer with the Timeline switch. In this case, the lights you add in After Effects can be used to create new shadows. Additionally, you can add new Ambient light to affect the color and overall lighting levels, or add new spot lights for directional lighting (**Figure 8.35**).

Figure 8.35 Switching an imported 3D model to be a 3D layer will alter its position. However, it will react to 3D lights and camera options like depth of field.

It's necessary to understand how the two lighting systems combine. You need to first get your base lighting right in Photoshop so the model has adequate lighting. Typically, we favor flat lighting in Photoshop. Once you move into After Effects, you can enhance the model by adding to that lighting (as long as the layer has been promoted to 3D). The two systems can either complement or contradict; it's up to you to manage the interaction.

Power Techniques for 3D in After Effects

The use of 3D space is one of our favorite features in After Effects (**Figure 8.36**). Whether it's designing title sequences, compositing shots, or creating complex effects, 3D is essential. It can also get a little confusing and intimidating from time to time. To help supercharge your workflow, we offer some practical advice. You may know a few of these tips already (which means you're smart and good looking), but a few new ones are worth the read.

NOTES

Working with 3D sources can start to hog RAM a bit. By lowering the resolution of the Composition panel, you can dramatically speed up the previews and redraw time. Switching from Full Resolution to Half Resolution speeds up previews by four times. In fact, previewing at half quality with the Composition panel set to 50 percent often provides a perfectly acceptable preview for most tasks (keying, particles, and glows being the exceptions).

Figure 8.36 3D Layers are much easier to use when you change your viewpoint.

Multiple Views

Imagine a real-world set. A top Director of Photography is on set, but he never takes his eyes away from the viewfinder. It kind of makes it hard to direct—and even harder to light the scene. In the real world, it's important to look through the viewfinder as well as poke your head up and look around the set.

The same holds true when you're working in 3D space in After Effects. You can have multiple viewers open at once (**Figure 8.37**) and click the View Layout button at the bottom of the Composition panel. From the panel, you can choose between multiple 2 View and 4 View layouts.

If you prefer working with separate floating windows, After Effects can accommodate. With the Composition panel active, choose View > New View. A new tab appears in the Composition panel. You can drag the tab away until it becomes a second, floating Composition panel in a separate window.

In both cases you can set separate angles for each window or view. We're big fans of the Custom View 1, Top, and Custom View 3 presets.

TIP

When you have your windows arranged the way you like, you can choose Window > Workspace > New Workspace to save the current setup.

To switch preview resolution quickly, try the following shortcuts:
- For Full Resolution, press Command+J (Ctrl+J).
- For Half Resolution, press Command+Shift+J (Ctrl+Shift+J).
- For Quarter Resolution, press Command+Option+Shift+J (Ctrl+Alt+Shift+J).
- You can also leave the preview resolution set to Auto so it will match the Composition panel settings.

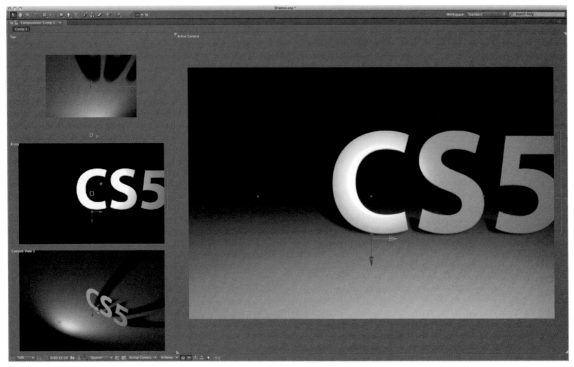

Figure 8.37 After Effects offers several view presets. Each can be fully customized.

Camera Controls

When you use 3D cameras in After Effects, there are a ton of choices to make. For example, you can choose advanced controls for geometric position, lens options, depth of field, and more. It can get pretty tricky. Sure, if you are a full-blown Director of Photography or a total 3D animation guru, you'll know your way around. But for the rest, the following sections contain some practical tips to make your workflow more efficient.

Simplified Camera Presets

When you create a camera, you're presented with an intense dialog box (**Figure 8.38**). Chances are it won't all make sense; that's why there are presets. These are great starting points and quickly let you explore the most relevant camera options.

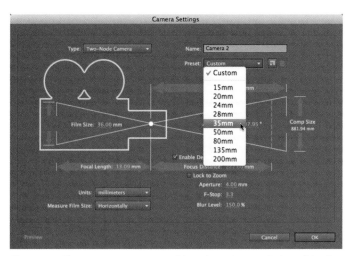

Figure 8.38 The camera presets are useful starting points to mimic traditional film and video cameras.

Here's a simple guide to what presets offer:

▶ Lower numbers (15mm, 20mm, 24mm) produce wide-angle lenses. They will take in more of the view but can become distorted at the edges.

▶ Higher numbers (80mm, 135mm, 200mm) will give you a narrow angle of view.

▶ A 50mm lens is a good default for a "normal" camera look. A 35mm lens is OK too.

Active Cameras Switching

Many don't realize that they have the ability to add multiple cameras to a 3D composition. This makes experimentation effortless because you can try out different camera moves without throwing the previous move away (**Figure 8.39**). As you design, you can look through any camera you want using the options in the 3D View menu.

Pose Your Subject

If you want to quickly pose layers in the Composition panel, there's a tool that works quite well. Press W to switch to the Rotation tool (V switches back to the Selection tool). Then in the Set menu you can choose to adjust Rotation or Orientation. Which one should you choose?

▶ Orientation is best for posing an object (setting its desired, static position). If you keyframe Orientation, it always takes the shortest path between two angles. For example, if you had a keyframe at 0 degrees and the second at 270 degrees, it would rotate only 90 degrees counterclockwise to get there.

▶ Rotation is the best choice when animating a spin. The Rotation property remembers the direction of the turn and can even store multiple revolutions.

TIP

Are you trying to move a layer in Z space? Dragging the scrubbable text doesn't move very fast. If you need to gear up, hold down the Shift key as you drag.

Figure 8.39 You can trim the layer handles for the camera to control when a camera becomes active.

The gotcha is that only the active camera will render. Which one's active? The answer is that it depends:

- If you have two overlapping cameras, the one on top of the layer stack takes precedence.

- If you want to edit between cameras, you can adjust the In and Out points in the Timeline. Then sequence the camera layers so you can cut between them.

Effect Cameras

Many effects (such as Shatter) have their own built-in 3D systems. This means by default that the effect has its own camera to use. This is because the effects are often used to quickly add 3D depth within 2D compositions.

You aren't limited here, however. You can choose to override the effects 3D system and use the one you've built instead. Just select the Use Comp Camera or Use Comp Lights option in the effect's property list.

Depth of Field

One of the main reasons to use 3D cameras is to be able to access the Depth of Field option. When turned on, objects that are too close or too far away from the camera appear out of focus. This behavior mimics how a real camera would behave.

Depth of Field is off by default because it adds complexity and render time. You can enable it in either the Camera Settings dialog box (**Figure 8.40**) or the Timeline panel. You can adjust its behavior by modifying properties like F-Stop, Aperture, and Blur Level.

Setting focus is pretty straightforward. Simply adjust the Focus Distance property. If you don't want to guess the distance, use a 2 or 4 View preset. When you look through any of the views that show you the camera, you get a bounding box that indicates Focus Distance. Drag the sliders until this frame surrounds your subject (**Figure 8.41**). Depending on the amount of blurring you've allowed, you may have some wiggle room before focus falls off.

NOTES

When using effects that have a 3D camera system, they typically remain as 2D layers. The 3D happens within the effect, not to the actual layer. Don't enable the 3D switch for the layer with the effect applied to it (e.g., the Card Dance layer).

TIP

By keyframing the Focus Distance property, you can create rack focus effects between objects.

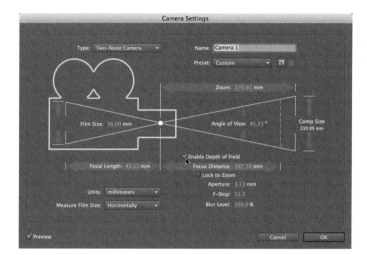

Figure 8.40 Using Depth of Field adds to render and preview time. We often leave it off until we near the end of our animation tasks.

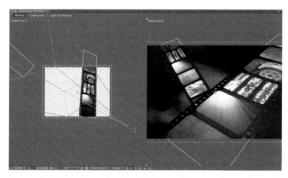 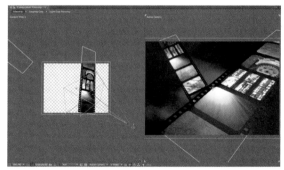

Figure 8.41 The bounding box for Focus Distance determines what is in and out of focus. Camera settings like Aperture and Blur Level will also influence depth of field.

Control a Camera with a Null

If you're trying to create a rotating camera, it can get a little complicated to build smooth sweeping effects. Think of it as the difference between trying to hold a camera while walk in a smooth arc versus putting the camera on a dolly and using a curved track.

The easiest way to do this is with a null object and parenting (**Figure 8.42**). Null objects are invisible layers that don't render or show visible properties.

Figure 8.42 A null object is used to orbit the camera around the imported 3D text created in Photoshop.

1. Create a null object by choosing Layer > New > Null Object.

2. Switch the null object's 3D switch.

3. Position the null at the center (or vortex) of your rotation.

4. Use the Parent column and pick whip in the Timeline to connect the camera and the null object.

5. Animate the null object by rotating to create your arcs. If you want to create a spiral, add keyframes to the camera's z-position so it moves closer to the null.

Lighting Strategies

If you talk to Directors of Photography, they'll quickly tell you that lighting is a key ingredient to good cinematography. Lights create perspective, they control depth of field, and they can dramatically impact emotional qualities of your shot. They also add to the number of details that you'll need to keep track of. Here are a few practical techniques to get better lighting results.

TIP

Lights can be parented just like other objects. We sometimes like to attach a light to the camera, so as it moves, the light goes with it (this works well for certain styles of shooting, such as perspective shots). You can also parent lights to a null object to make it easier to apply global positioning adjustments to all the lights at the same time.

Making Shadows

One aspect of lighting that is confusing to folks is that lights don't appear to cast shadows by default. Because shadows add complexity and render time, you'll need to enable them.

You'll first want to select the Casts Shadows option in the Light Settings dialog box (**Figure 8.43**). If you forget to do this, just select the light layer and choose Layer > Light Properties. Of course, you still won't see any shadows.

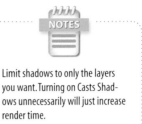

Figure 8.43 You can double-click a light in the Timeline to open its settings box.

Although layers are set up to receive shadows automatically, you need to specify which layers can cast shadows. If you stop and think about it, the mess you'd have if all layers made shadows would be quite time-consuming.

Select all your 3D layers that you want shadows applied to, and then twirl open the layer properties so you can access Material Options. Click the Off switch next to Casts Shadows to change it to On (**Figure 8.44**).

Figure 8.44 You'll need to set which layers cast shadows and which layers accept shadows using the Material Options for each 3D layer.

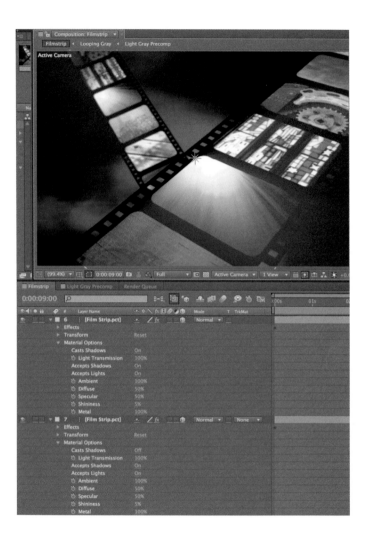

Controlling Light Transmission

Some of your 3D layers should be treated as being partially opaque. Perhaps the surface is glass or plastic, and you'd like to let some light pass through. The most basic example to visualize is a stained glass window. In this case, light should move through the layer and create shadows and colored light.

Start by enabling shadows for the light layer. You can then open the desired layer's Material Options. Enable Casts Shadows and adjust the Light Transmission property to 100% (**Figure 8.45**).

Figure 8.45 The default shadow (left). Changing Light Transmission to 100% (center). Adjust the Shadow Darkness and Shadow Diffusion properties for the Spotlight (right).

Often Overlooked Material Controls

In the rush to design, many motion graphics artists skip the advanced controls in the Material Options category. These are essential because they refine how a 3D light interacts with your 3D layer. The properties that affect appearance the most are Diffuse, Specular, Shininess, and Metal (**Figure 8.46**).

> **TIP**
>
> When you're first exploring Material Options, try lowering or raising their values one property at a time.

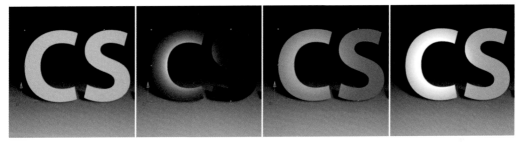

Figure 8.46 The only changes made to this scene were modifications to the Material Options. No other light settings were modified. The Material Options are indispensable controls that are often overlooked.

To use the advanced Material Options:

1. Drop all the Material Options values to 0% to remove the effect of the lights.

2. Slowly increase the Specular value. This will add a hot spot to your layer (it may get quite blown out). The Specular value controls how reflective the layer is. The higher the number, the brighter the reflection.

3. Raise the Shininess property, which will cause the light to show specular highlights. The higher the number, the smaller the highlight.

4. Use the Diffuse property to soften the results generated by the Specular and Shininess properties. This will soften the transition between lights and darks.

5. Raising the Metal property will lower the color distinction between the darker areas and the highlight, but the highlight will still be brighter. The Metal property also affects how much the layer's color influences the color of the reflection.

9

Designing with Audio

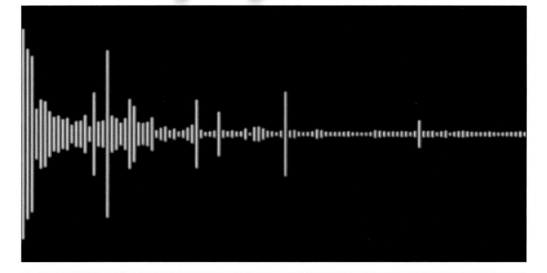

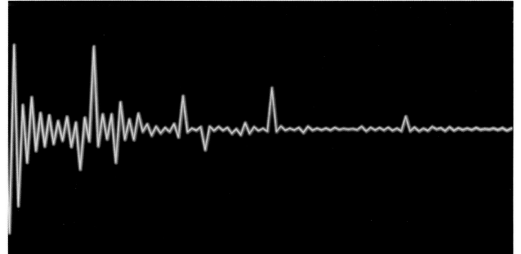

To me, movies and music go hand in hand. When I'm writing a script, one of the first things I do is find the music I'm going to play for the opening sequence.

—Quentin Tarantino

Designing with Audio

Creating motion graphics without audio is like cooking food without seasoning—pretty blah. Whether audio is used to inspire creativity in the studio or reinforce an emotion in your composition, it's an integral part to the creation and evolution of a project. Music crosses the bounds of language into a more guttural form of communication. There's something about sound that really changes how you think and process information.

In this chapter, we'll not only explore how to work with audio in Adobe After Effects, but also how to integrate Adobe Soundbooth into your everyday audio workflow. Sure, we'll look at the basics like adding markers and optimal file formats. But we'll also dig a little deeper into some of the other challenges like finding new audio sources, using audio to generate animated graphic elements, and working with audio seamlessly across multiple applications.

Using Audio Sources

Rarely do motion graphics end up being played back without music. Yet music often gets overlooked or short-changed during the design process (and instead gets slapped on at the end). Finding affordable, high-quality, and legal sources for music can sometimes be a challenge. Fortunately, Soundbooth has a variety of royalty-free music scores and audio effects that can be edited and mixed to match the style of your video.

File Formats

Adobe Creative Suite 5 supports five different audio formats, three uncompressed and two compressed.

CLOSE-UP

Finding Sources for Music

If you're looking for another place to find royalty-free or public-domain licensed music, you might want to check out http://freemusicarchive.org. It's a wonderfully forward-thinking site directed by WFMU-FM with the digital creative in mind. If you're looking for music for motion graphics or even samples cleared for remix and distribution, there are a variety of music licenses available. New artists and old, this site seems to have a little of everything available for download. Be sure to look at the terms of use for each song you want to use.

We recommend sticking with one of the uncompressed loss-less formats before working with compressed lossy formats. You should also check out the Adobe-specific ASND file format, which supports layered audio and multiple tracks for editing. Here are the five formats supported by CS5:

▶ **AIFF (Audio Interchange File Format).** This format is uncompressed and is the standard uncompressed audio format for Mac OS X. It has been widely adopted throughout the professional music and video industry. AIFF supports not only stereo, but can also be used for surround sound audio.

▶ **WAV (Windows Waveform).** This format is usually uncompressed and is the standard full-quality audio format for Windows. Although they are primarily uncompressed, you can embed compressed files into a WAV file (which you should try to avoid).

▶ **MP3 (MPEG-1 or MPEG-2 Audio Layer III).** The first most widely accepted lossy compressed audio format, MP3 rose to dominance shortly after its release in the early 1990s. MP3 was initially created by the German company Fraunhofer-Gesellshaft as part of the Moving Picture Expert Group's creation of MPEG-1 and later MPEG-2. Many companies helped refine the standard as it grew to dominance as the compression of choice for the first portable, digital, file-based music players.

▶ **AAC (Advanced Audio Codec).** Created as the successor to MP3, AAC is a lossy compression designed along with the creation of MPEG-4. Its biggest growth in popularity came when it was chosen as the default format for iTunes. It is a widely supported format as the default format used in the iPod, Nintendo DSi, and the Sony PlayStation 3.

▶ **ASND (Adobe Sound).** An amazingly flexible format, ASND supports layered multitrack mixes and has the ability to save history snapshots of your projects as you work. These snapshots save the settings of the project at that specific point in time, giving you the ability to go back to the snapshot at any time and edit the project from that point. In addition to the time abilities, ASND files can be imported directly into Adobe After Effects, Adobe Premiere Pro, and Adobe Flash Professional.

NOTES

There are two different kinds of AAC formats, protected and un-protected. The protected files have DRM (digital rights management) and cannot be copied digitally. If you have a problem importing an AAC file, look at the file information and make sure it's not a protected AAC file.

TIP

Do you want Adobe Media Encoder to automatically convert files as you work? Simply create a Watch Folder by choosing File > Create Watch Folder. In Preferences make sure "Start Queue Automatically when idle for: (xx) minutes" is selected. As long as Adobe Media Encoder is open, after the specified amount of time, any files in the folder will auto-matically be added to the queue and converted to the same settings as your last file conversion.

Additional Sample Rates

After Effects CS5 has removed support for some nonstandard fractional audio sample rates in the Render Queue. It also removed the ability to set arbitrary, custom values in the Output Module settings. These settings really only caused incompatible files, so the decision was to support only standard rates.

If you need to work with other sample rates or want additional controls, you can send audio to Soundbooth. Just choose Edit > Edit In Adobe Soundbooth to open the clip in Edit view in Soundbooth.

When working in Soundbooth, it is recommended that you work with a 32-bit project and down convert upon export.

If you're working with a video editor for a project, double-check to make sure your project's settings match the edit settings for the final project. Most of the time, you'll find that video projects are 16-bit audio at a sample rate of 48 kHz.

Sample Rates

A natural sound wave is perfectly smooth in its oscillation. Because digital audio is recorded using zeros and ones, that sound wave is recorded as a series of measurements over time; each one is known as a "sample." The higher the sample rate, the better the quality. You want a sample rate to be about double the frequency of the sound you're recording. It is widely accepted that the human ear can hear frequencies from 20 to 20,000 Hz. Most people can't hear that entire range, and the range changes as people age. To be able to reproduce the full range, you want a sample rate to be in the neighborhood of at least 40,000 samples. CD sound quality is recorded at 44,100 samples (44.1 kHz), whereas a standard, digital video file uses audio recorded at 48,000 (48 kHz). We recommend working with 48 kHz audio if you're designing for video or broadcast. If you're going to the Web, Flash typically prefers 44.1 kHz. If film is in your future, you may find that you'll be using higher-end audio down the road, such as 96 kHz.

Bit Depth

The sample rate is just one part of the equation when recording a sound wave. Bit depth controls the dynamic range, which is how closely each sample matches the amplitude of the original sound wave. The higher the value, the higher the dynamic range and the better the sound quality. CDs are 16-bit and DVDs are often 24-bit. Most video is edited at a bit depth of 16-bit, and this is fine when working in After Effects. If needed, you can work with up to 32-bit audio in After Effects.

Sample Rate Conversions

As you design, you'll often gather a variety of sources to use. You may find that you have 48 kHz material from a video camera intercut with 44.1 kHz audio from a stock music library. Don't worry; as long as you're importing a supported audio format, After Effects will attempt to automatically convert any audio source so the file's sample rate matches your project sample rate.

Sample rates in After Effects are set at the project level, not the composition level. To set the sample rate of your project, choose File > Project settings; the Sample Rate menu is at the bottom under Audio Settings (**Figure 9.1**).

We find that After Effects will successfully convert the sample rates of any imported audio in most cases. The notable exceptions are compressed sources (such as MP3), which can sometimes lead to strange audio sync issues. We recommend that you convert your audio to an uncompressed format with a sample rate to match your project before you import it into After Effects, which can be done using the Adobe Media Encoder.

The Adobe Media Encoder is fairly intuitive. Its straightforward interface makes it easy to specify conversion settings, load multiple files, start the queue of files to render, and let it do the heavy lifting (**Figure 9.2**).

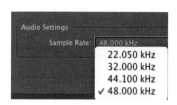

Figure 9.1 Select a sample rate in the Project settings under Audio Settings.

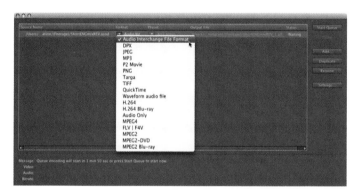

Figure 9.2 Drag and drop any files for conversion directly into the interface. Specify the new file format using the Format menu. To customize the conversion or see specific details about the conversion, click on the name of the preset to open the Export settings. When all the files are loaded and the settings are set, click Start Queue in the upper-right corner of the interface to start the conversions.

Creating Audio Sync Points

As you design, it's often much easier to ensure that graphic elements are properly timed to music or narration by using sync points. An audio sync point is nothing more than a marker applied to a layer or composition (we often create an empty adjustment or a null layer to hold them all). Typically, sync points (**Figure 9.3**) are added to indicate where different events are supposed to occur based on cues provided in the audio track. For example, a motion graphics designer would mark where the music reaches its peak to match the big reveal of the graphics. Similarly, a character animator would add markers to indicate areas for lip sync.

NOTES

In addition to marking key points in time, markers can be used to create chapter markers and cue points to add interactivity.

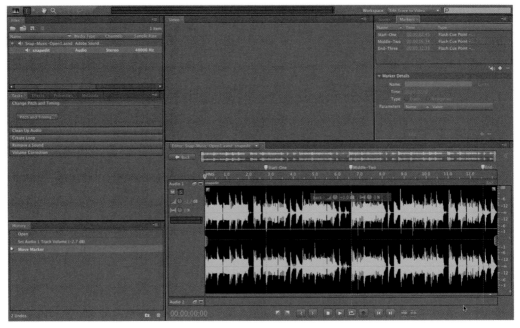

Figure 9.3 Soundbooth projects and their markers will seamlessly import into After Effects and Premiere projects.

TIP

To preview audio only within a specific range, set a work area. Position the current time indicator at the start of the desired work area and press B to set the Beginning of the work area. Move the current time indicator and press N to set the eNd of the work area. Then press Option+. on the numeric keypad (Alt +. on the keypad) to preview audio only within the work area.

Previewing Audio in After Effects

Before you preview anything in After Effects, you should check to see how you've set up previews to process. Choose After Effects > Preferences > Previews (File > Preferences > Previews) to specify the length of your audio previews. An audio-only preview is often preferable to a typical RAM preview because of real-time playback. When you have a complex project that a RAM preview cannot play in realtime, the video and audio can appear out of sync and can make adding markers very confusing. Audio-only previews are much easier for a system to load and ensure real-time playback.

To play an audio-only preview, press the decimal key (.) on your numeric keypad (Control+. on a Mac laptop). You can also load a preview by choosing Composition > Preview > Audio Preview (Here Forward).

If you don't need a full audio preview, you can just drag the current time indicator to find a cue point. Press the Command (Ctrl) key and drag the current time indicator across the Timeline to hear the audio track. To visually observe what's happening to the audio levels as you scrub, press Command+4 (Ctrl+4) to bring the Audio panel to the front.

Adding Markers

After Effects supports layer markers and composition markers. Both can also be added in realtime during any preview. When adding markers to music, invoke an audio-only preview, and then tap the multiply key (*) on the numeric keypad to the beat of the music. Once the audio is finished playing, all the markers just added will appear in the Timeline. Here are a few guidelines for adding markers:

▶ Add a Null to hold the markers. This gives you flexibility to slide markers without affecting footage and really comes in handy when you're working in a large composition with many layers. You can quickly move the Null up or down in the Timeline panel to maintain visibility when working with other layers.

▶ To apply layer markers, select a layer and press * on the numeric keypad (Control+8 on a Mac laptop).

▶ To apply composition markers, press Shift + 0–9 on the main keyboard.

Although we find tapping out to the music to be the easiest method, you can work other ways. If you're not feeling the rhythm, or if you just want to visually place your markers in the Timeline, here are a few helpful Timeline tips and key commands you should know (**Figure 9.4**):

TIP

To view more precise measurements in the VU meter, increase the height of the Audio panel.

Composition markers are an easy way to navigate a Timeline. To move the current time indicator directly to a composition marker, press the corresponding number on the main keyboard.

Time Navigator In   Time Navigator Out

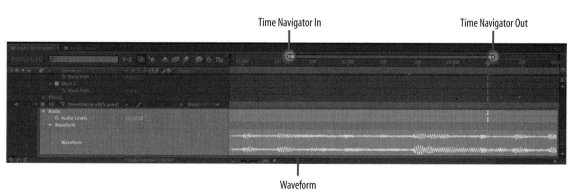

Waveform

Figure 9.4 Using the waveform can make it easy to line up markers visually to the peaks and valleys of the audio represented in the Timeline. Drag the Time Navigator brackets to view a specific area of the Timeline.

TIP

If you want to make markers truly useful, you can add labels to them. To edit a label, double-click the marker and type your label in the Comments field. Labels are also an easy way to communicate when moving a project between artists working in a group environment.

▶ Press LL to view an audio waveform in the Timeline panel.

▶ Drag the Time Navigator brackets to zoom into a specific area of the Timeline.

▶ Press = or − to zoom in and out on the Timeline around the current time indicator.

▶ Press ; to quickly zoom all the way into one frame (at the location of the current time indicator).

▶ Press Shift + ; to zoom out and see the entire length of the composition. Repeat the command and the Timeline view will change back to the duration specified by the Time Navigator.

To change the placement of a marker, drag directly on the marker in the Timeline panel. You can also be precise by opening the Layer Marker dialog box and entering a specific time value into the Time field.

Adding Soundbooth to Your Workflow

As motion designers, when creating a 30-second show open, we wouldn't think twice about moving the project back and forth between After Effects and Premiere Pro. Typically, we'd create the initial edit in Premiere Pro, taking full advantage of its real-time editing capabilities. Then we'd seamlessly move the project into After Effects using Dynamic Link. In After Effects we'd usually layer in more files created from Photoshop and Illustrator. So why not use Soundbooth when it comes time to either add or edit audio for the open? It only makes sense, and it's easy enough to send files out to Soundbooth while using either Premiere Pro or After Effects by selecting the audio file and choosing Edit > Edit In Soundbooth. Also, if you've designed an audio project in Soundbooth, both Premiere Pro and After Effects will flatten and import the entire project file natively as an ASND file. No prerendering—just import and go!

Creating Graphics and Audio

Although it's not known as a robust audio tool, After Effects has some interesting audio capabilities. In fact, it can generate tone-based sounds and create graphic elements that animate in response to sounds. All of this is made possible through the use of effects.

Audio Spectrum

Many designers want to actually see their audio on the canvas. This is especially true for those designing user-interface-style graphics or for projects where audio is a featured element. One great effect is the Audio Spectrum effect, which generates graphic lines that scale based on the frequencies present. The effect is limited to a single audio track (**Figure 9.5**), but you can pre-compose multiple audio tracks together if needed.

The overarching appearance of the spectrum generated is set under the display options (**Figure 9.6**). The rest of the options listed can help create highly stylized and unique versions of the spectrum. **Figure 9.7** shows the most useful controls.

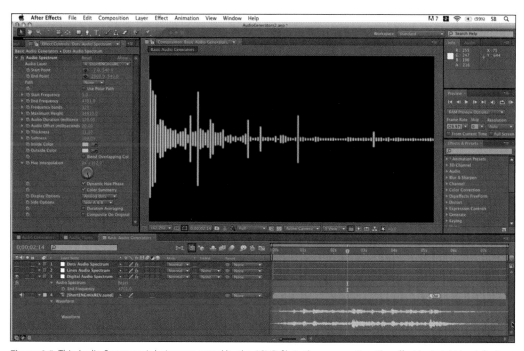

Figure 9.5 This Audio Spectrum is being generated by the ASND file in the composition. The effect is straight by default, but you can attach an Audio Spectrum to a custom path for a curve.

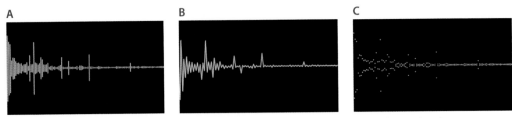

Figure 9.6 The three Display Options for Audio Spectrum are (A) Digital, (B) Analog lines, and (C) Analog dots.

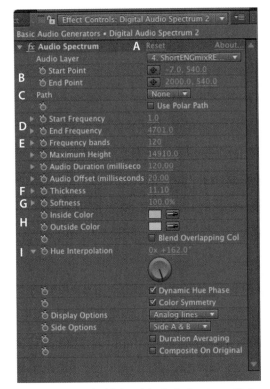

Figure 9.7 Some highlights of the Audio Spectrum effect.

A Audio Layer. Be sure to specify the source layer for the audio.

B Start Point, End Point. The easiest way to define the position is to click the target icons and then mark the desired position in the Composition panel.

C Path. You can use a custom path to generate the shape. Only paths applied to this same layer will populate the Path menu.

D Start and end frequency. You can set the frequency range for the effect. For example, you can limit the effect to only the bass portions of a track.

E Frequency bands. Use a higher number of bands to display the frequencies for a more complex effect.

F Thickness. Set the thickness for the lines of the spectrum.

G Softness. Set how feathered the lines of the spectrum will be.

H Inside Color and Outside Color. You can control the colors used to draw the line. Combining two different colors with softness can create a neon line effect.

I Hue interpolation. For any value greater than zero, the color will rotate through the hues based on the frequencies. Change your project to a 32-bpc color space to see the colors really light up.

Audio Waveform

The Audio Waveform effect produces a more wave-like shape than the Audio Spectrum effect. The setting options for Audio Waveform are very similar to the Audio Spectrum effect. Although it doesn't have the hue controls over the color like the Audio Spectrum effect, it does have the ability to react specifically to each channel in the stereo mix set under the waveform options. Like Audio Spectrum, Audio Waveform also has three Display Options (**Figure 9.8**).

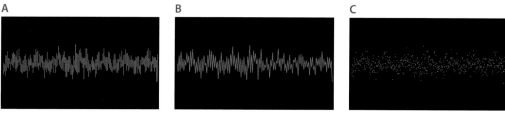

Figure 9.8 Display Options for Audio Waveform are (A) Digital, (B) Analog lines, and (C) Analog dots.

Using Tone to Create Sound

Although it sounds limiting at first, After Effects can create tone by applying the Tone effect to a layer. We know the anticipation is killing you. But the effect is surprisingly versatile. Instead of searching through libraries of various sound effects, Tone can generate simple sounds by mixing up to five different frequencies (**Figure 9.9**).

When you're using five frequencies to create one sound effect, the noise will distort rather quickly. To avoid distortion and clipping, divide 100 (for 100%) by the number of frequencies used to generate the sound. For example, if two frequencies are being used, you shouldn't set the level to a value higher than 50%. The biggest influence on the sound is the Waveform Options property that modifies how the frequencies are interwoven. Be sure to experiment with different methods to hear the effects.

NOTES

Tone will not function if placed on a placeholder layer. Be sure to apply it to a footage layer like a solid for it to function properly. If you apply it to a footage layer, the existing sound will be replaced.

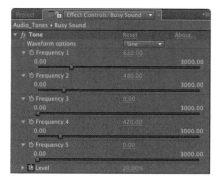

Figure 9.9 Adjust each of the five frequencies to create distinct results.

To really get the hang of the Tone effect, we recommend exploring the animation presets in the Effects & Presets panel. The Sound Effects category offers seven presets to choose from. When you apply a Tone preset, After Effects uses conventional keyframe techniques to manipulate the duration or repetition of the sound. For instance, with the Busy preset, if you want the sound to keep repeating, just copy and paste additional keyframes of the sequence of keyframes to continue repeating. If you want the beep to slow down and make noise a little longer, select all the keyframes by clicking directly on the name of the parameter, in this case, Level.

Once the keyframes are selected, you can change the spacing of the keyframes evenly by pressing Option (Alt) on the keyboard and dragging on the first or last keyframe (**Figure 9.10**). The Tone effect is directly tied to the presence of the solid layer. Trimming the layer will in turn trim the sound being generated. Just be sure to add fades at the beginning and end of the audio to eliminate any popping noise at the beginning or end of the layer.

Figure 9.10 Option (Alt)-dragging keyframes will keep the spacing between the keyframes in proportion to each other, no matter if they are tightened up or spaced farther apart.

To really hear the flexibility of the effect, combine Tone with other Audio effects. Options like Reverb, Flange & Chorus, and Modulator can create very complex sounds. You can use these to create digital effects or stingers to enhance your animation.

Using Expressions with Audio

If you've ever used expressions in After Effects, you know they can be easy to apply with the pick whip and can often provide solutions to animation problems that can't be solved any other way. However, many find the "math-like" scripting of expressions to be a turn-off.

But trust us; expressions are worth it and they don't have to be hard. With expressions and audio, you can literally drive the animation of a graphic element with the attributes of an audio channel. Using a simple pick whip, you can choose the parts of the sound you want to use and drive an animation. But before you can use the pick whip, you must prepare the audio by converting the audio into keyframes.

Converting Audio to Keyframes

When you first look at the properties of an audio layer, the only selectable item is the Audio Levels property. Unless you've already added keyframes, that value will remain flat and constant (which won't do much good for an animation).

To create parameters that are useful for animation, you need to convert the audio to keyframes. The easiest way to do this is with a keyframe assistant. Choose Animation > Keyframe Assistant > Convert Audio to Keyframes.

To see the results of this command, you need to view the layers in the Timeline panel. You'll find that a new Audio Amplitude null object has been created (**Figure 9.11**). Select the layer and press U to expand the animated properties of the layer. As you can see, the amplitude for the Left, Right, and Both Channels were converted into keyframes.

Now that keyframes have been created, the amplitude values can be tied to any property. Let's make the project blur to the beat of the music (**Figure 9.12**).

1. Open and select the Blurriness parameter of the adjustment layer.

2. Choose Animation > Add Expression.

3. Drag the pick whip to the slider under Both Channels and release it.

   By dragging the pick whip to the slider for Both Channels, you've created an expression where the value of the keyframes in the slider for the audio amplitude is tied to the blurriness of the adjustment layer.

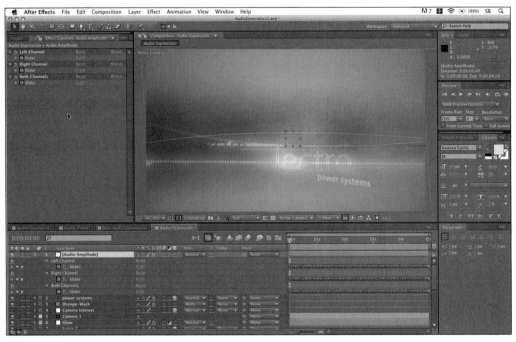

Figure 9.11 Three sets of keyframes created by the Convert Audio to Keyframes assistant. You can now use a pick whip to have the audio affect different parts of the scene.

Figure 9.12 To apply the expression, select the property and press Option+Shift+= (Alt+Shift+=). After the expression is applied, drag from the pick whip to the property you'd like to animate.

Shortcuts for Expressions

Expressions can get a bit cumbersome, so it's important to become familiar with them. We find these expression shortcuts helpful:

▶ To quickly view any expressions applied to a layer, press EE.

▶ To reveal all layers that contain expressions and key-frames, press U.

▶ To remove an expression, Option-click (Alt-click) the stopwatch of the parameter that contains the expression.

▶ To enable and disable an expression, click the = in the Timeline panel to the right of the parameter name.

Finding More Expressions

We haven't even scratched the surface of using expressions with audio. They can do much more than tie one parameter to another. Some expressions help animate cameras through 3D space or distribute layers in precise geometric patterns. If we've piqued your interests at all, you'll want to check out some of the following websites that specialize in teaching and/or selling scripts for use in After Effects:

▶ **www.tinyurl.com/aeexpressions.** The online After Effects help documentation for expressions is the perfect place to better familiarize yourself with expressions. More than just a typical help menu, the site is always kept current with updates and links to other relevant tutorials, articles, and resources.

▶ **www.motionscript.com.** An excellent resource to learn more about expressions and scripting, brought to you by Dan Ebberts.

▶ **www.aenhancers.com.** A site with message boards that cover everything from basic scripting and expressions to libraries, discussions, and even a board for script requests.

▶ **www.aescripts.com.** A very comprehensive site written by several of the industry's leading script writers. A multitude of searchable scripts are available for immediate download. The scripts cover many tasks, from placing layers in 3D space to setting up background renders. They even have an Expression toolbox designed to store and keep track of your scripts.

Using Soundbooth for Sound Design

Whenever you want to polish an animation and improve it from good to great, try adding sound design. By adding well-placed sound effects and environmental sounds, your animation will seem fuller and better timed. These sounds are often independent of the music track but can complement the music.

Soundbooth is the perfect tool for sound design because it has a little bit of everything. You'll find a searchable library of editable sources, single file editing, robust multitrack mixing, and effects that can add depth to the sound through simulating different environments.

Resource Central

Figure 9.13 Use the Workspace menu in Soundbooth to quickly change and optimize the interface for specific tasks.

To jump start sound design in Soundbooth, we recommend a quick trip online. Resource Central is the section of Soundbooth where you can browse through a range of audio resources. To view Resource Central, make sure you're connected to the Internet, and in the Workspace menu choose Find Sound Effects and Scores (**Figure 9.13**).

The Sound Effects and Scores features have very similar interfaces. So once you understand how to browse and import sources from Sound Effects (**Figure 9.14**), the same techniques will apply to Scores (**Figure 9.15**).

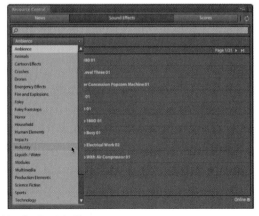

Figure 9.14 Search within specific categories to save time looking for the right files.

Figure 9.15 The Play button and the Download button are next to the names of the files. Click the Play button to preview the audio file; click the Download button to download the file to a shared folder on your hard drive.

After you've downloaded a file, drag it to the Project panel in the upper-left panel in Soundbooth to add it to your project.

Custom Scoring Motion Graphics

How would you like a collection of royalty-free music tracks? These tracks can be easily retimed or have their mix of instruments adjusted. You'll even receive a bunch to start (and others are affordably priced). Interested? Well then check out Scores.

The Scores you'll find in Soundbooth are amazingly flexible sources to work with. To browse through Scores, click the Scores button in the Resource Central panel.

1. As you browse through the different categories, press the Play button to preview the score.

2. When you've found the music you like, click the Download button to the left of the score's name to download it (**Figure 9.16**).

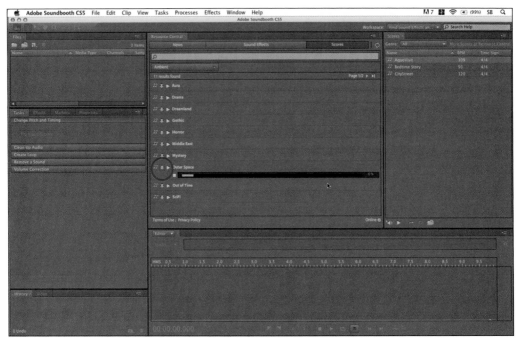

Figure 9.16 To use a score you like, download it by clicking the Download button.

3. Once the file has been downloaded, you will see a check mark to the right of its name in the panel. Even though the file has been downloaded, it still needs to be extracted. Drag on the name of the file to move it to the Scores panel on the right to extract the score and add it to the Scores library that's stored locally on your machine (**Figure 9.17**).

Figure 9.17 You must extract the file after download before it can be edited or used in a project. Drag the score to the Scores panel to extract the score into the local Scores library.

4. To edit and see the features of a score, it needs to be added to a multitrack project. Select the score and click the Add Score to Multitrack button (**Figure 9.18**).

5. Up to this point, you've just been using Soundbooth to browse through a library of sources. You couldn't actually save a file until it was visible in the multitrack project, but now it's ready to be saved.

After the project is saved, go back to the upper right of the interface and change the workspace to Edit Score to Video (**Figure 9.19**).

Now Soundbooth is ready to add a video track to the project. Import the file into the Files panel and drag it onto the audio tracks to add it to the project. Any additional tracks required for the footage will automatically be created (**Figure 9.20**). Soundbooth supports Flash Video, QuickTime, Windows Media, MPEG-4, and MPEG-2 files. Both AVI and MPEG-1 files are also supported for Windows.

Figure 9.18 If a score currently resides in your local Scores library, you can add it to a multitrack project by clicking the Add Score to Multitrack button at the bottom of the Scores panel.

Figure 9.19 Switching the workspace makes it easier to edit the score by automatically bringing the most used panels forward in the workspace.

Figure 9.20 This time-lapse shot of Seattle does not contain any audio.

TIP

Audio can be extracted from any video file imported into Soundbooth by clicking on the yellow words Extract Audio in the upper-right corner of the video track.

Figure 9.21 The Outer Space score on track 1. You can edit a score's length using the Properties panel.

To edit the audio to this video, you need to customize the score.

1. Select the score on Audio track 1 and select the Properties tab on the left to access the options for this score (**Figure 9.21**). Before you change any options, take a quick look at track one. The score has been divided into sections: an intro, an ending, and three parts. Since this clip is short, we don't need quite that many sections.

2. Instead of trying to edit the parts directly in the Timeline, go back to the Properties panel, click the Variation menu, and choose the 36 Seconds variation (**Figure 9.22**). Now the score is just composed of the Intro, Part3, and the End (**Figure 9.23**).

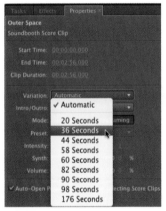

Figure 9.22 The Variation menu contains different lengths of the same score, so if you just need music for a 30-second spot, you can avoid more involved editing by choosing the shorter variation.

Figure 9.23 Look in the Timeline to see the different sections of music that make up a score. This makes the style of music predictable and modular, so overall it's easier to edit.

3. To quickly zoom the scale of the Timeline, click the Zoom Out Full button in the upper-right corner of the Timeline or use the keyboard shortcut (\) (**Figure 9.24**).

Figure 9.24 **Figure 9.24** The Zoom Out Full button displays the entire length of the audio clips in the Timeline.

4. Press Home and the spacebar to watch the project from the beginning.

5. To edit the score to match the length of the video, select the score in the Timeline. Then in the Properties panel, change the Intro/Outro setting to None and change the duration to 00:00:33.200 (**Figure 9.25**).

In addition to changing the length and parts of the score using the Properties panel, you can still edit the instrumentation of the score. To view all the different options, click the Parameters menu in the Timeline and choose Show All (**Figure 9.26**). To better view the different variables, click the Maximize Clip button in the upper-right corner of the score layer (**Figure 9.27**).

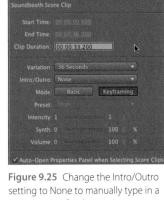

Figure 9.25 Change the Intro/Outro setting to None to manually type in a new duration for the score.

Figure 9.26 Parameters in a score can show you all the editable parameters to either add or remove instruments from the score.

279

Figure 9.27 Use the Maximize Clip button in the upper-right corner of the score layer to optimize the view of that score on your screen.

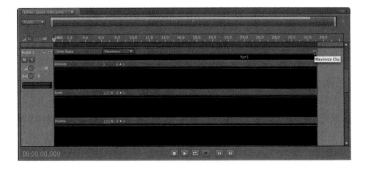

Each score will have slightly different variables to customize. In this specific score, Synth is the variable; Intensity and the Volume are present in all scores. The following explains what the Intensity and Synth settings are actually controlling in this score:

▶ **Intensity.** Intensity controls the amount of instrumentation used in the score. As the number increases or decreases, instruments will be added to or subtracted from the score.

▶ **Synth.** Synth is a specific parameter that controls how much synthesizer gets mixed into the score. Since this is unique to this score, the other variables could be other instruments or even control over different melodies.

To adjust any of the variables, drag directly on the yellow values. As the value changes, a keyframe will automatically be added at the location of the current time indicator (**Figure 9.28**).

Figure 9.28 All the variables in a score can be keyframed in the Timeline. Adjusting any of the values will automatically create a keyframe where the current time indicator is placed.

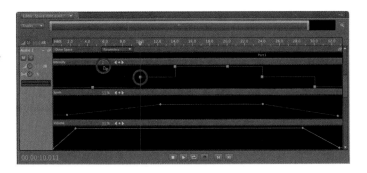

Keyframes in the Intensity layer will default to adding hold keyframes instead of linear keyframes like the other layers. To gradually mix in or mix out instruments in the Intensity layer, right-click on the hold keyframes and choose Linear (**Figure 9.29**).

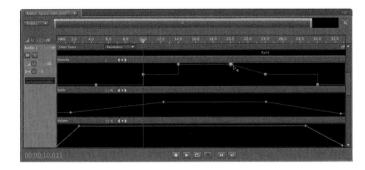

Figure 9.29 To change keyframe interpolation, right-click on the keyframe to choose Linear or Hold.

The music track is all set. To create a new mood for the animation, layer in some other sounds. Because this animation flickers a lot, some kind of rain background noise might work. As you add different tracks you can also add effects to the audio to distort it and make it sound more interesting.

To look for effects, change the workspace to Find Sound Effects and Scores in the Workspace menu.

When all the major edits are complete, shift your mind and think about how all of the sources are mixing together. Even if they don't mix well right off the bat, adding a few different effects can sometimes do the trick. The enhancements to the rest of this project are purely subjective, so we encourage you to experiment with different filters and settings.

TIP

When dragging a new audio source into a multitrack project, pay close attention to where you drop the file. If the cursor is over the middle of the track, the audio will start right there in the middle of the track. To avoid this, drag the file to the head of the track in the large gray area to the right of the Mute button.

1. To add filters to a track, you need to send it to edit by clicking Edit in the upper-right corner of the track.

2. Whenever a track is in edit, it's represented twice visually. The top version is the waveform; the bottom version shows the frequencies.

3. To apply an effect, click the Effects panel and then click the fx button in the lower-right corner of the panel to open the menu of effects (**Figure 9.30**).

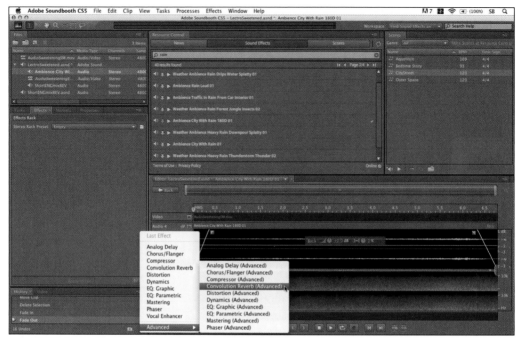

Figure 9.30 To place an effect on a track while in edit, select the track and click the fx button in the lower-right corner of the Effects panel to access the effects menu and apply the effect.

4. The Convolution Reverb effect is one of the most processor-intensive effects in Soundbooth (**Figure 9.31**). It's also the easiest to use to simulate different environments. Once a filter is applied, click Settings in the Effects panel to open its options. Play the track as you make adjustments to hear a preview in realtime.

5. Pitch and Timing will increase or decrease the frequency or change the length of the clip. Let's bring the pitch down just a touch. To apply the effect, choose Processes > Pitch and Timing (**Figure 9.32**).

Figure 9.31 Use the Convolution Reverb effect to simulate different audio environments.

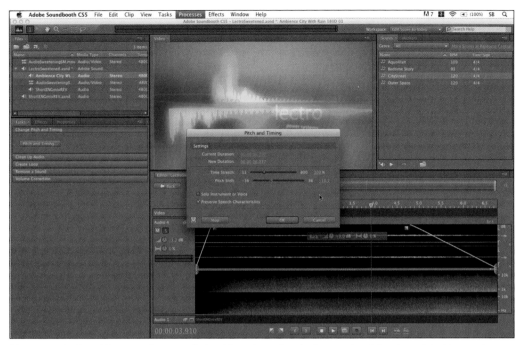

Figure 9.32 Pitch and Timing are being applied to this track to adjust the frequencies of the rain track. In this case, the frequencies decrease as the Pitch is adjusted down.

6. When you're finished applying filters to tracks, click the Back button in the upper-left corner of the Timeline to go back to multitrack editing. Click the Loopable button to the right of the Play button, and play the project (**Figure 9.33**). Adjust the fades and the levels on each track to choose a mix you like (**Figure 9.34**).

7. When you're happy with your new mix, save your project. As soon as you save a Soundbooth project, since projects are ASND files, it's already prepped and ready to use in the rest of the Adobe Creative Suite Production Bundle.

8. To create a single file of the entire mix, choose File > Export > Multitrack Mixdown. Saving a single mixdown is a good idea for a few reasons: to create a library of completed projects, for archiving purposes, or to send the file to others for feedback.

9. If you need to create a file from just one track, you can do that as well by right-clicking directly on the track and choosing Export Clip Mixdown.

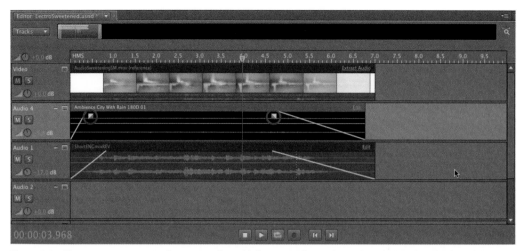

Figure 9.33 The two-tone squares in the upper-right and left corners of an audio track control the length of any fade in or fade out on that track.

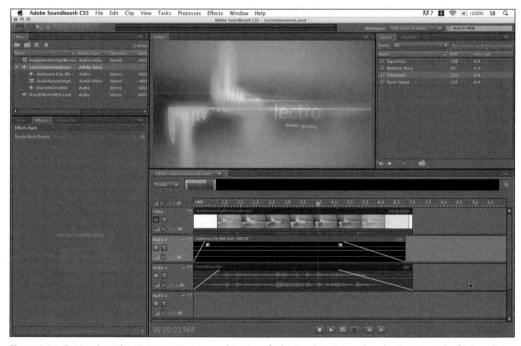

Figure 9.34 Getting the right mix is sometimes a combination of adjusting, listening, and readjusting to get the final results.

10

Designing Vector Shapes

I found I could say things with color and shapes that I couldn't say any other way—things I had no words for.
—Georgia O'Keeffe

Designing Vector Shapes

Throughout this book, we've talked about putting together the ultimate motion graphics toolbox. If you think about it, vector shapes are like a Swiss Army knife, versatile and essential. You have tools for just about every task in one small, lightweight package.

Vectors can be used in everything from masks to motion paths. They are flexible, yet precise; rarely does a project get completed without one. In this chapter we'll share the techniques we use most often when using vector shapes to create motion graphics.

Many Paths Lead to Vector Art

Neither art nor production is known for its predictability. Fortunately, the Adobe Creative Suite is designed to help make it easier to deal with changes as they arise. The Edit Original command in Adobe After Effects makes it effortless to jump back to Adobe Photoshop or Adobe Illustrator to quickly update a file.

We find that the versatility of tools like the Pen tool (as well as vector paths) make Illustrator and Photoshop worth visiting frequently. So when you create that perfect mask in Photoshop, you can paste it directly into Illustrator to apply some vector effects or import it into After Effects for animation. Throughout this chapter we'll discuss some of the finer points of working with vectors across Illustrator, Photoshop, and After Effects for creating motion graphics (**Figure 10.1**).

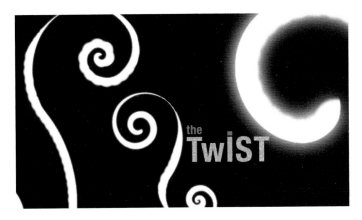

Figure 10.1 This design was completed using tools from Illustrator, Photoshop, and After Effects.

You'll find valuable, effective vector tools in all four graphics applications in the Creative Suite. How do you know which one to use? Here are some tips to help you choose:

▶ **Illustrator.** The words vector and Illustrator are practically interchangeable. Vectors are to Illustrator what photos are to Photoshop. With precise control over strokes, fills, and vector filters, Illustrator is the answer for anything vector. It's really the king of vectors. We use it most often to create graphic eye candy, flowing swooshes, dashed strokes, or any kind of repeating pattern (**Figure 10.2**).

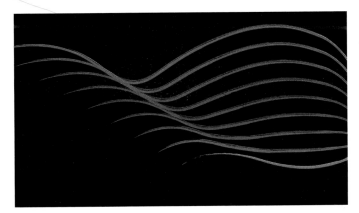

Figure 10.2 These lines were originally only two paths, accented with different brushes. This group of flowing lines was created using a blend between the two paths.

▶ **Photoshop.** Photoshop is the best application to create, edit, and save selections from bitmap files. We usually convert selections to paths and save them for use in

TIP

If you'd like to learn more about Flash and After Effects integration, you can read a free excerpt called "Flash Essentials for After Effects Users" from Adobe Press at www.peachpit.com/store/product.aspx?isbn=0321606078.

NOTES

If you need to create Flash animation, remember that After Effects can export a vector SWF file. Just be sure to use only vector sources and avoid rasterizing layers. This means no filters or motion blur. Following all of these guidelines will keep your files nice and tiny for the Web.

After Effects. Its tight integration with After Effects means that any vector shapes in Photoshop will import as layer masks in After Effects. This is quite a time-saver when you're moving a project from storyboards in Photoshop to animation in After Effects.

▶ **Flash.** Flash is a popular tool among character animators due to its vector drawing and Timeline capabilities. Options like the Bones tool also offer Inverse Kinematics animation tools, which allow for animating items with parenting-type controls (although the interactions use a different model than After Effects). For experienced After Effects users, the Flash Timeline takes a little getting used to.

▶ **After Effects.** Many designers fall into the trap of trying to do everything in After Effects. Just remember that After Effects is also known for its capability of easily working with a variety of sources. We'll often copy and paste paths into position keyframes to create perfectly smooth camera moves. But of course, we create plenty of graphics directly in After Effects with Shape Layers, as well as create and modify paths or masks with the Pen and Point tools.

The Pen and Point Tools

With all the different Pen and Point tools, creating and editing paths can appear more complicated than they really are. In this section, we'll provide essential keyboard shortcuts to all but eliminate the temptation to switch to other tools. These shortcuts function the same in Illustrator, Photoshop, and After Effects. Master these and you'll gain confidence and speed across the Creative Suite.

Creating Anchor Points

To break down vector paths and shapes to their core, they store position information in two dimensions. Whether it's the precise edges of a shape or points along a path, you can store that data within a vector path. And with an infinite number of lines and shapes possible, paths only use two kinds of points: smooth points and corner points (**Figure 10.3**).

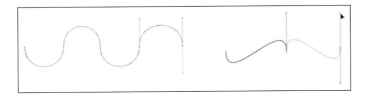

Figure 10.3 Other than using the Shift key to keep the handles straight, only the corner point in the middle of the second path required a keyboard shortcut to break the handles and redirect the curve.

The difference between smooth points versus corner points is that smooth points have straight direction lines, often referred to as handles. When you adjust direction lines attached to a smooth point, the curved segments on both sides of the point are affected simultaneously. On the other hand, if you change a direction line attached to a corner point, only the curve on the same side of the point as the direction line is affected.

The positions of the direction lines and points will affect the size and shape of a curved segment between the points. To adjust the direction handles after a point has been set, use the Convert Anchor Point tool (pressing Option [Alt] while using the Pen tool will toggle to the Convert Anchor Point tool). As you draw paths, you can leave them open (such as a curved line or spiral). This works well for motion paths you want to create for the Position property. You can also make closed shapes (such as circles, ellipses, or custom shapes). These work well as design elements or for masks applied to layers in the After Effects Timeline.

Selecting Paths and Points

When you create paths, you'll undoubtedly want to move the paths and points around the scene for final placement. There are primarily two tools you can use to select paths and points: the Selection tool and the Direct Selection tool. What makes them different is exactly what is selected by default:

- ▶ The **Selection tool** selects an entire path and its points with one click, so it's the tool to use for repositioning an entire path.

- ▶ The **Direct Selection tool** selects individual points and sections of paths. When using this tool, you must click directly on points or drag a selection around the anchor points to select them.

TIP

As you create a path with the Pen tool, if you want to stop without closing the path, press Command (Ctrl) on the keyboard to quickly switch to the Selection tool. Click anywhere in an empty part of the canvas to deactivate the last point and set the path.

Using Smooth Points

Smooth points are a drag, literally. To create a smooth point as you're creating a path, just drag as you set your points. If you hold down the Shift key right after you start to drag, the direction handles will snap every 45 degrees (**Figure 10.4**).

Figure 10.4 These two lines were created using the Shift-drag technique. Drag the handles in the same direction for each point to create the tight waves or in the opposite direction for the large curve shapes.

TIP

As you're dragging out handles in Illustrator and After Effects, you can reposition the anchor point. Hold down the spacebar and drag around the canvas to relocate it.

Creating Corner Points

Creating a corner point as you create a path is a two-click process. Click once to set the position of the path point. Then, before you click that point again, in Photoshop and Illustrator hold down the Option (Alt) key, in After Effects hold down the Command (Ctrl) key, and then drag to determine the direction of the path after the corner point (**Figure 10.5**).

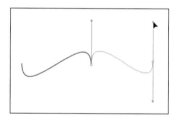

Figure 10.5 Changing direction of the control handles across a path point creates a corner point.

Pen Tool Auto Switching

When you're working with the Pen tool, pay close attention to the lower-right corner of the icon. The tool will dynamically update and change functions to try to anticipate your next intended action (**Figure 10.6**).

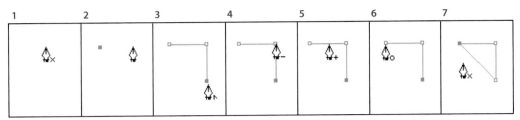

1 The tool is ready to create a new path.

2 An icon does not appear because new points are being added to the path. The closed anchor point will be attached to the next anchor point set.

3 When you set a point, move away, and hover back over the active point. The tool anticipates a drag to create handles for a smooth curve point.

4 Over the open point, the tool switches to delete path points.

5 Over any other section of the path, the tool changes to add anchor points.

6 Over the original anchor point, the circle indicates that the tool will close the path.

7 With the path closed, the Pen reloads. The x indicates that the tool is ready to create another separate path.

Figure 10.6 The Pen tool displays its function in the lower-right corner.

Some find this Auto Switching useful (unless it's offering the wrong choice). If you don't like the Auto Switching behavior, you can disable it. Each tool treats Auto slightly differently:

▶ In Illustrator, you can disable switching completely. Choose Preferences > General, and then select Disable Auto Add/Delete.

▶ In Photoshop, deselect Auto Add/Delete in the Options bar to disable switching.

▶ Although there is no option to disable Auto Switching in After Effects, the RotoBezier option automatically sets the direction handles for you. This can make creating paths easier and faster to draw (although it's a matter of personal taste).

Setting Up Vector Documents for Motion Graphics

Although it's easy to think of artwork as artwork, it's important to remember that Illustrator serves several design communities. Print designers use it for CMYK artwork and illustrations. Web designers use it for user interface design. Motion graphics designers tend to use it to make art elements and fluid shapes.

TIP

If you want After Effects to automatically create and adjust direction handles for you, you can convert any manual path or shape into a RotoBezier path after it's already been created. Simply select the path and choose Layer > Mask And Shape Path > RotoBezier.

While you're in Illustrator, if you're more comfortable with the layout of the interface in Photoshop, use a new workspace setup. Choose Window > Workspace > Like Photoshop and Illustrator will look surprisingly similar to Photoshop.

Of course, when three different camps get together, the potential for problems is high. If you don't set up your AI files correctly, they may be difficult (if not impossible) to effectively use with After Effects.

Creating Illustrator Files

Illustrator has several features to help designers create elements for video, but it all starts with the document settings. Even though Illustrator is vector based, it's important to set up your documents using one of the Video and Film presets in the New Document Profile.

Yes, you can create vector elements any size you want, and then scale them in After Effects; however, this requires selecting the Continuously Rasterize switch. Although this may not be a big deal for a few elements, once you start duplicating those elements and animating them, render times can start to increase.

In Illustrator CS5 there are more options for video in the Advanced settings at the bottom of the New Document dialog box (**Figure 10.7**). Here are a few we find essential:

NOTES

It's important to remember that many vector files are designed for professional printing (especially logos). As such, they'll use the CMYK color space. You need to convert these files before bringing them into After Effects. Open the file and choose File > Document Color Mode > RGB.

Figure 10.7 When you use one of the new document video presets, the technically important settings are already configured for you.

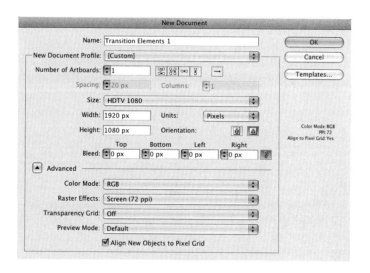

▶ We recommend selecting Align New Objects to Pixel Grid to help keep hard edges sharp.

▶ Change Transparency Grid to Off if you want Illustrator to use its traditional white background.

▶ If you want to see how your Illustrator files will look
   when rasterized, change the Preview Mode to Pixels.

Designing with Multiple Artboards

You can use multiple artboards to make Illustrator function
like a big table. Instead of pieces of paper on a desk, it's
your designs virtually living in one Illustrator document.
This approach will seem familiar because it's much like
having multiple compositions in an After Effects file.

If you are designing artwork such as a title treatment or
anything that benefits from the spatial reference to its
environment, artboards make it a breeze to create multiple
versions within one document. Instead of creating one
huge document with a bunch of different versions strewn
all over the place, use multiple artboards to add some
organization to an otherwise rather unorganized process.
Artboards can be created at anytime, so of course, there's
more than one way to create them (**Figure 10.8**).

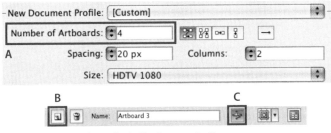

Figure 10.8 You can create new
artboards in three different ways.

A When you start a project under the New Document Profile.
B When you press Shift+O to select the Artboard tool; in the tool options menu click the
   New Artboard button.
C When you click the Move/Copy Artboard button in the Artboard tool options menu. By
   default it moves the artboards around. Hold down Option (Alt) on your keyboard and
   drag to make a copy (the same command you use to copy elements in the canvas).

In addition to their functions as an organizer, artboards
are quite functional as well. It's convenient to have all the
designs and elements in one document, ready to save out
at any time. This kind of workflow works well for graphics
waiting for approval as well as for a toolkit of elements.

To import each of these elements for animation in After
Effects, you'll need to create separate files for each. Simply
choose File > Save As. Make sure the Use Artboards option

TIP

When you need to create multiple variations of a graphic, create one version of the graphic and copy it to the clipboard. With that copied, choose Edit > Paste On All Artboards. You can then modify each graphic independently.

Using multiple artboards is an easy way to create frame-by-frame animation. Create an element to animate and position it in the frame. Duplicate the artboard and its contained artwork by Option (Alt) dragging on the artboard to create a duplicate of the board. Repeat the process for each frame, and be sure to save each to a separate file.

is selected at the bottom of the window. You can then choose to use All or specify a range.

Illustrator's Vector Tools

Building shapes for motion graphics can be a lot like making tile for a mosaic. You have to take care of the little things in order to create the big picture. Illustrator is the perfect place to start building elements.

Illustrator is the best application for creating complex shapes, patterns, and brush strokes. With new tools like the Width tool and refined Dashed Line controls, Illustrator CS5 gives you more precise control over the details. Add new paint features like the Bristle brush, and you can add highly stylized looks to your graphics without the extra render times sometimes caused by heavy effects filters.

Importing these elements into After Effects is a straightforward process. However, there are some tips and tricks that can help extract the best information from the projects for use in After Effects.

Creating Fluid Shapes

One hallmark of modern motion graphics design is the use of flowing vector shapes. When you need these, look no further than Illustrator. Let's create a fluid shape from scratch. We'll use a two-step process. We'll first create the base shape with the Spiral tool (Illustrator offers many other Shape tools as well, such as the Arc tool and the Polygon tool). We'll then use the Width tool to add the finishing accents to the curves.

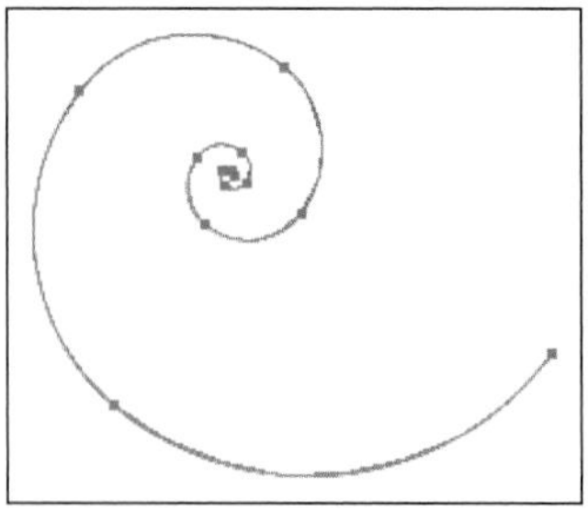

1. Select the Spiral tool from the Tools panel. It can be found in the same well as the Line tool. Drag anywhere in the canvas to create the shape (**Figure 10.9**).

2. As you're dragging out the shape, there are two sets of keys you can use to affect the shape of the spiral:

   ▶ Use the up and down arrows to add or subtract segments.

   ▶ Hold down Command (Ctrl) as you drag to control the decay of the spiral.

Figure 10.9 Use the arrow keys as you drag to add or subtract segments from the Spiral tool.

3. To complete the shape, create another spiral that's slightly different. Rotate and position it so the two pieces are tail to tail.

4. Combine the two tails by executing both the Average and Join commands in one step with a handy keyboard shortcut. Select both end points with the Direct Selection tool and press Command+Option+Shift+J (Ctrl+Alt+Shift+J) to move (Average) and combine both end points (Join) in one action (**Figure 10.10**).

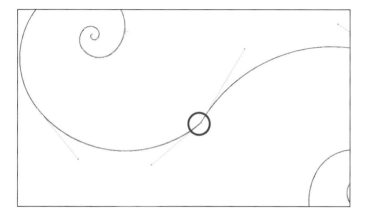

Figure 10.10 The two end points are moved and joined together, creating one continuous shape.

5. Use the Convert Point tool (Shift+C) to smooth out the anchor point.

With the two spirals joined together, you've created an initial shape. Let's use the Width tool to take things a step further and accent the curves with precision (**Figure 10.11**).

1. Select the Width tool (Shift+W). Drag anywhere on a path to pull out the width.

2. Press Option (Alt) as you drag to bring the shape out of one side of the path only.

You can save the profiles created by the Width tool to reuse on any path. Select the path and view the profile either in the Control panel or the bottom of the Stroke panel. Click on the profile and click the disc icon in the lower-left corner to save the profile.

TIP

If you've used Illustrator for a while, you might be used to opening different panels to modify things like Stroke and Fill. With the new Appearance panel (Shift+F6), you can access controls for fill, stroke, and effects in just one panel.

Figure 10.11 Press Shift+W to select the Width tool and drag on any path to change its width. Press Option (Alt) and drag to add width to one side only.

Creating Flowing Lines with the Blend Tool

Let's continue our journey to create smooth lines and flowing shapes. We like to use the Blend tool for creating flowing lines that can add depth to just about any project. The key to working with this tool is really in After Effects. All you need to do in Illustrator is to create the paths in the artboard. Once the lines are created, you can select the paths and copy them in Illustrator. Then, in After Effects, you can paste only the raw path data of the strokes. Paths can be pasted into either a shape layer or onto a layer solid to then apply effects to the paths.

So, let's create our flowing lines in Illustrator, understanding that only the path will be imported into After Effects.

1. Draw two smooth paths across the screen with the Pen tool. For a slightly busier look, have them overlap at some point in their curves (**Figure 10.12**).

2. Press W to select the Blend tool, click on the first path, Option-click (Alt-click) on the second path to create the blend, and open the Blend Tool dialog box. With the dialog box open, you can change the default settings for the Blend tool and specify your own options. To see the strokes, change the spacing to Specified Steps and choose the number of steps in between the two strokes you created (**Figure 10.13**). We'll set this example project to eight specified steps.

NOTES

If you're pasting paths from Illustrator into After Effects, in Illustrator choose Preferences > File Handling and Clipboard and make sure AICB Preserve Paths is selected. This will ensure that the path data will be properly interpreted through the clipboard.

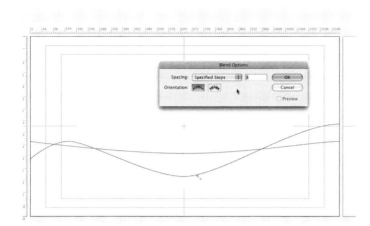

Figure 10.12 Two basic lines drawn in the canvas set the outer boundaries for a ribbon of lines you'll create using the Blend tool.

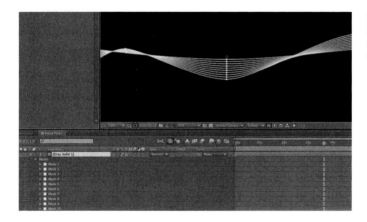

Figure 10.13 Use the Blend tool between two different shapes to create copies that will blend from one shape to the other.

Creating Grids

Let's take a creative break from flowing lines to create a graphic that is precise. An unsung hero in many designers' toolkits, the Grid tool creates pixel-perfect grids. Found under the Line tool in the Tools panel, the Grid tool can create even divisions or weighted divisions where each row or column is a different size (**Figure 10.14**).

Figure 10.14 You're able to create and color a grid quickly using the Grid tool and the Live Paint Bucket tool.

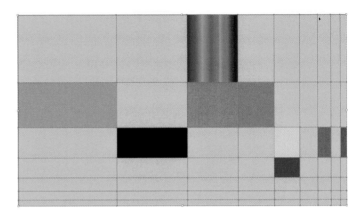

Make a grid to cover the entire artboard, and then drag from one corner diagonally across to the other. To dynamically modify the appearance of the grid as you're dragging, press X, C, F, or V to skew the grid off center. Think of those keys like the direction arrows on a keyboard: X is left, C is right, F is up, and V is down. While still dragging out the grid, using the arrow keys will increase or decrease the overall number of divisions (**Figure 10.15**).

Figure 10.15 The same shortcut keys for the Grid tool also work with the Polar Grid tool.

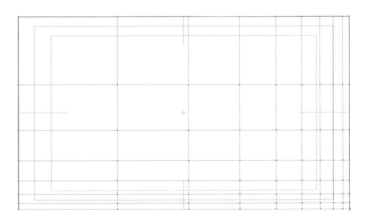

After creating the grid, add color to the different squares using the Live Paint Bucket tool. With the grid still selected, select the Live Paint Bucket tool (K).

Select a swatch from the Swatches panel to choose a color. Use the arrow keys to choose different colors. Notice that the colors are being chosen directly from the Swatches panel (**Figure 10.16**). You can fill with any swatch in the Swatches panel, even gradients and patterns.

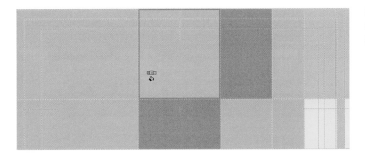

Figure 10.16 Selected closed shapes can be filled using the Live Paint Bucket tool.

Outlining Type with Offset Path

The Offset Path effect is the best way to create an outline for any path created in Illustrator. We use it most often to create a thick border around type. Let's use Offset Path to create a border around some type we'll continue to stylize later with the Blob brush (**Figure 10.17**).

1. Create a duplicate of the type layer, and choose a different color for the fill of the type on the upper layer so you can clearly see the results of the effect.

2. Select the type on the lower layer and choose Effect > Path > Offset Path. Select preview and change Offset to **15**. Once a filter is applied, it can always be edited in the Appearance panel (Shift+F6).

Effects in Illustrator are divided into two sections, Photoshop and Illustrator. Illustrator effects are vector and should be applied to vector graphics. Photoshop effects can be applied to bitmap and vector graphics. Their effect will generate bitmap results. You can specify the resolution of the raster effect by choosing Effect > Document Effect Raster Settings.

Figure 10.17 Duplicate the entire type layer so the offset and the type layer will be ready for animation; that is, they will already be on two separate layers.

It's easiest to create variations on a shape by using Effects. As effects are applied, they remain fully editable in the Appearance panel. Although this makes it easier to go back and make changes, it makes it harder to use that new shape as a starting point for more changes without rendering the effect into actual geometry. The function used to render effects into actual geometry is Expand (**Figure 10.18**).

Figure 10.18 Expanding an object will render effects or blends, or even convert strokes to fills. The Pathfinder is the tool to use when you want to combine multiple overlapping shapes into one object.

To properly prepare this offset path graphic, you need to use the Expand function. Choose Object > Expand. Since we're not planning on animating each letter individually, we should fix the overlapping paths and merge all the letters into one final shape. Choose Window > Pathfinder, and then choose Unite to merge all the overlapping paths together into one object.

Adding Texture with Brushes in Illustrator

Brushes in Illustrator are slightly different from brushes in Photoshop in that each stroke is recorded as a vector path. This is useful because it means that you can go back and edit the stroke. However, it's not useful when you end up with a lot of strokes in a project because they can bog down Illustrator's performance as you work on a project. Fortunately, creating motion graphics doesn't normally require extensive use of vector brush strokes in Illustrator.

In this section we'll add some texture behind a graphic using the new Bristle brushes. We'll also paint directly within some text using the Blob brush and the new Draw Inside drawing mode.

Using Bristle Brushes

The Bristle brush is a new feature in CS5 that is designed to simulate the true characteristics of an actual paintbrush. With the Bristle brush you can create natural-media brush strokes with precise control over the bristle settings. To achieve the full effect of the Bristle brush, we recommend using a Wacom tablet. The tablet works with the Bristle brush to determine the angle and the pressure of the brush. Without the tablet, painting with the Bristle brush will draw a continuous even stroke (**Figure 10.19**).

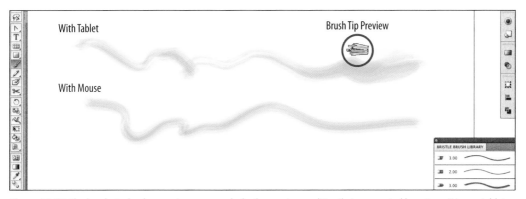

Figure 10.19 The brush stroke drawn using a mouse lacks the varying qualities that are created by using a Wacom tablet.

To load a Bristle brush, choose the Brush tool, and in the Control panel open the brush definition menu by choosing New Brush > Bristle Brush. Or, you can open the Bristle Brush Library from the Brushes panel menu by choosing Open Brush Library > Bristle Brush > Bristle Brush Library. Any traditionally trained artist will appreciate these preset brushes and custom options because each tip is modeled after specific real-world brushes (**Figure 10.20**). Here are some tips for choosing and working with the Bristle brush:

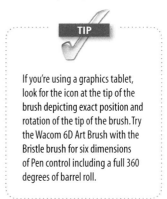

TIP

If you're using a graphics tablet, look for the icon at the tip of the brush depicting exact position and rotation of the tip of the brush. Try the Wacom 6D Art Brush with the Bristle brush for six dimensions of Pen control including a full 360 degrees of barrel roll.

▶ Angled brushes are great for accenting dimension and calligraphic styles. Use straight brushes to paint a constant, even stroke. Tips with points are good for general use; hold them more vertically for sharp lines, and angle your pen on its side for thicker strokes.

Figure 10.20 There are 14 Bristle brushes to choose from.

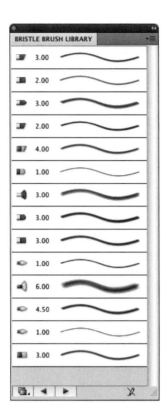

▶ When painting, use the [key to make the brush tip radius smaller and the] key to make the brush tip larger.

▶ Use the number keys across the top of your keyboard to change the brush opacity in 10 percent increments (1 = 10%; 10 = 100%).

Each Bristle brush can be customized. Double-click the brush in the Brushes panel to open its options. The different settings are literally named after each characteristic associated with actual paintbrushes. Here are some tips for customizing a Bristle brush (**Figure 10.21**):

▶ Set a low Bristle Density to create a stroke with more variance in the stroke.

▶ Longer bristles create softer brush strokes.

▶ Combine adjustments to the width of the bristles with the length of the bristles to intensify the adjustments. For example, choose very thin bristles with long bristles to create very soft strokes.

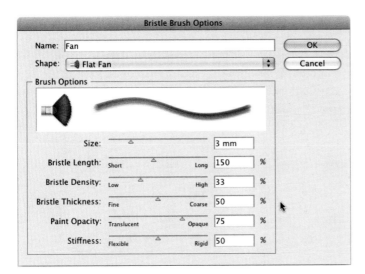

Using the Blob Brush

Using the Blob brush is another way to paint in Illustrator. But instead of painting individual strokes, the final result is always outlined, creating a solid shape or "blob." Combine the Blob brush with the new drawing modes in CS5, Draw Behind and Draw Inside, and you'll have countless ways to treat type or any shape in Illustrator (**Figure 10.22**).

1. To paint inside each letter, you need to activate the new Draw Inside mode found at the bottom of the Tools panel. Select an individual letter using the Direct Selection tool. Click the Drawing Mode button at the bottom of the Tools panel and choose Draw Inside. Dotted-line corner brackets appear around the letter to indicate you're using Draw Inside mode.

2. Be sure to deselect the letter before you continue so you don't accidentally change the letter's fill or stroke. Press Shift+B to choose the Blob brush, and paint inside the top part of the letter.

3. Choosing Draw Inside with a letter selected automatically creates a clipping mask for that letter, which is visible in the Layers panel.

4. Select the shape made by the Blob brush in the Layers panel and apply an inner glow to discolor the edge of the blob. In this example we used a dark brown color and chose Multiply to darken the edge of the shape and add some dimension to the paint.

Figure 10.22 The Blob brush makes it simple to create any organic shape like dripping paint without the headache of multiple brush strokes because it creates a filled shape as its result. Combine the Blob brush with the new drawing modes to paint organically within rigid structures like these letters.

Building Complex Shapes

There are primarily three techniques we use regularly to create more complicated shapes. When you combine these techniques with all the tools available in Illustrator, there really isn't much that can't be created.

Copy, Repeat Transform

One of the easiest ways to build complex shapes in Illustrator is by repeating a transform function. Whenever you transform vector shapes in Illustrator, you can always repeat the transformation by pressing Command+D

TIP

When performing transforms on a rotation, rotate the shape by a number that divides evenly into 360 to avoid any irregularities in the created pattern.

(Ctrl+D). The key is to specify the anchor point before completing the transformations (**Figure 10.23**).

1. To create a flower pattern from the single oval in Figure 10.23, select the oval and the Rotate tool.

2. To specify the anchor point for the rotation and open the Rotate dialog box, Option-click (Alt-click) at the bottom of the oval.

3. Choose a number that divides evenly into 360 (for example 20 or 30) and click the Copy button.

4. Because you created a copy of the shape and transformed its rotation when you clicked the copy button, Illustrator will automatically repeat the same functions again when you press Command+D (Ctrl+D). That key command will repeat the previous function each time it is used, so repeat the command multiple times until the shape is completed.

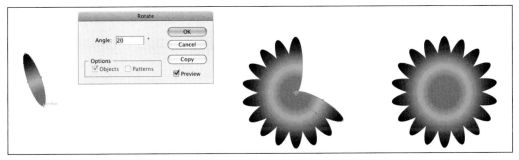

Figure 10.23 Pressing Option (Alt) as you set an anchor point for the rotation allows you to choose a specific value for each rotation. As you create copies of your shape, the flower in steps 1-4 fills out. This Option (Alt) technique works with many more tools than just Rotation.

Pathfinder

Using the Pathfinder is a way to create new shapes by using overlapping shapes. For example, you might want to cut a circular shape out of a square. With the overlapping shapes selected, choose Window > Pathfinder and look closely at the buttons in the upper row to see the function each button will perform. Click a button to apply that function; undo and try another to see how each function is applied (**Figure 10.24**).

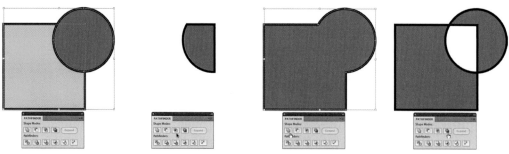

Figure 10.24 When using the Pathfinder functions, the object in the foreground is what determines the color of the resulting shape. The illustrations on each button in the Pathfinder clearly depict each function.

TIP

When you're using the Shape Builder tool, you can specify the fill and stroke of the new shapes with the colors loaded into the Fill and Stroke in the Tools panel.

The Shape Builder tool performs the same functions as the Pathfinder in a more visual and interactive manner (**Figure 10.25**). To use the Shape Builder tool, the shapes must first be selected. Drag through any of the shapes to combine them. Then hold down Option (Alt) and drag to subtract any geometry away from the shape.

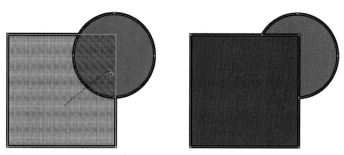

Figure 10.25 The Shape Builder tool performs the same basic functions as the Pathfinder in a more direct, interactive manner. Unlike the Pathfinder, you can specify a revised shape color from the fill in the Tool Panel.

Creating Libraries of Shapes

If there is a vector graphic you need to use on a regular basis, you should consider saving it as a symbol. To save a graphic, simply drag it directly into the Symbols panel (**Figure 10.26**). Here are some of the finer points to consider as you create your own symbols:

▶ When saving a symbol, the Type setting is ignored in Illustrator. That option is used when saving graphics for use in Flash.

▶ Name the symbol, set the registration point, and click OK. The registration point is like setting the anchor point of a symbol.

▶ To save a symbol permanently, save a library. In the Symbols panel menu choose Save Symbol Library. Any symbol in the panel will be saved into that library.

▶ All saved libraries will appear in the User Defined section of Symbol Libraries.

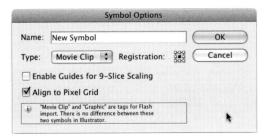

Figure 10.26 The Symbol Options panel for saving a symbol. The Type setting has no effect on a symbol being saved in Illustrator. It only pertains to symbols in Flash.

Organizing Layers for Animation

When you're working with flattened vector files, you'll need to separate the elements into layers so they can be independently animated in After Effects. If you need a refresher, we covered multiple ways to release artwork to layers in Chapter 4. Here are some of the key commands we've found useful in Illustrator for selecting, grouping, and ungrouping objects:

▶ **Select all objects on a layer.** Option-click (Alt-click) on the layer name

▶ **Switch between the Selection and Direct Selection tools.** Command+Option+Tab (Ctrl+Alt+Tab)

▶ **Toggle between Direct and Group Select tools.** Option (Alt)

▶ **Ungroup.** Command+Shift+G (Ctrl+Shift+G)

▶ **Group.** Command+G (Ctrl+G)

▶ **Create a new layer.** Command+L (Ctrl+L)

Using Symbols for Quick Designs

As you design in Illustrator, there's a secret source of vector artwork you need to know about: Symbols. To view Symbols, choose Window > Symbols. Use the Symbols panel menu to load the different libraries. To use a symbol, simply drag it to your artboard.

Symbols are vector graphics that are stored in a library within Illustrator. They can be used with the Symbol Sprayer tool to spread them around, much like particles. The interesting thing about Symbols is how they are linked back to their library. When you drag a symbol into an artboard, it's just an instance of that symbol. So if you apply a change to the symbol, you'll have the option of spreading that adjustment across all the different instances of that symbol used in your Illustrator file.

To be able to edit a symbol and break it apart for animation, right-click and choose Break Link to Symbol. Once the link is broken, you can separate any elements onto their own layers.

If you want more symbols, check out the Adobe Exchange website for Illustrator to find many more symbols and a bunch of other presets and goodies.

Expanding Objects

Some elements in Illustrator need to be expanded before they can be separated into layers for animation. When you're working with blended shapes, there is an option to expand the blend. This will preserve the strokes and any brushes applied as individually editable. Usually, to prepare these elements for animation, we'll follow expanding the blend with the Release To Layers command and move the group of layers out of their parent layer so each element resides on its own layer (**Figure 10.27**).

To Expand a blend, choose Object > Blend > Expand. Use Release to Layers, Sequence to move each ring onto its own layer. Then select all the new layers and drag them to the top of the layer hierarchy so they can be imported into After Effects as separate elements.

Figure 10.27 Once this blend of rings was expanded into individual objects, each ring was assigned a different brush and color. They were then released to layers and moved out of their parent layer, so each element would be on its own layer in After Effects.

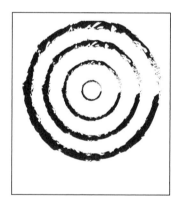

NOTES

You can save a layered Photoshop file directly from Illustrator by choosing File > Export > Photoshop psd. This is helpful when creating graphics that will be further treated and composited with other graphic elements in Photoshop.

Combine Expand with Simplify to create the shape and control the number of vertices required to trace a shape in After Effects (**Figure 10.28**). Sometimes just using Expand will create many unnecessary vertices, which is why it's so important to use Simplify to reduce those numbers and keep things simple.

Use the following two steps to create the actual outline of the shape (step 1) and limit the number of vertices used to create that shape (step 2).

1. Use Expand to trace the outer edges of the shape and notice the high number of vertices generated. To apply Expand, choose Object > Expand.

2. With the new path selected, choose Object > Path > Simplify, select Preview, and drag the sliders to make adjustments. Use a high number for Curve Precision to stay true to the original shape.

Figure 10.28 Use Expand to convert the variable width stroke into a filled shape. Use the Path > Simply function to trim down the number of path points required to recreate the shape.

Designing Vectors with Photoshop

Photoshop's vector capabilities have continued to grow exponentially with the release of each new version. Many artists, editors, and photographers unfamiliar with Illustrator have found this very helpful. They can take advantage of vector graphics' scalability and flexibility without having to learn a slightly different interface and a number of new tools.

There are three different modes for using and creating vector paths in Photoshop: Shape Layers, Paths, and Fill Pixels (**Figure 10.29**).

▶ **Shape Layers.** Creating vectors using this mode automatically creates a solid-color filled layer and applies the path as a vector mask to that solid color layer. The opacity and color of the fill can be adjusted in the Layers panel using the Fill option.

▶ **Paths.** Paths mode creates a path without a fill or stroke that is not visible in the Layers panel but is shown in the Paths panel as a Work Path.

▶ **Fill Pixels.** The Fill Pixels mode can only be selected when a nonvector layer is selected in the Layers panel. It creates bitmap fills and strokes using vector paths like the Custom Shape tool.

Figure 10.29 Shape Layers and Paths use the same basic paths to create vectors; they are just saved in different places.

When you're using any vector Shape tool, click on the arrow just to the right of the Custom Shape tool to view its options. You can create a star in the Polygon shape options and add arrow heads to the Line tool.

Using the Custom Shape Tool

To quickly view all the vector tools available in Photoshop, press U to select the Custom Shape tool and look in the Control panel. You should recognize most of the usual suspects: the Pen tool, the Direct Selection tool, and some Shape tools (Line, Rectangle, Ellipse, etc.). The shape farthest to the right that looks like a blob is called the Custom Shape tool. When a Custom Shape tool is used in a Photoshop document, by default it creates a shape layer with a solid color fill. Here are some things to consider when working with the Custom Shape tool:

▶ With the Custom Shape tool selected, click the Shape thumbnail to the right to open the Custom Shape Picker.

▶ To add more shapes into the picker, click the arrow in the upper-right corner and scroll down to choose a library.

▶ When you choose a library, add the new shapes to your current selection by choosing Append, or replace the current library with the new library.

- To use a custom shape, drag it directly onto the canvas. Hold down the Shift key to keep its original proportions. Its color is determined by the foreground color in the Tools panel.

- To change colors, select the layer, load a new color into the foreground color, and press Option+Delete (Alt+Delete) to fill from the foreground color.

- Because custom shapes create a vector shape layer, they can be edited just like any other vector shape with the standard Pen and Point tools.

Any vector shape in Photoshop can be saved as a custom shape. Select the vector path and choose Edit > Define Custom Shape. Add a name and click OK to save the shape.

Understanding Work Paths

Whenever a path is created in Photoshop, it is either a Work Path or a shape layer. Work Paths are special in that they can be created from a selection. This can come in handy when you need to create a vector shape from an object in footage or a picture. Use the superior selection tools in Photoshop to create a selection, and then convert the selection to a path. Then import that path into After Effects to use as a source to generate an animated graphic effect (**Figure 10.30**). Follow these three steps to create and save any path in Photoshop from a selection.

Figure 10.30 Work Paths can be created from selections, converted to selections, and permanently saved through the different commands in the Paths panel menu.

1. Load any selection you want to use as a source to create a new path.

2. Create a new blank layer in the Layers panel, select that layer, and open the Paths panel.

3. In the Paths panel menu, choose > Make Work Path.

When you're saving a Work Path, consider these factors:

▶ The smaller the tolerance number, the more closely the path will match the selection. Don't choose a number that's too small, or the path will be very jagged.

▶ When the path is listed in the Paths panel as *Work Path* in italic type, that means it is temporary and will not be saved permanently in the file.

▶ To permanently save a Work Path, double-click its layer in the Paths panel and name the newly saved path.

▶ Paths can also be converted to selections in the Paths panel menu by choosing Make Selection with the source path layer selected.

Using Vector Elements in After Effects

Vectors are very useful in After Effects and can be used in many different graphic elements from shape layers to layer masks. There are a variety of effects that can be used with paths to create elements like brush strokes and strobing lights. Although vectors can be created directly in After Effects, it's often easiest to create complicated shapes and paths using other applications like Illustrator.

Vector paths are unique in how they can be imported into After Effects because a path can create a stroke and a fill, and because each application treats paths slightly differently. Sometimes, to ensure the best translation and flexibility between applications, it's best to copy and paste vector paths directly to specific parameters within an After Effects project.

NOTES

Just because an element is vector doesn't mean it's ready to animate. We recommend opening all EPS and SVG graphics in Illustrator. Be sure to check that the color mode is set to RGB. You can also convert the vector file into layers (using the Release to Layers command in the Layers panel). Be sure to save the file as a native AI file for maximum flexibility upon import.

Shape Layers

Shape Layers is a great tool to use to generate repeating graphic shapes and elements. We discussed Shape Layers pretty extensively in Chapter 7, "Designing Backgrounds." What's important to grasp in this chapter is the ability to use an external path as a source for a shape layer. To paste a path from anywhere, Photoshop, Illustrator, or even from a layer mask in After Effects, just copy the Path property (**Figure 10.31**).

To create a new shape layer, choose Path from the Add menu in the shape layer. Twirl open the Path disclosure triangle and select the word Path next to the stopwatch. Then paste the path, and it will be added to the shape layer as a new shape.

NOTES

When you're creating a shape layer using the vector tools in After Effects, there are two buttons to watch out for just to the left of the fill options: Tool Creates Shape and Tool Creates Mask. Tool Creates Shape creates a typical shape layer where you have control over every parameter of the fill and stroke. The Tool Creates Mask option creates a layer mask applied to the shape layer. That way, you can apply effects that only interact with layer masks, like Vegas and Stroke.

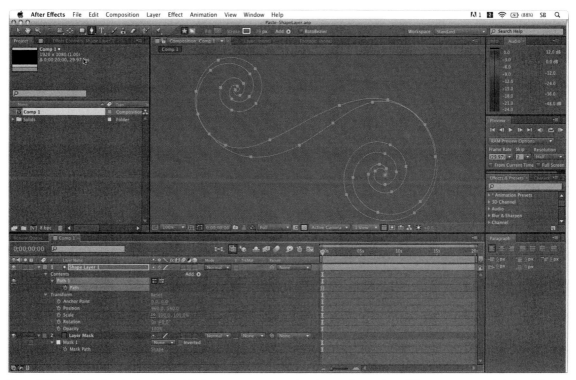

Figure 10.31 Specifically selecting the Mask Path to copy or paste a path makes moving masks to different parameters relatively painless.

Custom Animation Paths

Vector paths can be created and pasted directly into the Position property of a shape (or any layer) as a motion path to control an object's position with precision (**Figure 10.32**).

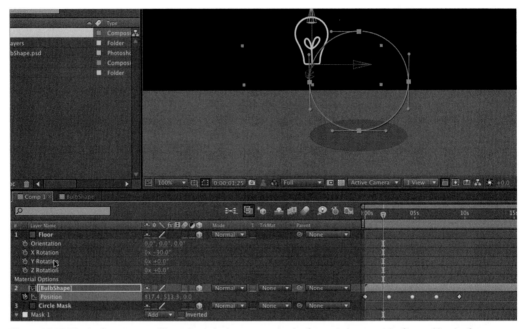

Figure 10.32 The keyframes created from the path shape are roving keyframes in between the first and last keyframes. This way, you can change the duration of the move by dragging only the first or last keyframes; the middle keyframes will slide around accordingly to ensure a smooth animation.

It doesn't matter if the path shape is a mask inside an After Effects project or simply a path directly copied from Illustrator. The example in Figure 10.32 shows a circle path shape that happens to be a mask applied to layer 3. To make the lightbulb graphic element move in an exact circle, you can literally copy the path from layer 3 and paste it into the position parameter for the lightbulb element. Follow these steps to do just that:

1. Select the Mask Path on the Circle Mask layer 3 and choose Edit > Copy.

2. To make the bulb travel in a perfect circle, twirl down the Position parameter for the BulbShape layer and click on the word Position to make sure it's selected.

3. With the Position selected, choose Edit > Paste.

Now the bulb will move in a perfect circle, mimicking the same shape as the mask.

Morphing Shapes

In After Effects, you can actually paste different path shapes into the same mask and create a morph between the two shapes. The layer named Morph already has a layer mask applied with the stroke effect. That's the layer we'll use to create our morph animation. The key is to select the actual mask shape by clicking directly on the text named Mask Path that appears under the Mask layer.

1. Open the masks on all three layers. Be sure to twirl open the Mask 1 layer to select the mask layer for each layer. Select the mask layer from layer 3 and copy it.

2. On the layer named Morph, select the Mask Path under Mask 1 and paste the new shape. Be sure to click the stopwatch to add a keyframe to the new mask shape (**Figure 10.33**).

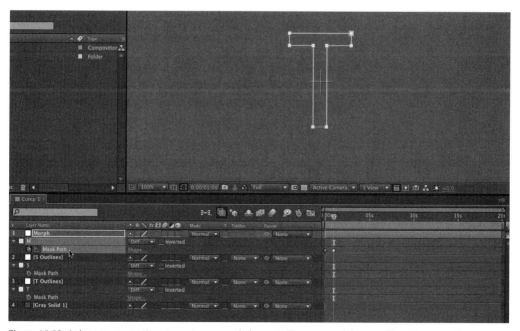

Figure 10.33 As long as you continue to paste new mask shapes to the same mask layer, you'll continue to add more keyframes and variations to your morphing shape.

3. Move the current time indicator down the Timeline to around the one second mark.

4. Select the Mask Path in layer 2 and copy it. Then select the Mask Path on the Morph layer and paste.

There should be one mask and two keyframes on the mask in layer 1. If you load a RAM preview, you'll see the animation and morph between the two shapes. Now each shape is represented by a keyframe in the Timeline. If you want the shape to cut back and forth between the different shapes, paste more keyframes to build the repetition, and change the keyframes to Hold keyframes by right-clicking and choosing (toggle) Hold keyframe to make the shape cut instead of morph.

Importing Artboards

To work with Illustrator files that contain multiple designs in multiple artboards, they need to be saved out as individual files using the "Save each artboard to a separate file" option found in the Save As options. In this project we saved out three artboards from one Illustrator file and imported each as a composition into After Effects. Even though the files imported properly, you still need to be aware of one detail—layer management:

NOTES

When you use the Video and Film presets, even when you specify one artboard for the project, the file created will automatically contain two artboards. One artboard will be the appropriate size, and a second larger artboard will be created to ensure that the larger artwork is not cropped upon import into After Effects.

▶ Regardless of the graphic that exists within the specific borders of an artboard, all the layers will be created and saved across all artboards. For example, you might have a graphic element that exists on layer 5 in artboard number one but not in artboards two or three. When they are saved out as separate files, both artboards for two and three will still contain layer 5; it will just be an empty layer.

▶ To avoid having unnecessary layers, open the Illustrator document and delete any extra layers. Even if there are multiple empty layers above sublayers, move the graphics up in the layer hierarchy and delete any extra unnecessary empty layers before trying to import into After Effects.

Importing Vector Shapes and Paths

Layered Illustrator files can be imported into After Effects as compositions. Any vector shapes or strokes are always imported as vector graphics without any specific path information. Half the fun of working with vector information in After Effects is the flexibility of working with actual vector path data. To import vector files with flexibility in After Effects, we recommend importing the Illustrator file as a composition and any path information that might be useful when animating.

To launch Illustrator while in After Effects, select a layer from the Illustrator document in the Project panel and press Command+E (Ctrl+E) to use Edit Original.

1. To import shapes from Illustrator, select the shapes and copy them.

2. In After Effects, create a new solid by pressing Command+Y (Ctrl+Y). With the new solid selected, paste.

3. After Effects automatically outlines any shapes with variable widths in Illustrator (**Figure 10.34**).

Figure 10.34 After Effects will trace a path around any generated effects in Illustrator, like the Offset Path effect.

4. If After Effects creates too many vertices on the new outline path, use the Expand and Simplify technique covered earlier in the section "Expanding Objects" to lessen the number. Then recopy and paste the new path.

5. Any strokes with a normal profile in Illustrator will just paste as a path without any shape waiting for an effect to be applied (**Figure 10.35**).

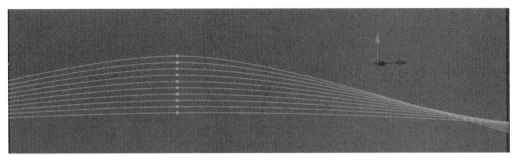

Figure 10.35 A mask or path without an effect applied appears as a path when the layer is selected. When you apply the Stroke effect, you can specify properties like stroke width and color.

After Effects automatically imports paths from Photoshop documents that contain either shape layers or vector masks. Any paths saved in the Paths panel in Photoshop can be copied directly into After Effects. To copy a path for use in After Effects, select the layer containing the path in the Paths panel and just press Command+C (Ctrl+C) to copy it. Once it's copied, you can paste it to shape layers or masks as described in the preceding steps.

Generating Path Effects

Once a path is applied to a layer in After Effects, it's ready to animate. There are four different effects that we use most often: Stroke, Vegas, Beam, and Scribble. They all function in a similar fashion in how they're applied and in their general stroke settings, but each has its own benefits. Below each effect's description in the following list we've added some key options and features to consider when using each effect.

Stroke. Stroke is a very reliable, simple solution to animating paint along a path (**Figure 10.36**).

▶ To have a stroke draw across the path, keyframe the Start and End percentages.

- ▶ Spacing changes the solid lines to dots as the value is increased.

- ▶ Adjust the Paint Style to have the stroke draw on the current layer, reveal its layer, or draw over a transparent background.

- ▶ The Hardness setting adjusts how soft the path appears.

- ▶ The Stroke effect supports the stroke of multiple masks in sequence, which is a great way to generate flowing graphic shapes in a background.

- ▶ The Stroke effect can do much more than just create flowing graphic lines. It is the perfect effect to use for map animations when you need to draw an illustrative path depicting movement through a map down a specific road, trail, river, and so forth.

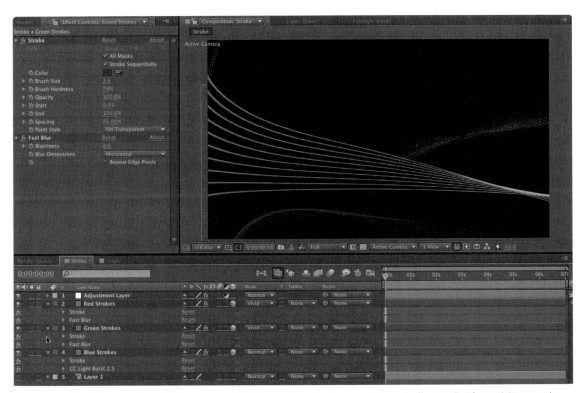

Figure 10.36 Stroke is a good overall effect to start with when you're not quite sure which mask effect is called for. Its ability to stroke multiple paths sequentially is very handy for creating animated line elements.

Vegas. Surprisingly different than Stroke, Vegas has controls geared to flowing shapes along a path, very much like lights popping on and off around a sign in Las Vegas (**Figure 10.37**).

▶ To use this effect quickly, only keyframe the Rotate parameter to control the speed of the shapes around the path.

▶ All the parameter adjustments in Vegas are straightforward; adjust the Segments, Length, and Width to impact the shape of the effect the most.

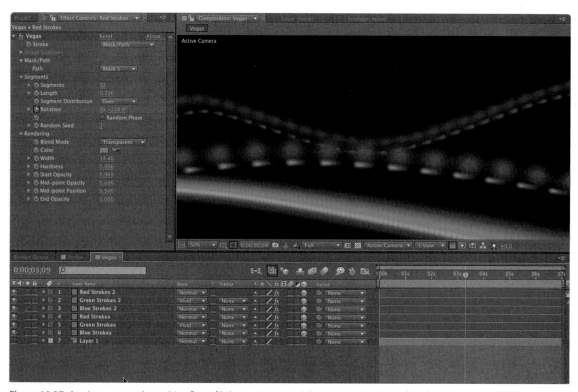

Figure 10.37 Anytime you need a strobing flow of light moving around the scene, try the Vegas filter first.

Beam. Most often, Beam is used for creating light sabers and laser blasts in a scene. We think it's an unsung hero in motion graphics because of its precise controls for the Start point and End point of the effect (**Figure 10.38**).

▶ Apply expressions to the Start and End points of the Beam effect, tying them to the position parameters of different graphic elements in a project for Beam to dynamically draw a line connecting the two graphics.

▶ Use the Time parameter to adjust the offset of the beam along the path.

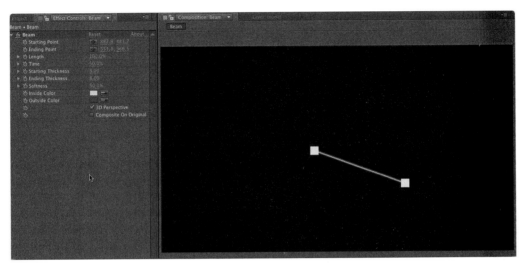

Figure 10.38 With a few expressions created with the pick whip, the Beam filter is perfect to draw a line between two animated graphics.

Scribble. Scribble is used to create highly stylized animations that look like someone creating a graphic element by scratching back and forth with a pen or crayon (**Figure 10.39**).

▶ Changing the Fill Type will control exactly where the Scribble will occur, inside, outside, or directly along a path shape.

▶ Control the speed and feel of the animation by adjusting the Wiggle Type and Wiggles/Second.

▶ Use the Stroke options to control everything from the curviness to the overlap and variation along the stroke.

Figure 10.39 Scribble is an effect that works best when you have a keen eye for detail. You can very quickly go over the top with this effect.

SECTION III

Design Exploration

11

Motion Control 2D and 3D

In this lesson, we look at several shots that were built for a feature-length documentary. The film is called *Bedford: The Town They Left Behind*. It's a documentary about a town that lost more people per capita in World War II than any other. The film was directed by Joe Fab and Elliot Berlin of the Johnson Group (www.bedfordthemovie.com). Our challenge was to bring photos, documents, and maps to life to engage the audience in a rich history.

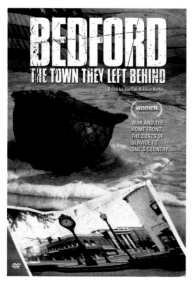

Everything we hear is an opinion, not a fact.
Everything we see is a perspective, not the truth.

—Marcus Aurelius

Motion Control 2D and 3D

Documentary-style motion control photography is becoming increasingly popular for use in all styles of video production. Of course, photos are a mainstay for narrative pieces, but we've seen them become a key part in advertising, editorial, and entertainment projects as well. Why just show photos statically and full screen? Putting elements into motion helps guide the viewers' eyes and can engage them.

Traditionally, photos have been animated in three ways:

▶ The first method involves sending the images to a motion control camera operator. This is an expensive process and must be adequately budgeted for both time and money. A robotic camera is controlled by joysticks and moves are programmed in. The signal is then recorded to videotape or captured to a digital file. Images cannot be color corrected or enhanced unless new prints are made.

▶ The second method involves setting up a camera and a card stand. An operator can then use a video camera and a tripod to shoot the photos. This method is prone to keystoning (due to the tilting to avoid light reflections) and does not allow for photo restoration or precise movement.

▶ The third method involves importing the photos into a nonlinear edit system and enlarging (zooming) them. This method tends to produce softening and has very limited results. Moves tend to be stiff and rigid. Many plug-ins have recently been developed that work within edit systems that improve upon this technique, but there is still a better way.

The Approach

We love the challenge of creating graphics that engage a viewer. To truly bring your photos to life, we can think of no better solution than Adobe Photoshop and Adobe After Effects. These two applications seamlessly interact and offer several benefits over traditional methods (**Figure 11.1**).

Figure 11.1 The following stills are excerpted from the opening title sequence for the feature film *Bedford: The Town They Left Behind*. The shot relies on Photoshop and After Effects entirely. All the 3D work was completed using only these two tools.

Photoshop allows for photos to be restored; damage caused by age or wear can be removed. Additionally, you can enhance color, improve tone, and even stylize images to a desired look. Photoshop makes easy work of combining images into larger panoramic photos, which is particularly useful for both wide-angle views and large images that need to be scanned in parts.

By combining Photoshop with After Effects, extremely high-quality motion control is possible. You can achieve results that outperform those done on expensive motion control rigs. You can achieve natural, realistic camera moves that engage the viewer. But why stop there?

Imagine if you could introduce the illusion of motion in the third dimension into a static image. Harnessing the power of Photoshop and After Effects makes this possible. You can add subtle motion and bring your photos to life, making your audience do a double take to determine if the images are really moving (**Figure 11.2**).

Figure 11.2 Through the use of the z-axis and a phenomenon known as parallax, subtle movement is created. Compare the position of the window and awning over the group's shoulders as the 3D camera moves through the scene.

By splitting up the image in virtual space, each element comes to exist on its own layer. Shift the layers in conjunction with one another or rack focus from foreground to background. The delicate movement created within the frame creates an unusual and attention-grabbing effect.

Go further and really work in a 3D space. You can add perspective by creating virtual worlds with Vanishing Point Exchange (**Figure 11.3**), integrate 3D models (**Figure 11.4**), or extrude your own shapes with Repoussé. You can even create particle effects in 3D space (**Figure 11.5**).

Figure 11.3 Vanishing Point Exchange lets you build three-dimensional scenes by using a perspective grid. After Effects then reassembles the photo as 3D planes.

Figure 11.4 True 3D models were resurfaced with textures from the original photographs in Photoshop Extended. The models were then imported into the After Effects scene.

Figure 11.5 Trapcode's Particular plug-in lets you create realistic particles that take on true dimensionality. The plug-in works well for smoke, rain, snow, and haze.

These techniques are not for the meek. They build upon several skills that take time and practice to master. However, the rewards are bountiful. You'll master 3D cameras, learn how to use 3D lights, and discover techniques that are as adaptable as your imagination.

Preparing Photos for Motion Control

Not every photo is ready for movement or the television or cinema screen. Problems can range from composition to resolution to damage (**Figure 11.6**). In some cases, you won't have a choice as to whether an image should be used (that's why clients were invented). You'll need to prep whatever photos your clients want to use.

But since you've likely been hired because of your good judgment, sophisticated taste, and artistic abilities, you should speak up and have some input. The sections that follow provide some general guidelines to consider and problem areas to avoid.

CLOSE-UP

Essential Skills

Creating two-dimensional motion control is far easier than its three-dimensional cousin. However, doing either well is not for "newbies." To do these techniques properly, you must have a solid foundation in these areas:

▶ Photo restoration
▶ Color correction
▶ Advanced selections
▶ Layer masking
▶ Cloning and healing
▶ Content-Aware Scale and Fill
▶ Organizing and importing layered comps
▶ Using 3D cameras
▶ Using 3D lights
▶ Keyframe interpolation
▶ Cinematography

Figure 11.6 The contrast of this image needed to be enhanced. The sky was replaced with a stronger image. The water was rerendered to create actual waves using the Psunami plug-in from Magic Bullet. The two boats were isolated so they could be brought closer together and "bob" on the waves.

Resolution Requirements

Your first concern to balance is adequate resolution. This holds true whether you are scanning photos or working with digital images. You'll need enough pixels if you intend to do a zoom or a pan. Dots per inch bog down many artists, but that measurement is useless when it comes to

NOTES

Images that have very high-pixel counts can get a little cumbersome in After Effects. Be sure your computer has enough RAM as you work with high-resolution sources. You may also need to lower the image quality and scale your images a bit.

screen graphics. The simplest way to understand resolution is to think of a zoom ratio. Here's a simple formula:

Screen size x Zoom ratio = Pixel count

For example, let's say you are creating files for a program being produced in 1080p. This equals a screen dimension of 1920 pixels by 1080 pixels. If you wanted to do a zoom or pan with a four times magnification, you would need an image that is 7680 pixels wide and 4320 tall.

With 7680 pixels, you can perform a pan across four screens. Don't worry about cropping or sizing for the screen; just make sure that you have enough pixels for additional movement. The goal is to have extra pixels when you shrink the image. In other words, you scale down the image to zoom out (or see more of the viewable area) and restore it to 100% to zoom in. These extra pixels also come in handy when you work in 3D space and want to pan or zoom with an After Effects camera (**Figure 11.7**).

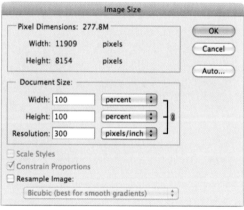

Figure 11.7 With a width of nearly 12,000 pixels, After Effects has plenty of resolution for camera zooming. The shot can be framed very tight with no pixelation, allowing for a dramatic camera move.

A Need for Focus

Out-of-focus pictures lower the quality of the final shot. We recommend a few basic approaches to prevent soft focus from ruining a shot. The method you choose will depend on your working scenario.

Scan It Right

Whenever possible, we prefer to do our own scanning, not because it's fun, but because it's the best way to ensure that we have what we need. Several problems can be introduced by those with a distinct lack of skill using antiquated scanners. Here are a few scanning tips:

▶ Ensure that the scanner is lying flat, or you may get misregistered scans.

▶ Use a gentle glass cleaner whenever smudges appear. Spray the cleaner on the soft cloth, and then wipe down the scanner bed. Make sure your photos are also clean before scanning; if they're not, wipe them with a soft cloth.

▶ Place your photos on the scanner straight. Use the edges of the scanner to help you maintain parallel edges on your photos. If you get crooked photos, choose File > Automate > Crop and Straighten Photos in Photoshop.

▶ If you are scanning in previously printed items such as newspapers, magazines, or books, you will likely get a moiré pattern. Scanning the small spaces between the previously printed dots causes this. Most scanners have a Descreen filter in their software.

▶ Save to uncompressed or lossless compressed formats such as TIFF or PSD for maximum image quality.

If you're dealing with digital files, be sure to zoom the images to 100% and check focus. This is easy to do in Adobe Bridge when browsing. If you select a photo, a thumbnail will appear in the Preview pane. Click in the pane and a loupe appears. You can then drag and look at areas at 100% magnification (**Figure 11.8**).

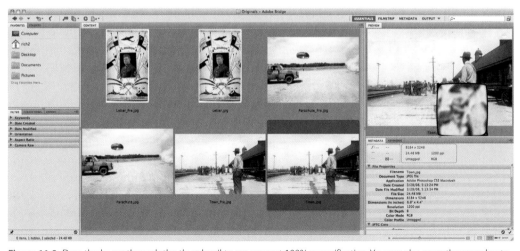

Figure 11.8 Drag the loupe through the thumbnail to see areas at 100% magnification. You can also press the spacebar to zoom an image full screen. Click when zoomed to magnify the image to 100%; you can then drag to pan. Press Esc when you're finished.

TIP

Remember that not every area in a photo will be in focus. But we recommend looking at details like people's eyes as well as tiny patterns or architectural details.

NOTES

Although After Effects offers sharpening effects, you are better off using filters in Photoshop. It's much faster to process an image that is not being scaled or animated over time.

TIP

The Clone Stamp tool works very well, especially if a lower-opacity brush is combined with multiple sample points. Using multiple strokes helps you avoid too much repetition in the pixels (creating an obvious pattern).

If you're working with traditional photos, such as prints, slides, or negatives, be sure to magnify the image by using projection, a light box, or a traditional optical loupe. The smaller an image, the more likely it will appear sharp because out-of-focus details will be minimized.

If you have no choice and must work with an image, be sure to sharpen it. Apply a filter such as Smart Sharpen in Photoshop. You can enhance soft details and enhance edges. Just be careful not to overdo it.

Aspect Ratio and Composition Concerns

Rarely do photos line up with a television or cinema screen. Still cameras have different aspect ratios, so even if the picture is in a landscape orientation, you'll still have gaps in the image. Of course, there's also portrait images and photos that will be cropped too tight or lack headroom. Mostly likely, you'll need to manipulate a photo to get it to work for the screen.

There are three primary ways of accomplishing this task:

▶ Use the Clone Stamp tool
▶ Use Content-Aware Fill
▶ Use Content-Aware Scale

Clone Stamp Tool

The Clone Stamp tool (S) is an old favorite of Photoshop users. It's been a part of Photoshop since the first version, but it's still quite relevant and can produce predictable and accurate results. The Clone Stamp tool works by sampling pixels from one area and painting them to another. This technique goes beyond copy and paste, however, because it uses the flexibility of the Photoshop Brush panel.

Experiment with the Aligned option when cloning. If Aligned is selected, the sample point and painting point move parallel as you move. If you click and start over, the sample point picks up at the same distance and angle from the painting point. If Aligned is deselected, the initial sample point is used (even after you stop and resume cloning). The second method ensures that you're always sampling from the same area.

We'll often clone to an empty area for more flexibility. Just select the Use All Layers option to clone from any visible layer. You can then make an empty layer at the top of your Layers panel and select it before cloning (**Figure 11.9**). Isolating your strokes to a new layer makes it easier to see the before and after versions (just toggle the visibility of the layer). You can also change your mind and erase parts of the cloned layer.

Figure 11.9 Cloning to an empty layer is the best option when patching a scene. Here we added more headroom so the camera could point up into the sky during the camera move.

Content-Aware Fill

The Content-Aware Fill option is a new addition to Photoshop CS5. It works by automatically generating new textures to fill in a selected area. The new textures are created through a computer-assisted synthesis that works by analyzing surrounding pixels.

Start by making a selection. This can be done using a Marquee or Lasso tool, the Magic Wand or Quick Selection tool, or the Color Range command. Press Shift+Delete to bring up the Fill dialog box and choose Content-Aware Fill from the Use menu. Click OK and Photoshop generates similar content to fill the area based on the source image. The new image content is based on the surrounding image content, with a little bit of randomness added to prevent the new pixels from looking like obvious copies of the surrounding area. This is a great way to remove an object or blemish from a scene. It's also an essential technique when you cut out an object to make a layered file for three-dimensional motion control (**Figure 11.10**).

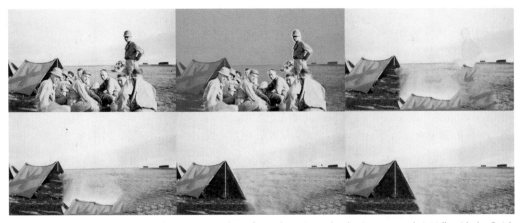

Figure 11.10 Several tools were used to remove an object from a layer. A rough selection was made initially with the Quick Selection tool (W). The selection was then examined and refined using a Quick Mask (Q). The Content-Aware Fill command was then used to create a new texture; the area was very large, so the texture needed refinement. Smaller selections were made and the Content-Aware Fill command was applied again. To finish the image, the Spot Healing Brush (J) was used to remove minor blemishes and damage.

NOTES

Each time you use the Content-Aware Fill command, it generates a new texture. If you don't like the first attempt that Content-Aware Fill generates, just choose Edit > Undo. Then re-run the Content-Aware Fill command to create a new pattern.

In many cases, the Content-Aware Fill command completes a job in one step. Even if the results aren't perfect, you're still much further along. Think of it as a great jump start that can be touched up with a little use of the Clone Stamp or Spot Healing Brush tool.

Content-Aware Scale

The Content-Aware Scale (Edit > Content-Aware Scale) command was introduced in Photoshop CS4. It attempts to combine scaling with a feature that allows images to automatically be recomposed. When used correctly, the image will automatically adapt to preserve vital areas during the scale (**Figure 11.11**).

The Content-Aware Scale command is different than Free Transform because it attempts to leave certain parts of an image as they are while selectively scaling others. There are two ways you can tell Photoshop which areas to ignore:

▶ Click the Protect Skin Tones button to tell Photoshop to attempt to preserve regions that contain skin tones. This works well if you're dealing with a color photo that has people in it.

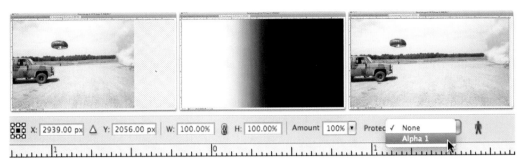

Figure 11.11 We first double-clicked on the *Background* layer to make it a floating layer and then extended the canvas to the desired width (left). Next, an alpha channel was added, in which white defines the area to be masked and gray is a gradual transition (center). The Content-Aware Scale command was set to protect the alpha (lower) and then was stretched to fill the canvas (right).

▶ You can also create an alpha channel if needed to protect a selected area. Simply add a new channel and paint over the areas you'd like to define as the frozen area. Then choose the alpha channel from the Protect menu in the Options bar.

Captured Action

The final characteristic we look for is a sense of captured action. We look for photos that tell a story—those in which there appears to be something happening in the frame. We evaluate which way people are looking or where activity is taking place in the frame.

By studying the image, you'll find the story within:

▶ Look for areas where your eye is drawn. These are great starting points or landing points for camera moves.

▶ Are there distractions in the frame? You may need to remove or defocus certain elements so the viewer's experience is uninterrupted.

▶ Is there "captured movement" within the shot? If so, go with it (**Figure 11.12**).

▶ What angles exist in the frame? Try to remember where the real camera was in the frame when the photo was shot. Let the reality of the photo influence the new reality you're creating.

Figure 11.12 The parade of soldiers is moving from left to right. The corresponding pan of the camera should move in the opposite direction to create a sense of the group passing.

Panning and Scanning Photos

Before we explore working in three dimensions, we need to quickly set the stage and get the regular pan and scan variety moves covered. The bulk of the moves you'll do will be traditional ones that involve flattened images and keyframes. This is the case for two reasons: First and foremost is budget. We've never seen a documentary or program that had enough cash to bring every photo into a 3D world. The second reason is overkill. Not all photos benefit from a three-dimensional effect (**Figure 11.13**).

Before you skip this section, answer this question. Which three animation properties should you use with photos to create a sense of movement? Easy right? Scale, Rotation, and Position.

Wrong.

The secret is Anchor Point. This is the default center point of a layer, and when you animate it, a new phenomenon occurs. You'll see much smoother moves and avoid gaps at the edges as you're changing the point of interest. When working in two dimensions, keyframing the Anchor Point is much more realistic. Keep reading for more practical tips.

NOTES

If you're working with several files that are numbered, be careful not to import them as an image sequence.

Figure 11.13 Using a few keyframes, you can create an animation to guide the viewer through a photo.

Moving to After Effects

After your images are prepped, you'll need to import them into After Effects. We recommend organizing your images into folders using Adobe Bridge. Create folders by scene or script block to make navigation easier.

Once you have the images in After Effects, you'll need to create compositions for each image. An easy method is to select multiple photos and drag them onto the new composition icon at the bottom of the Project panel (**Figure 11.14**).

After Effects provides you with the Multiple Compositions option, which will place each photo into its own composition. You'll need to set the duration and dimensions for the composition by choosing Composition > Composition Settings. Stick with the composition presets offered by After Effects unless you're dealing with a unique playback screen.

Figure 11.14 When you drag, you have a choice of putting photos into one composition or creating a unique composition per photo.

Animating Your Images

Although After Effects offers five animation properties, you'll need only three of them. Stick with Anchor Point (A), Rotation (R), and Scale (S). Using an Anchor Point is like moving the camera; using Position is like locking down the camera and moving the picture instead.

Here's the approach simplified:

1. Open a composition and highlight the first photo layer.

2. Press S to call up the Scale properties. Then hold down the Shift key and press A for Anchor Point and R for Rotation.

3. Turn on all three stopwatches to add keyframes (**Figure 11.15**).

Figure 11.15 The use of Anchor Point and Scale is essential. Rotation is an optional property that works on certain images.

4. Adjust the composition window so you can see the entire image. If needed, use the , (comma) key to zoom out or the . (period) key to zoom in.

5. Adjust Anchor Point, Scale, and Rotation to set a starting position for the image. Remember that you can drag the number values to change them.

6. Move toward the end of the composition by dragging the playhead until you get to a desired duration for the camera move. You may need to adjust the duration of the composition.

7. Adjust the ending values for the animation (**Figure 11.16**).

NOTES

If your image is an odd number of pixels wide or tall, you'll get an Anchor Point value with a .5 decimal. Change the number to remove the decimal; otherwise, you'll get subpixel resampling and unneeded softening.

Figure 11.16 You can use guides to help you check alignment. Turn rulers on by pressing Command+R (Ctrl+R) and then dragging them out from the side or the top.

8. Preview the animation by clicking the RAM Preview button. The animation caches to disk and then plays back in realtime when it's ready.

TIP

If you're working with high-resolution images, you can change the Resolution menu to a lower quality to speed up RAM previews.

Flicker Fix

When animating photos, you'll likely see flicker (which is generally caused by thin lines). The truth is that it may or may not be real. Be sure to preview the animation at full quality (you may even need to render a short portion). Then watch the clip back in realtime on a broadcast-quality monitor.

If flicker is still present, we recommend a trip back through Photoshop. Open the Actions panel and click the submenu (the triangle in the upper-right corner). Load the set of actions called Video Actions in the Actions panel Preset menu. Run the Interlace Flicker Removal action on your pictures. If needed, you can run the action a few times or try running the Motion Blur filter (Filter > Blur > Motion Blur) at a value of 1–4 pixels at an angle of 90 degrees.

If you don't like the effects of Exponential Scale, just choose Edit > Undo. In some cases the effect is very pleasant (especially when creating a gradual scale). In others it may be too dramatic.

Enhancing the Animation

Although your initial animation looks good, After Effects offers advanced controls to improve it. The biggest change is to modify the velocity curves for the keyframes. This can create a more natural start and stop movement. The goal is to make the moves look like they were shot with a real camera, not done on a computer.

1. Right-click on the first Anchor Point keyframe and choose Keyframe Assistant > Easy Ease Out.

2. Repeat step 1 for the first Rotation keyframe. You've now created a more natural "drag" or resistance as the animation moves out from the first keyframe.

3. Repeat the keyframe assistant for the last Anchor Point and Rotation keyframes, but this time choose Easy Ease In.

   Now let's try modifying the Scale property so it behaves more like a true camera zoom.

4. Click on the word Scale to highlight both keyframes. Choose Animation > Keyframe Assistants > Exponential Scale.

   This powerful assistant will accurately simulate the ballistics of a camera zoom.

5. Click the Graph Editor button to see selected keyframes in greater detail.

   The Graph Editor shows a natural curve for the Scale keyframes, which indicates a more natural speed change that simulates a camera zoom (**Figure 11.17**).

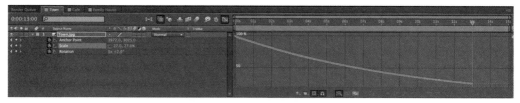

Figure 11.17 The Exponential Scale keyframe assistant makes it easier to simulate a natural zoom.

6. Preview the animation by clicking the RAM Preview button.

7. You can adjust the keyframes with the Graph Editor to smooth out keyframes and animation (**Figure 11.18**).

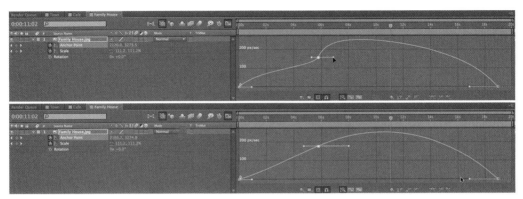

Figure 11.18 Adjust the handles to remove any bobbles in the motion path. After each adjustment, preview the animation to check its effect.

Expanding Photos into the Third Dimension

Now that you've explored the use of simulated zooms and pans, it's time to graduate to a real 3D camera. In this section we'll build on your existing knowledge as well as the material covered in Chapter 8, "Designing and Working in 3D." Here we'll explore specific techniques that relate to motion control 3D projects.

Determining Captured Perspective

Take a close look at your photo and try to identify different areas of depth. Be sure to identify a minimum of two planes in your photo. For the best results, however, you'll want to look for three planes: foreground, subject, and background (**Figure 11.19**).

These planes will get isolated to their own unique layer (**Figure 11.20**). Once the layered file is expanded in 3D space, you'll essentially end up with a "shoebox diorama" (**Figure 11.21**). As you animate your camera, the different distances between objects will create a parallax effect.

Figure 11.19 Depending on your shot, the foreground or the subject may be closest to the camera. Don't worry, both will work well.

Figure 11.20 Splitting the shot into three layers required multiple techniques that we'll explore later in this section.

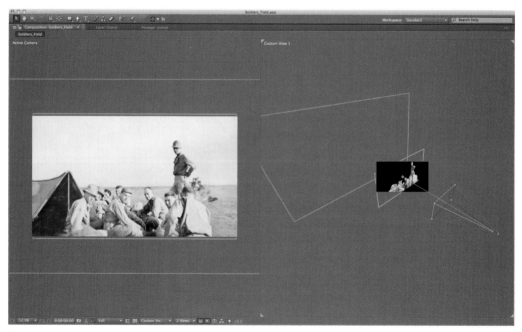

Figure 11.21 By positioning layers in 3D space, you can create entire scenes.

Planning the Shot

Just as directors storyboard their shots, you may want to block out your moves before moving into After Effects. On a piece of paper or blank canvas, create a staging diagram (**Figure 11.22**). Try to roughly determine how much separation there is between your foreground, subject, and background. The more distance (within believable reason), the better depth of field and ability to harness parallax to create a sense of movement. Parallax is the concept of "apparent motion" of a nearby object against a distant background. By increasing the distance between subject and background, and then moving the 3D camera, you get a greater sense of photorealistic motion.

Making Accurate Selections

To extract an object in Photoshop, it must be selected with one of the many available selection commands or tools. You have to tell Photoshop what you want selected and what should happen to those selected pixels.

When you have a selection, you can isolate individual pieces of a composition to their own layer. It's possible to place only what you want on an isolated layer. Transparency is the foundation of compositing, and since there are many different situations, there are many approaches to selecting and extracting images.

Quick Selection Tool

The Quick Selection tool (W) is a major improvement on the Magic Wand tool. It's similar in that you can click on a region of color to make a selection. But there's a reason the Quick Selection tool takes priority over the Magic Wand in the Tools panel.

The Quick Selection tool allows you to create a selection quickly based on color and contrast. You can press the right bracket key (]) to make the selection brush larger, and press the left bracket key ([) to make it smaller.

Simply click and drag in the image to make an initial selection (**Figure 11.23**). If you want to add to the selection, click and drag again. If too much of a selection is made, hold down the Option (Alt) key to subtract from the selection.

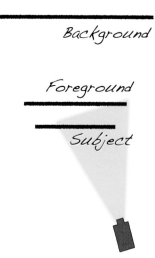

Figure 11.22 A quick sketch or diagram can help you plan your camera moves. You can easily experiment in a composition by adding more than one camera.

Figure 11.23 The Quick Selection tool does an excellent job of detecting edges, even on a sepia-toned image.

CLOSE-UP

Better Selections—Now Faster!

Here are a few important commands and modifier keys related to selections. Three standard modifier key combos are used when building selections:

▸ Holding down the Shift key before making a second selection adds to the initial selection.

▸ Pressing the Option (Alt) key lets you subtract from an item.

▸ Holding down Shift+Option (Shift+Alt) creates the intersection of the two selections.

▸ By employing these three modifier keys, you can use the basic tools and build up a selection. But don't try to build your selection all at once.

▸ You can add the Shift key after you've begun drawing with the Marquee tool to constrain the selection to a perfect square or circle.

▸ Holding down the Option (Alt) key enables you to draw from the center with the Selection tool. This is particularly useful when selecting a circular area.

▸ You can combine the two key combinations above to both constrain and draw from the center simultaneously.

Color Range Command

Another command that is frequently overlooked is the Color Range command. You'll find it in the Select menu (Select > Color Range). The Color Range command makes it easy to select large areas of color or color ranges (**Figure 11.24**). To begin, use the eyedropper on the desired color or area.

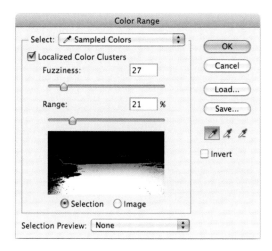

Figure 11.24 The Localized Color Clusters option makes it effortless to isolate a selection.

▶ To add to the selection, hold down the Shift key or use the plus eyedropper.

▶ To subtract from the selection, hold down the Option (Alt) key or use the minus eyedropper.

▶ The Localized Color Clusters option adds a tolerance option to constrain the command near where you click.

▶ The Fuzziness control softens your selection by increasing tolerance for stray pixels.

▶ You can preview the selection as a mask by using the Selection Preview menu.

TIP

The Color Range command can also be accessed with the context menu when a selection tool is active.

Refine Edge Command

With the Refine Edge command, Photoshop offers a great option for controlling a selection. The Refine Edge command can be accessed two ways. It's available in the Options bar for all selection tools, or you can choose Select > Refine Edge. This command is very intuitive, and its sliders provide

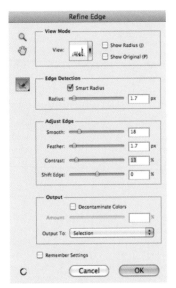

Figure 11.25 Although it offers many sliders, you should work your way from top to bottom in the Refine Edge dialog box.

TIP

You can select the Show Radius and Show Original check boxes to make it easier to see the changes created with the Edge Detection options.

quick feedback as you refine a selection (**Figure 11.25**). This command is similar to the Refine Mask command covered earlier in the book.

You can click the View button to change the viewing mode for how the selection is displayed (or use the corresponding keyboard shortcut). Try the different modes to see the results. We favor the following options when working on transparency:

▶ **On Black (B).** Previews the layer over black, which is good for light edges.

▶ **On White (W).** Shows the selected region over a white background, which works best for dark edges.

▶ **On Layers (L).** Composites the image over any other layers (or transparency if it's a single-layer image).

The Edge Detection option can be used to clean up the edges further. These controls work best for areas of partial transparency. Experiment with Edge Detection to improve the selection. Use the Radius slider to refine the edge. The Smart Radius option automatically evaluates contrast in the edges and attempts to correct for better transitions. If your object lacks uniform hardness and softness, use this option (which is the case for most photographs). You can also use the Refine Radius tool to paint over any edges that need additional refinement. In addition, you can hold the Option (Alt) key to switch to an erase mode to undo any unwanted refinements.

The next group of sliders allows you to adjust the edge globally. You can remove jagged edges, feather a selection, or improve contrast. If you have a uniform fringe around the edges, use the Shift edge commands.

The last category, Output, determines how the processed selection is treated. If you're working with strong background colors that are being removed, use the Decontaminate Colors option. This will apply color correction to remove any color spill from the background onto the selected object. You can also choose what Photoshop will do with the new selection. You can have Photoshop exit to a standard selection, apply a layer mask, make a new layer from the selected pixels, and more (**Figure 11.26**).

Figure 11.26 After applying the selection as a layer mask, we took a brush with 25% opacity and painted in a soft area at the edges for the ground. When there's a contact zone between the subject and the ground, you need to make a transition zone to avoid having the subject appear to float.

Masking Layers

To perform motion control 3D, you'll need to mask your images. This nondestructive technique is the best way to extract parts of an image to their own layers. These layers will then be reassembled in 3D space to create a "shoebox diorama."

Layer masking is an extremely flexible technique that supports multiple levels of transparency (via shades of gray or blurring). Most important, you can continue to touch up your mask throughout the postproduction process. If you're working in After Effects and you're not happy with an edge, you can choose to Edit Original by pressing Command+E (Ctrl+E) to switch back to Photoshop. With a little bit of paintwork, you can refine problems in the layer's transparency. When you're done, just close and save the PSD file and it will update in After Effects.

To add a mask, make sure the photo you want to mask is a layer (as opposed to a locked *Background)*. You cannot mask the background of an image, because it is not a layer. You must convert it to a layer by double-clicking and naming the layer. You will likely want to duplicate the layer two to four times so you have enough copies for foreground, subject(s), and background. Disable the visibility of the other copied layers as you're working on a specific layer.

Start by making a rough selection, much like an initial cutout with a pair of scissors. Try tools like the Polygonal or

Magnetic Lasso, the Color Range command (Select > Color Range), or the Quick Selection tool. If you need to add or subtract, you can always jump into Quick Mask mode by pressing Q and painting with your brush (**Figure 11.27**). With the selection active, click the Add Layer Mask button at the bottom of the Layers panel or use the Refine Selection command first and then add a layer mask.

Figure 11.27 The Quick Mask command is very useful for refining edges. If you double-click the Quick Mask icon (the last on the Photoshop Tools panel), you can access the Quick Mask options window. You can change the color and opacity of the Quick Mask to make it easier to work with.

Here are a few practical tips when it comes to masks:

▶ Use the Brush tool with a soft edge to touch up the layer mask. Be sure to load the default colors by pressing the D key. White will be used for areas that are opaque (solid), and black will be used for areas that are transparent. You can then toggle between black and white by pressing the X key. A good mnemonic for this shortcut is Devil's Xylophone.

▶ Zoom in so you can better see your pixels. Use the Navigator panel to keep a "global" view and move around your canvas.

▶ Press [for a smaller brush and] for a larger brush. To create a harder or softer brush, use the Shift key. Pressing Shift+[will make the brush softer; pressing Shift+] will form harder edges.

▶ We suggest placing a high-contrast, solid color directly behind the masked layer. This is a temporary step, but it makes it easier to see stray pixels.

- Use the Smudge tool with Lighten or Darken mode to touch up the layer mask. This is a great way to move the mask in only one direction while pushing. Adjust the Strength to taste; a lower value usually works best.

- You can also use the Blur tool or a filter to slightly soften the edges for a believable feather.

- If you need to "choke" a mask, try applying a Levels adjustment directly to the layer mask. By adjusting the midpoint, you can expand or contract the mask as needed.

- The Refine Mask command and the Masks panel give you very flexible controls. The interface is nearly identical to the Refine Selection command, but you can use it to touch up masks in significant ways.

- Leave the layer masks live for import into After Effects (don't merge or flatten). This way you can easily switch back via Edit Original for quick tweaks.

- As you create masks, remember that you can load them by Command-clicking (Ctrl-clicking) on the thumbnail. Once you've masked a layer, loading it and then inversing it (Select > Inverse) can be a quick way to mask your remaining layers.

- You can also use the loaded selections to remove objects in the background plate. We suggest expanding the selection a few pixels (Select > Modify > Expand) and then running the Content-Aware Fill option (**Figure 11.28**).

NOTES

When working with layer masks, be sure you click on the mask's thumbnail in the Layers panel so your strokes are modifying the layer mask, not the pixels of the original layer.

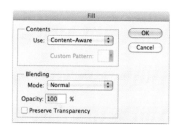

Figure 11.28 Getting a clean background plate is much faster with the Content-Aware Fill command.

Prepping the Layers for After Effects

Before sending your layered document to After Effects, you need to do a little organization work. Be sure that every layer has a unique and descriptive name that clearly identifies what the layer is. Background copy 2 isn't as meaningful as, say, Tent or Soldiers. While you're looking at layers, be sure to reduce the total number to only the essentials. We find that three to five cutout layers are usually plenty for this effect.

You also may need to downsample your image and save a new copy. Once we've determined how much zooming will occur or how wide we'll pan, we reevaluate the size of the image. Although extra resolution is good, there's no need

CLOSE-UP

Background Removal

Although the foreground and subject will use masks, your background layer does not. Rather, you must "remove" all the elements you extracted to their own layers (the foreground and subject). To do this, you have several options:

- Clone Stamp tool
- Healing Brush tool
- Spot Healing Brush
- Patch tool
- Content-Aware Fill

to bog down After Effects. Simply choose Image > Image Size and resize with the Constrain Proportions option selected. Then choose File > Save As to make a new copy and to preserve the original resolution in another file.

When your layers are prepped, we recommend placing a merged copy on the topmost layer. In the Layers panel add a new, empty layer and place it at the top. Make sure all the layers you want to use are visible. Then hold down the Option (Alt) key and choose Layer > Merge Visible to make a flattened copy. This new layer should contain no masks; it will be used to check composition later (**Figure 11.29**).

Figure 11.29 These three layers plus the Reference layer are ready for the move to After Effects. The masks are easy to modify throughout the workflow, and the layers have simple, yet descriptive names.

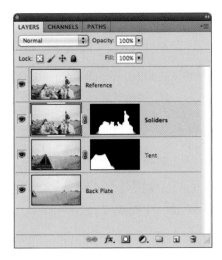

Animating in 3D Space with After Effects

Now that your files are prepped, it's time for the fun part: creating the 3D scene. Truth be told, you've done all the hard work. Your workflow gets much easier going forward. We'll continue with the same image from the previous section for illustrative purposes (but you'll find several more examples on the DVD). We'll also explore advanced techniques at the end of the chapter.

Converting a Photoshop File to 3D Space

You're now ready to bring in your Photoshop file. The process we recommend is simple but specific. Choose to import the PSD file as a composition (*do not* choose the Composition – Retain Layer Sizes option). In the next dialog box, just click OK to accept the default import values. Go ahead and keep the Composition panel set to Quarter quality to reduce your overhead.

Open the layered composition you just imported and change its settings to match the shot duration and delivery standard you are using for the project. You can press Command+K (Ctrl+K) to call up the Composition Settings (**Figure 11.30**).

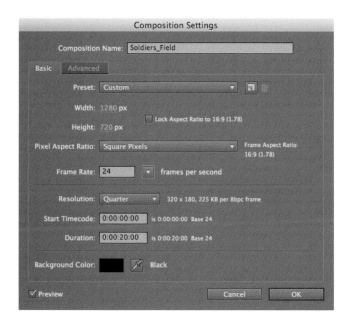

Figure 11.30 Discuss delivery standards with the project's editor or producer. You don't want to waste time having to rerender because of the wrong frame rate or frame size.

Now you're ready to promote all the layers (except the Reference layer) to 3D space. Click the 3D layer switch for each layer (**Figure 11.31**). Add a 3D camera by choosing Layer > New > Camera. Knowing which setting to choose can be tricky (unless you happen to have metadata information about the actual photo). For historical photos, we tend to use the 35mm or 50mm preset cameras (**Figure 11.32**).

Figure 11.31 If you can't see the 3D switches, click the Toggle Switches/Modes button at the bottom of the Timeline.

Figure 11.32 The 3D camera dialog box offers several controls (and the ability to create your own presets). For more on 3D cameras, be sure to see Chapter 8.

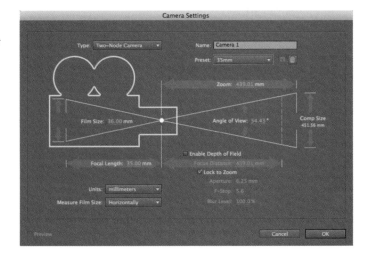

TIP

For a great script that can automate some of this expansion process, check out pt_Multiplane. Paul Tuersley sells it for $20 at http://aescripts.com/pt_multiplane.

Blocking the Scene

Now you'll expand your objects along the z-axis. Start by turning off the visibility of the Reference layer. You'll toggle this layer off and on in the future to check your composition. Switch your view in After Effects so it's easier to design in three dimensions. Choose the 2 Views – Horizontal from the menu at the bottom of the canvas (**Figure 11.33**). Set the Left Viewer to Active Camera and the second to either Top or Custom View 1 (whichever you find easier) (**Figure 11.34**).

Select your bottommost layer, which you'll position first. Press P for position, and then adjust the Z slider (the third number) to move the image away from the camera. Try a positive number between 1,000 and 25,000 to simulate the apparent distance in the original image.

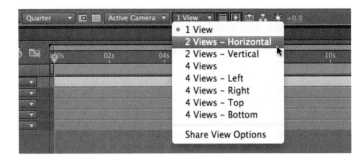

Figure 11.33 If you have a very large monitor, you may want to try the 4 Views options for more control.

Figure 11.34 We find that Custom View 1 provides a nice view of the "set." Your view is 45 degrees to the left and 45 degrees off the floor.

You now need to scale the layer back up so its apparent size matches the original. Press S for Scale and scale the layer up so it matches the other layers (when the edges match the edge of the others). You may need to zoom your canvas window to see your edges (**Figure 11.35**). Toggling the visibility for the reference image off and on, or leaving it set to a low opacity for onion-skinning, makes this task easier.

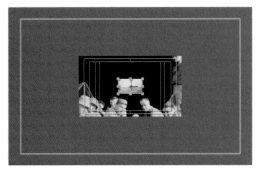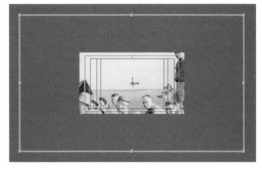

Figure 11.35 The scaled layer should line up with the others. You can change the label colors of the layers to make them easier to see.

Repeat the scaling and positioning for the next layer. Depending on the image, you may move this object farther away or closer to the camera. You're just trying to create a sense of depth. Remember that you can switch views to make it easier to see the arrangement of layers in Z space (**Figure 11.36**). Don't put as much distance between the foreground and subject layers as you would between the foreground and background layers. This effect should be subtler. Remember to use your reference image (layer 2) for checking alignment.

Figure 11.36 The Top and Custom View 1 show the relationship between Z-positions differently. Try using both for an accurate assessment of the scene.

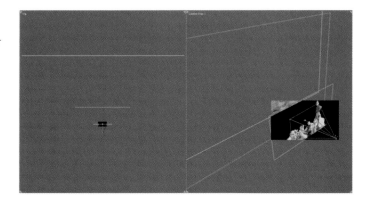

Using 3D Cameras

Animating the 3D cameras is pretty straightforward. In fact, compared to other motion graphics projects motion control 3D is much less abstract. You have a clear subject and a reference source, which makes framing and composition much more clear-cut.

Here are a few suggestions for getting the best results:

▶ Creating moves is much simpler when you're using two composition views. In one viewer you can see through the viewfinder; the other lets you see your physical camera. You can choose to use 2 Views - Vertical or 2 Views - Horizontal depending on your monitors.

▶ When you select the camera layer in the Timeline panel, you can see it in the second viewer. You can drag and manipulate the camera right in the viewer.

▶ Set your starting frame first. Use the Camera Position and Zoom controls. To move the camera, use a combination of sliders and camera control handles. In the canvas, you can grab the green arrow to move the camera on the y-axis. Use the red arrow to move along the x-axis and the blue arrow to move along the z-axis (**Figure 11.37**).

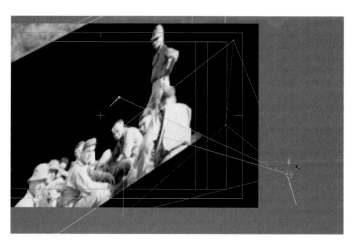

Figure 11.37 The camera handles offer smooth control over camera position and point of interest.

▶ You'll notice a line with a small crosshair circle. This is the point of interest. Adjust this to affect where the camera is pointed.

▶ Under the Camera Options category, you can keyframe Zoom and Focus Distance (for zoom or rack focus effects). You can also adjust the aperture and blur level to affect the depth of field. Be sure Depth of Field is turned on for the most photorealistic results (**Figure 11.38**).

TIP

You may need to press the , (comma) or . (period) keys to zoom out and see all. Hold down the spacebar to move around the window by dragging.

NOTES

You may want to lock your layers to avoid accidently moving them when manipulating the camera.

▶ Avoid more than a 45 degree move, or the scene will likely fall apart. In fact, only subtle moves are needed to get the most from this effect.

▶ RAM preview from time to time to see your results and get a sense of timing and composition. To expedite the experimental process, the initial preview should be done at Quarter quality (Resolution setting in the Preview panel or the Auto setting to match the resolution set in the Composition panel).

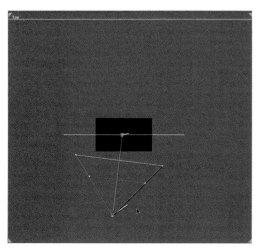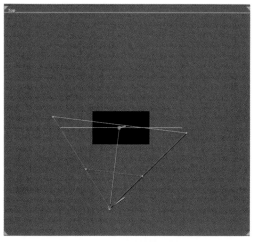

Figure 11.38 Once Depth of Field is enabled, you'll need to adjust the Focus Distance property. This will likely need to be keyframed to compensate for a moving camera. You can see an actual box in the composition window that indicates where it is set.

TIP

To create arced camera moves, select a keyframe in the Timeline. Then in the canvas, you can click with the Convert Vertex tool (nested with the Pen tool) to create Bezier handles. Adjust the curve to taste.

▶ Create traditional camera moves like dollies and pans to take advantage of the depth of field. To really achieve parallax, be sure to introduce a slight angle to the movement (which is caused by differences between the camera position and the point of interest).

▶ You can add multiple cameras to a scene to try different moves. Only the topmost camera will be used, or you can control which one is active with visibility switches.

Advanced Techniques

The journey of creating motion control 3D is a bit of a never-ending wormhole. As soon as you master one technique, you'll discover new ones. The key to your sanity and budget is to combine techniques. Keep some shots simple and push others to new heights. Here are three key technologies that you can further explore to create fantastic effects.

Vanishing Point

Vanishing Point is truly a partnership feature (you'll need both Photoshop Extended and After Effects to pull off this technique). It allows you to draw perspective planes in Photoshop. Those planes should define major surfaces or fields of view. You invoke Vanishing Point by choosing Filter > Vanishing Point. Normally, you'd use it for perspective cloning, but with After Effects a cooler option exists.

The Vanishing Point Exchange feature relies on a visual effects technique called *photogrammetry*, which is commonly used to simplify 3D scenes. It assists in that not every object has to be modeled. This significantly reduces the complexity and time needed to create, render, and output a 3D animation (**Figure 11.39**).

Figure 11.39 The ground and train station were turned into a simple 3D scene. The people were then inserted into the scene at appropriate distances. Notice as the camera moves how elements interact differently due to their distance. The people are perpendicular to the ground and can cast shadows.

Open a photo that you want to work with in Photoshop, and then choose Filter > Vanishing Point. The Vanishing Point interface opens. Start by drawing your first grid inside the image. This should be the largest surface of the object. Define the four corner nodes of the first plane surface. The Create Plane tool is selected by default. Click the preview image to define the four corner nodes.

Here are some general pointers for using Vanishing Point:

▶ Look for a straight line to use as a reference.

▶ Extend a bit beyond the boundaries to deal with peaks or extruding objects.

TIP

We've found that Vanishing Point Exchange works best when a photo has an angle of about 45 degrees with the subject. You should also try to keep the frame as unobstructed as possible. You can open the files created by Vanishing Point Exchange (VPE) into Photoshop to clone or erase unwanted details.

▶ You can tweak the first plane as much as needed.

▶ Try to use a rectangular object in the image as a guide when creating the plane. You can zoom in with the zoom controls in the bottom-left corner. Be sure to line up each edge of the plane with the perspective of the photo. Take your time on this step, because it's the most crucial part.

TIP

You can also use this technique to create surfaces for the floor and sky when you're dealing with a horizon.

Once the first plane is created, you'll need to generate the second for the other surfaces. You can create a new plane by holding down Command (Ctrl) and dragging from the center of a plane's edge. It's critical that you "tear off" planes rather than creating new ones so the model can stay attached. Drag the handle so the plane extends beyond the edge of the object. You'll likely need to adjust the angle so the second plane lines up. You can change the angle with the controls in the top bar.

You can tear off planes for the floor or ground. If you're using multiple ground planes, be sure to adjust them so they overlap. For this task, you'll find it easiest to zoom out and see some of the gray canvas space. Drag the handles and resize the planes as needed (**Figure 11.40**).

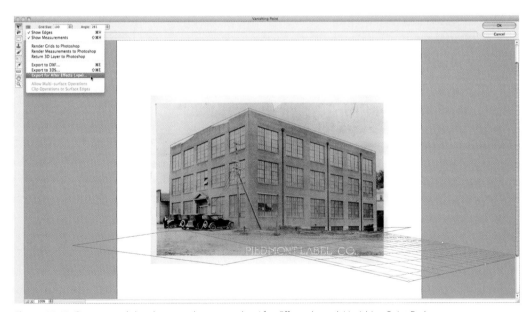

Figure 11.40 Once created, the planes can be exported to After Effects through Vanishing Point Exchange.

When you're finished, click the submenu in the upper-left corner, and then choose Export for After Effects (.vpe). Create a new folder, which will serve as a destination for the PNG files and 3D data that Photoshop will generate. After the export is completed, click OK to store the Vanishing Point information. You can then close and save the Photoshop file. If you need to revisit the planes for tweaking, just open the PSD filter and run the Vanishing Point filter again; your previous planes will be there for editing.

Switch to After Effects and create a new project. Then choose File > Import > Vanishing Point (.vpe). Navigate to the folder you created, select the VPE file, and click Open. After Effects creates a new composition, reassembles the 3D objects based on the VPE data, and arranges all the planes (each an individual layer in the PNG format) in 3D space (**Figure 11.41**).

Figure 11.41 Vanishing Point Exchange was used to create a plane for the ground and the sky. The soldiers and tents were then added back into the scene. Because they are perpendicular to the ground, the camera feels like it is moving across a surface as it dollies.

You can use the Orbit Camera tool (C) to rotate around your scene:

▶ You can rotate about 40 degrees left or right before a scene looks too fake.

▶ Be careful not to pull the camera too high in the frame, or the object will look like a cutout doll.

▶ The individual PNG files can be cleaned up easily in Photoshop. Select them one at a time and press Command+E (Ctrl+E) to edit them. In Photoshop, use cloning and erasing to clean up unwanted pixels or blank areas. After fixing the files, close and save them to return to After Effects.

▶ When you're ready to animate, change the After Effects composition settings to match your needs. Animate the camera or null object to create the desired animation.

▶ Use the different views in After Effects to place multiple elements correctly in the scene (**Figure 11.42**).

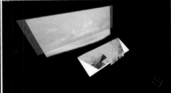

Figure 11.42 Changing the 3D view makes it simpler to see your scene. Use multiple views as you position cameras, lights, and objects.

Puppet Tools

The Puppet tools can be used to quickly add natural motion to photos or vector artwork. The tools use an effect (called the Puppet effect), which will automatically be applied when you use the tools. The Puppet effect warps the image based on the positions of pins that you place (**Figure 11.43**). You can use pins to define which parts of an image should move (or shouldn't) and which parts should be in front when other parts overlap.

Figure 11.43 The Puppet effect warps the position of the hands and allows the fingers of the statue to bend over time.

▶ **Puppet Pin tool.** Use this tool to place and move Deform pins.

▶ **Puppet Overlap tool.** Use this tool to place Overlap pins, which indicate which parts of an image should appear in front of others when a distortion causes parts to overlap.

▶ **Puppet Starch tool.** Use this tool to place Starch pins. These stiffen parts of the image so they are distorted less by the warp.

Placing Pins

When you place the first pin, it applies the Puppet effect. After Effects will automatically attempt to break the image into a triangular mesh. You can see this mesh when a Puppet tool pointer is over the area that the outline defines (**Figure 11.44**).

The mesh and the image pixels are interconnected, so moving the mesh will move the pixels. Here's how the controls work:

▶ If you move a Deform pin, the mesh changes shape. After Effects attempts to keep the overall mesh as rigid as possible to produce natural, lifelike movement.

▶ A layer can have multiple meshes. Add meshes if you want to control distortion independently.

▶ The meshes do not recognize moving footage (such as video) and will not update.

Puppet Overlap Controls

You can use the Puppet Overlap tool to apply Overlap pins. This is a simple way to control apparent depth. You must apply Puppet Overlap pins to the original outline. You have two controls:

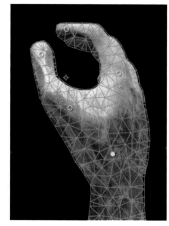

Figure 11.44 Place pins at logical points. In this image a vise was made using five pins. A pin was placed at each fingertip, each joint where the fingers connect to the hand, and one in the bend of the wrist.

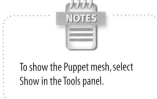

▶ **In Front.** Shows the apparent proximity to the viewer. In Front values are added together for places for the mesh where extents overlap. You can also use negative In Front values.

▶ **Extent.** Specifies how far from the Overlap pin its influence extends. The fill is dark if In Front is negative; the fill is light if In Front is positive.

Puppet Starch Controls

When you're distorting one part of an image, you may want to prevent other parts from being distorted. The Puppet Starch tool is used to apply Starch pins to keep parts rigid. You must apply Puppet Starch pins to the original outline (**Figure 11.45**). You have two controls:

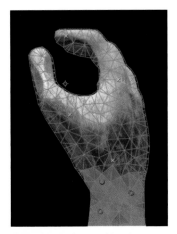

Figure 11.45 The use of Starch pins keeps the wrist from bending as the fingers move. Be sure to adjust the Amount and Extent settings to control rigidity.

▶ **Amount.** Specifies the strength of the stiffening. The Amount values are added together for places on the mesh where extents overlap. You can use negative Amount values. Small Amount values are best for preventing image tearing without introducing much rigidity.

▶ **Extent.** Specifies how far from the Starch pin its influence extends. The Extent is indicated by a pale fill in the affected parts of the mesh.

Sketching Motion with the Puppet Pin Tool

With Sketch, you can animate the motion path of one or more Deform pins in realtime (or a specified speed). This makes it effortless to create natural movement and to sync it with audio or other elements. A quick way to invoke Sketch is to hold down the Command (Ctrl) key and sketch in realtime when you click and drag on a pin (**Figure 11.46**).

Be sure to click Record Options in the Tools panel to access the following options:

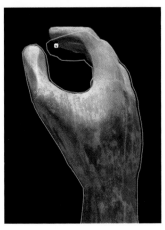

Figure 11.46 The Sketch option takes a little practice but is very organic.

▶ **Speed.** This is the ratio of the speed of recorded motion compared to playback speed. If Speed is 100%, the motion is played back at the same speed at which it was recorded. If Speed is less than 100%, the motion plays back faster than it was recorded. This is a useful way to draw elaborate paths.

- **Smoothness.** Try using a higher value to remove extraneous keyframes from the motion path. It is in fact better to have fewer keyframes if you want smoother motion.

- **Use Draft Deformation.** If your system is lagging, try this option. It will ignore Starch pins when sketching, which improves system performance.

Enhancing the Scene

Would you like to take the techniques discussed in this chapter further? There's no end to the possible refinements. Just remember to balance reality with created reality. Here are a few modifications we make to truly make the shots engaging.

Adding Lights

The use of lights in a scene can really add to the 3D nature. You can use lights to enhance your scene and draw the viewer's eye to the area of interest. It's important to remember that lights add significantly to the render time. We generally add them after the first draft renders have been cut in by the editor and the timings are locked down. Try introducing these types of light:

- **Ambient light.** Be sure to lower the overall lighting of the scene before you add other lights. We typically set an ambient light to around 80% to create a slightly "darkened studio" effect that we can build on.

- **Directional light.** You can add other directional lights to the scene that are motivated by existing lights. Think about where the sun is, and then put a point or a spot light there. Are there windows in a scene? Put a light on the outside and have it shine through. Do you need to cast shadows? Do so with lights (**Figure 11.47**).

- **Volumetric light.** If you want to create lights that you actually see (such as sunbeams) as opposed to lights whose results you see (like shadows), check out Trapcode Lux. This advanced plug-in works with the After Effects lighting system and creates light that you can point and see its beams.

Figure 11.47 As the hands bend and cross each other, the light causes realistic shadows. Be sure to adjust the Cast Shadows and Accepts Shadows properties to avoid unwanted shadows on your background.

Using Footage Plates

If you want to put a little more reality into your motion control 3D, you'll want to build up your footage library. Be sure to build a healthy library of stock clips, especially skies. We've also found that wide shots or urban areas work well. The key here is to get some subtle motion into the background that complements rather than distracts (**Figure 11.48**).

Figure 11.48 Shooting time-lapse shots is a great way to make your own background plates for skies. Time-lapse motion offers a subtle animation that complements motion control.

Creating your own time-lapse shots is pretty simple. You can pick up an intervalometer to attach to a DSLR camera for about $125 (**Figure 11.49**). This lets you set timings for how often the camera records a shot. By locking down a camera and shooting in manual mode, you can record a new still. Typically, these stills are shot every 2–30 seconds and can then be imported into After Effects as an image sequence. These stills create gentle time-lapse shots that work well for the background. You can stretch layers and apply frame blending to smooth out the slowdown effect.

TIP

You can visit http://tinyurl.com/aetimelapse for a video tutorial on using After Effects to assemble time-lapse movies. The technique is explored in depth in the book *From Still to Motion: A Photographer's Guide to Creating Video with Your DSLR* (Peachpit Press, 2010).

Figure 11.49 Intervalometers are often made for specific camera models. Be sure to check for compatibility before ordering one.

Creating Depth with Particles

A subtle element that we love to add to motion control shots is particles (**Figure 11.50**). Although After Effects offers several particle effects, we find the investment in Particular from Trapcode to be worthwhile. We use the effect to add smoke, atmosphere, haze, and clouds. These effects should be added after you've finished all other elements in the shot because they take a while to render. The addition is slight but often well worth it.

NOTES

We've included several of the shots in this chapter on the book's DVD. You'll find both project files and rendered movies. You're also welcome to check out the finished movie. See the website www.bedfordthemovie.com for screening and ordering information. The film is available on Amazon.com as well.

Figure 11.50 Columns of smoke were added to this scene for the smoke stacks and the burning buildings after a bomb attack. The smoke has actual dimensionality, so as you rotate past it the clouds have depth.

12

Building with
Panoramic Images

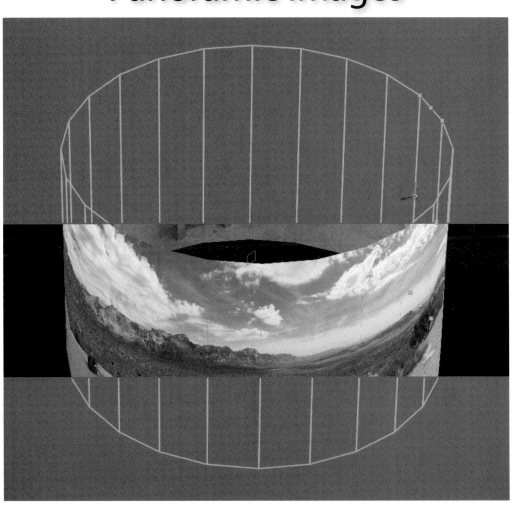

I knew the wild riders and the vacant land were about to vanish forever... and the more I considered the subject, the bigger the forever loomed. Without knowing how to do it, I began to record some facts around me, and the more I looked, the more the panorama unfolded.

— Frederic Remington

Building with Panoramic Images

Panoramic photography is the practice of shooting multiple photos and then stitching them into a larger photo. If enough photos are taken, a large panoramic image can be made. This process traditionally has used highly specialized camera rigs and a lot of training.

At RHED Pixel, we got involved with panoramic photography more than a decade ago. The ability to capture wide vistas, enormous high-resolution photos, and sweeping views was just too enticing. We also started to explore QuickTime VR technology and focus on creating virtual tours and interactive movies.

What does panoramic photography have to do with motion graphics and visual effects? As it turns out, a lot. We first began using our panoramic images to make large photos for documentary-style motion control projects (**Figure 12.1**). We started panning and scanning photos for long shots used in video productions. But then a lightbulb went off.

Figure 12.1 The Photomerge command can bend images to create a composite image that lines up several photos into a larger photo (left). The images can also be seamlessly blended together (right) to hide exposure variance.

We discovered that these images made great looping textures for seamless backgrounds or installation-style graphics. When working with immersive environments (such as nightclubs or retail), the images could be played on large video walls as content.

Then Hollywood got in on the action as the green screen frenzy took off for special effects. Entire scenes were being created using photographic plates—sometimes as reference for 3D models, other times used "as is." Panoramic photos could then be brought into Adobe After Effects to serve as a backdrop for chroma key footage. In fact, they could even be turned into immersive environments for 360-degree sets.

What used to be a meticulous process is now ridiculously easy. The Photomerge command in Adobe Photoshop is incredibly effective and easily merges multiple images into a seamless panorama.

Acquiring Panoramic Photos

Creating a panoramic photo requires multiple exposures. Ideally, those photos will be taken from a stationary position and be evenly distributed across an arc or circle as you pan the camera. Pulling this off takes the right gear and the right techniques.

Essential Gear

There are dedicated panoramic rigs that position the camera so it is suspended above the tripod (so it floats over its nodal point). They are designed to minimize distortion and keep the camera precisely rotated. These rigs are quite useful, but are not cheap. Although they are nice to have, we find that Photoshop can easily correct for many of these issues and the highly specialized gear is not needed.

However, what is essential is a tripod. You'll want a tripod with adjustable legs so you can easily level the tripod. Some users merely tilt or cant a video-style tripod to level a camera, but that won't work when you're shooting a wide-angle image. As the camera pans, you'll get a noticeable tilt to the image. Being able to adjust the height of each leg becomes essential (**Figure 12.2**). You'll know you've leveled the camera by using a bubble level (many tripods have one built in) (**Figure 12.3**).

Figure 12.2 Using adjustable legs lets you quickly level the camera. For faster adjustments, we prefer latch-style lags as opposed to couplings that have to be screwed (and unscrewed).

Figure 12.3 A bubble level can quickly indicate if the camera is level. This is essential to ensure that the panoramic image doesn't lean or tilt as you pan the camera.

Ideally, you'll want to shoot in portrait mode. This allows for the least amount of bending as you rotate the camera. Essentially, you are creating a circle out of several rectangles. A portrait orientation allows for more sides to the shape, hence a smoother curve. Unfortunately, most cameras mount to their tripods in landscape mode.

One option is to look for a tripod with a tilting plate (**Figure 12.4**). This works well but does introduce a slight distortion to the image. A better option is to get an L-plate for your camera. This makes it easy to rotate the camera 90 degrees. We use a plate and tripod mount (**Figure 12.5**) from Really Right Stuff (www.ReallyRightStuff.com). Although they are a premium grade, they offer plates made to fit specific camera models precisely. Camera controls and ports are not blocked by the L-plate.

Figure 12.4 Titling the tripod plate can create an unstable camera and can add additional distortion because the camera is off center.

Figure 12.5 An L-plate is a good compromise between a dedicated panoramic rig and a standard tripod.

Pros know that it's better to only slightly move the camera to create overlapping images. There are specialized tripod heads that you can purchase from companies like Kaidan (www.kaidan.com) and Really Right Stuff that make leveling and rotation even more precise. It is preferable for the tripod head to have degrees marked on it to make your shooting more accurate as you rotate the camera (**Figure 12.6**).

Figure 12.6 We usually rotate 15 degrees when shooting panoramic photos with a standard lens. This produces 24 exposures for a full 360-degree panoramic and has plenty of overlap for the Photomerge command.

Shooting Techniques

Capturing a professional-looking panoramic image is easier than you might think. With a little practice, you can make the technique repeatable and effortless. Fortunately, modern DSLR cameras are very forgiving and even show you their results before "developing."

Great panoramas start with great photos. For the Photomerge command to work properly, we've provided some guidelines for you to use when shooting. Here's our recipe to success:

1. **Set up your tripod.** Set up your tripod and make sure the legs are spread wide enough for a stable base. Then make sure the tripod is level. Photoshop can handle a slight variance in angle, but more than a few degrees can confuse the Photomerge command.

2. **Go manual.** Your camera should be in Manual mode. You want to minimize changes in exposure as you pan the camera. Be sure to keep your exposure constant throughout all shots of the panorama. We recommend taking a few test shots from around the arc and then adjusting your settings.

3. **Shoot raw.** Camera raw formats offer much greater control over exposure and significantly more image detail to work with. If you have a tough exposure (like strong directional lighting), raw files will help facilitate a good result.

4. **Shoot in portrait mode.** You may need to get a special bracket or tripod head to do this easily, but it's well worth it. Shooting in portrait mode minimizes horizontal distortion and produces a panorama with the maximum image quality.

5. **Avoid distortion from the lens.** You'll want to avoid using fish-eye lenses or other types of lenses that excessively bend the image. If you do use a lens of this type, choose the Auto layout option to minimize distortion (**Figure 12.7**).

Figure 12.7 The merged image on the left uses the Perspective method and creates very different results than the Auto method (right).

6. **Focus on infinity.** Be absolutely certain that you put the camera into manual focus. You'll want to focus at infinity so everything stays the same through each shot.

7. **Keep an eye on moving objects.** If people or other objects are moving through the frame, be sure to avoid duplicating them in multiple exposures. If the scene is quite busy, you should shoot each angle a few times. You can always merge multiple exposures to remove an object from a shot.

8. **Overlap shots.** The Photomerge command prefers an overlap of 25–50 percent. Although some overlap is good, too much can also be a problem. If Photoshop encounters more than a 70 percent overlap, it may have difficulty blending exposures.

9. **Avoid focal length adjustments.** Do not change your focal length while shooting. If you're using a fixed lens, this is simple. However, you can still shoot with a zoom lens. Just be sure you don't adjust the lens while shooting.

10. **Precisely pan the camera.** You'll want to turn the camera a consistent amount for each shot. The number of exposures you'll need will depend on your shooting style and equipment.

Capture Your Shots

Remember that the goal while shooting for a panoramic image is to have consistent overlap from one shot to the next. Photoshop detects these details so the shots can be joined by the Photomerge command. Make sure there is at least a 15 percent overlap between each shot. Depending on the type of lens you use, you will need between 2 and 24 exposures. More exposures mean less distortion and cleaner panoramic photos.

Portrait Aspect Ratio

Do your best to shoot in portrait mode (**Figure 12.8**), as you'll be able to minimize distortion by creating sizable overlap. If you're shooting a full 360-degree panoramic image, turn the camera in 15-degree increments. This means you will need to take 24 pictures for a complete loop.

Figure 12.8 Using 24 images, this panorama has plenty of overlap and results in a high-resolution photo.

Landscape Aspect Ratio

If a landscape orientation is your only option, you won't need as many exposures because of the wider images (**Figure 12.9**). You can try shooting in 20-degree increments (18 pictures) or 30-degree increments (12 pictures).

Figure 12.9 In this shot, everything was done incorrectly. The camera was in landscape orientation, the shots were hand-held, and the camera was in Aperture Priority mode. Still, the Photomerge command worked correctly and saved the day.

Handheld Shooting

What about handheld shooting for panoramic photos? The official answer is no; don't do it. However, at times we've been inspired by a great view without having all our gear with us. If you must shoot your panoramic images without a tripod, you'll need to adjust your handheld shooting technique. In this case, use your body as a tripod.

Try wrapping the camera strap around your elbow or shoulder (**Figure 12.10**). This allows you to place tension on the strap so it is taut. The tension is a useful way to constrain the camera movement and make it more an extension of your body. Here are some guidelines for producing the best handheld results:

Figure 12.10 Use your body and camera strap to stabilize the camera.

1. Hold the camera in front of your body so its strap hangs downward.

2. Slip your arm through the strap so it goes just past your elbow.

3. Wrap your hand around the outside edge of the strap and grab the camera body.

4. Press your elbow into the strap to increase tension on the strap and stabilize the camera.

   To pan the camera smoothly, you'll need to properly position your body.

5. Square up your body with your subject.

6. Spread your feet shoulder-width apart.

7. Rotate at the waist and twist your body while keeping your shoulders and camera in close to your body (making sure there's overlap between shots).

We've seen the Photomerge command deftly handle shots that lacked a tripod's support. Although we prefer to use our gear, Photoshop has freed us to work without it when necessary.

Photomerge Command

Photomerge is a specialized "mini-application" within Photoshop that assists in combining multiple images into a single photo. You can access it from either Photoshop or Adobe Bridge. Depending on the resolution of your sources and the speed of your machine, it can take a while for Photomerge to complete stitching a panorama.

Organizing Images

As we've discussed throughout the book, using Bridge is a great way to organize your photos (**Figure 12.11**). You can readily group, rename, sort, and sift your images. We typically use Bridge to navigate to our panoramic photos, and if needed to make selections between multiple exposures.

NOTES

Chances are, you don't need a panoramic image that's 30,000 pixels tall. If you're shooting with a high-resolution DSLR camera, don't be afraid to preprocess your photos. Use the Image Processor script (File > Scripts > Image Processor) to convert a group of images to lower-resolution TIFF files. We usually cap the image height to 3,000–5,000 pixels when we're working in HD.

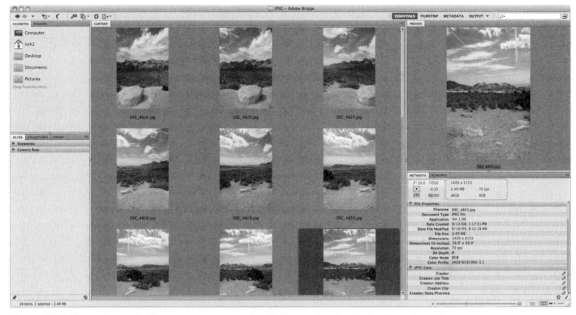

Figure 12.11 You can invoke the Photomerge command from Bridge by choosing Tools > Photoshop > Photomerge.

After you've selected all the images, it's time to process. Hold down the Command (Ctrl) key to select multiple images as you click on Bridge. You can also use the Shift key to select a range of images. In Bridge, choose Tools > Photoshop > Photomerge to open the selected images and send them to Photoshop for processing.

Choosing a Layout Method

The Photomerge command offers six different layout options when creating a panoramic photo (**Figure 12.12**). Each method interprets the panoramic photos differently. We often try to run multiple methods to see which produces the best results. A good place to start is Auto, which attempts to align the images but will bend them as needed. Here is a rundown of all six layout options:

Figure 12.12 The layout methods produce dramatically different results. When creating a 360-degree image, we stick with Auto for the first attempt.

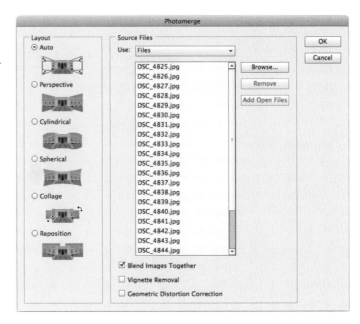

- ▸ **Auto.** With the Auto method, Photoshop first analyzes your source images. Next, it applies the Perspective, Cylindrical, and Spherical layout options. Photoshop then attempts to choose the method that will produce the best Photomerge.

- ▸ **Perspective.** The Perspective method creates a composition by designating one of the source images as the center of the panoramic image. Photoshop generally picks the middle image, and then transforms the other images around it. Photoshop will stretch and skew images as needed to overlap the layers and blend them together.

- ▸ **Cylindrical.** The Cylindrical layout option works best for creating very wide panoramic images. The source images are overlapped in a way that looks like an unfolded cylinder.

- ▸ **Spherical.** The Spherical option is best suited for 360-degree panoramas. The images are mapped to the inside of a sphere and can create a seamless image for use in specialty applications like multimedia or animation.

▶ **Collage.** The Collage method changes only the rotation or scale to overlap the content.

▶ **Reposition.** The Reposition method changes only the alignment of images but does not transform (stretch or skew) any of the source layers.

Aligning Images

Once you've chosen your images and sent them to Photoshop with the Photomerge command, you're on your way. We're using the Auto layout method in this case, because we're creating a 180–360-degree panoramic image.

The other option you should choose is blending. Select the check boxes next to the Blend Images Together property in the Photomerge dialog box to have Photoshop automatically generate masks and blend exposures together. Another option, Vignette Removal, is useful if your images have been darkened, usually by the lens hood. Both options will attempt to blend the edges of the photos together (**Figure 12.13**) and hide subtle differences in exposure.

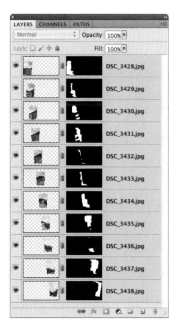

Figure 12.13 By blending images together, variations in exposure are hidden and a more seamless image is created by masking.

When you click OK, Photoshop opens all the source files and attempts to build the panoramic image. Photoshop assembles the panorama based on your choices in the Photomerge dialog box. Because layers are preserved, however, you can still make small tweaks to individual layers. Nudge any layers with the Move tool if your alignment is off. You can also paint to touch up the layer masks to help blend the photos together.

When you're happy with the photo, you need to finish it. Flatten the layers so you have a large, single layer file by choosing Layer > Flatten Image. We also recommend cropping the image to remove unwanted areas at the top and bottom (avoid removing too much from the left or right edges or the seamless loop may be broken).

Making a Seamless Loop

The resulting image after applying the Photomerge command is quite large but is not a perfect loop. All the interior overlap of the images has been blended, but there are still extra pixels at the left and right edges. The outside edges need to be blended together.

This process could be done with lots of compositing and cloning, but that would be a waste of perfectly good design time and require a pile of monkey work. Instead of performing several tedious steps, we offer a Photoshop action that will finish processing the full 360-degree panoramic image:

1. Choose Window > Actions to call up the Actions panel.

2. Click the Actions panel submenu and choose Load Actions (**Figure 12.14**). A new browser window opens.

3. Navigate to the Chapter_12_Media folder on the accompanying DVD.

4. Select the action Panoramic_Loop.atn and click Load.

5. In the Actions panel, locate the Panoramics set (folder) and choose the Seamless Loop action.

6. Click the Play selection button in the Actions panel.

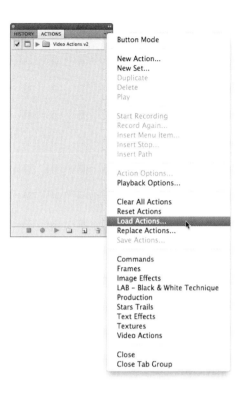

Figure 12.14 To store a set of actions for quick reference, you can copy it into the Presets folder in Photoshop.

7. The image is now seamless on the left and right edges. A new dialog box invites you to crop the image as needed. Click Continue.

8. Crop as needed (**Figure 12.15**).

Figure 12.15 The action cleans up the edges of the image and creates a seamless wrap using the same technology as the original Photomerge command.

9. Choose File > Save As and name the file. Save it to your project folder. We recommend saving as a TIFF file. You can apply LZW image compression to reduce the file size.

Cleaning Up Unwanted Objects

Chances are, you'll end up with a few unwanted objects in your photo. It might be a power line that's sagging in the frame or an unwanted tourist walking through the shot. Fortunately, Photoshop offers a suite of tools for removing objects and hiding blemishes.

Content-Aware Fill

The Content-Aware fill option is a new command in Photoshop CS5. It allows you to select an area and then fill it with a texture that is automatically generated based on pixels surrounding the selection. What happens is that Photoshop randomly synthesizes similar content to fill the area based on the surrounding source image data. This is a great way to remove an object or blemish from a shot. In some cases it completes the job in one step; in others it offers a great jump start that can be touched up with cloning or healing (**Figure 12.16**).

Figure 12.16 A rough selection was made with the Lasso tool (left). The Content-Aware fill command does a good job of removing the object (center). A quick use of the Clone Stamp tool completes the touchup (right).

To use the command, you'll need to make a selection. We find that the Lasso tool or the Quick Selection tool works well. You'll want to make the selection slightly larger than the targeted area. To create a gentle transition zone, be sure to choose Select > Modify > Feather and enter a value of 5–25 pixels to blend the selection.

To access the Content-Aware Fill command, you'll need to open the Fill dialog box. Choose Edit > Fill to bring up the Fill dialog box (**Figure 12.17**). Choose Content-Aware fill from the Use menu and click OK. The command may take a few moments to process if you're working with a high-resolution image. If you don't like the first attempt Content-Aware fill generates, just choose Edit > Undo and then repeat the Content-Aware fill command.

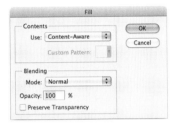

Figure 12.17 To access the Fill dialog box (and Content-Aware fill), just press Shift+Delete.

Clone Stamp

If you've used Photoshop for a long time, you've surely come to rely on the Clone Stamp tool. It can produce predictable and accurate results with just a little practice. It works by sampling pixels from one area of an image and painting them in another (**Figure 12.18**). What makes the tool so useful is that it relies on the flexibility of Photoshop's Brush panel, which allows you to adjust the size and hardness of the brush as well as the opacity of the stroke. When cloning, be sure to use a soft brush. You can quickly adjust the hardness of a brush by holding down the Shift key and pressing [(for a soft brush) or] (for a harder brush).

Figure 12.18 The Clone Stamp tool is a quick way to remove distracting blemishes from an image.

The most useful option when cloning is to specify the desired alignment of the brush. In the Options bar, you have two choices:

▶ **If Aligned is selected,** the sample point and painting point move parallel as you brush. If you click again and start over, the sample point picks up a sample relative to the current brush position.

▶ **If Aligned is deselected,** the initial sample point is reused. This method ensures that you are always sampling from the same area. But the other method (when Aligned is selected) produces more visual variety if you have a large textured area to clone.

To set the source point for cloning, simply Option-click (Alt-click) within the current document. You can also use another open document as a source (just be sure that it is set to the same color mode). This defines the source point for sampled pixel data.

To get the best results, follow these performance tips:

▶ Try cloning at a low opacity from several different places to fill in a problem area. This way you can avoid too much repetition in the pattern.

▶ Try to "follow the line" by looking for edges to follow in the image. Try to follow the natural curves and linear paths that are present.

▶ You can clone from all visible layers by selecting the Use All Layers option. This option is useful if you want to clone to an empty layer at the top of your document while sampling from the layers below.

Healing Brush

The Healing Brush is designed to correct imperfections in a photo. Similar in handling to the Clone Stamp tool, it successfully hides blemishes by taking cloned pixels and matching the texture, lighting, and shading of the sampled area to the original pixels. This can generally produce results in which the repaired pixels blend seamlessly together (**Figure 12.19**).

Figure 12.19 The Healing Brush takes a short while to process and blend, but the results are usually seamless.

You can use all the Clone Stamp tool shortcuts with the Healing Brush tool. Be sure to specify the tool alignment in the Options bar. If Aligned is selected, the sample point and painting point move parallel as you brush. If you click again and start over, the sample point picks up relative to the current brush position. If Aligned is deselected, the initial sample point is reused. The latter method ensures that you are always sampling from the same area, but the former method produces more visual variety if you have a large textured area.

Here are a few Healing Brush tips to get better performance:

▶ Because the sampled pixels are drawn from an area before you click, it may be necessary to release and start over occasionally to avoid sampling the problem area.

▶ Release the mouse to merge the sampled pixels. The stroke will most likely look strange until then.

▶ To get better results on an area with strong contrast, make a selection before you use the Healing Brush tool. The selection should be bigger than the area to be healed and should follow the boundary of high-contrast pixels. Then, when you're painting with the Healing Brush, the selection will prevent color bleed-in from outside areas.

▶ You can clone from all visible layers by selecting the Use All Layers option. This option is useful if you want to clone to an empty layer at the top of your document while sampling from the layers below.

NOTES

The Spot Healing Brush works well if you don't want to manually set a sampling point. Just be sure to avoid using too big of a brush when painting, or you'll get poorer texture sampling.

Panoramic Photos in After Effects

When you've completed your panoramic photo, it's ready for After Effects. Remember that panoramic photos do not *have* to be 360 degrees (just the most useful ones are). You also may want to downsample the image resolution:

▶ If you're using the photo for a virtual set, keep a higher-resolution file (we do). A vertical height of 3,000–10,000 pixels is adequate. Use the higher numbers if you're trying to simulate distance for depth of field effects.

▶ If you're using the photo in a seamless loop, you won't need as much resolution. For things like DVD menus or installation graphics, resize the photo in Photoshop so its height is no more than 2X your target finishing size (such as 2160 pixels for a 1080p composition).

Creating a Seamless Loop in After Effects

One of the easiest ways to use a seamless image is to create a looping texture with the Offset effect. When applied to a layer, After Effects can shift the pixels and wrap them seamlessly around one edge to the next. The result is essentially a perfect pan, with the original pixels entering from the opposite side.

The only control you'll need is the Shift Center To option. When you add a keyframe, the values are expressed as pixels. While precision in keyframing is nice, in this case it is not that useful because it requires doing a lot of math. A better option is to double-click the keyframe. In the dialog box, you can change the Units of measurement to % of source (**Figure 12.20**).

Figure 12.20 Measuring in percentages makes it easier to achieve precision.

The default Shift Center To value is 50%, which indicates that the image is centered in the Composition panel. Add a second keyframe and set it to 150% (which equates to one full cycle of pushing the pixels out one direction and wrapping them to the other side). This generates one seamless loop (**Figure 12.21**). You can adjust the timing by spreading the keyframes apart. You can also create multiple loops by using 100% increments as you change values.

If you keep the layer set to Best quality, the Offset effect uses subpixel precision, which produces a very clean pan result.

Figure 12.21 This looping background creates a seamless movement thanks to the wrapped panoramic image. Use longer duration times to create slow pans.

Creating a Virtual Set

Another panorama option is to use the panoramic photo as a large cylinder. To do this, we'll turn to an After Effects script. The use of scripts allows programmers to customize After Effects and create complex effects. In this lesson, we'll add a third-party script that coverts a panoramic photo into a cylinder and adds a 3D camera to the scene. The script called pt_Panorama.jsx was created by Paul Tuersley.

To get the latest script, visit http://aescripts.com/pt_panorama. You can donate any amount to purchase the script.

To install a script, you must quit After Effects. Download the latest version of the pt_Panorama script. Navigate to the After Effects application folder. Open the folder Scripts, and then open the folder ScriptUI Panels. Copy the file pt_Panorama.jsx to the ScriptsUI Panels folder. You can then relaunch After Effects.

Using the script is pretty straightforward:

1. Add the panoramic image to a composition sized to your output format.

2. Select the panoramic image, and then choose Window > pt_Panorama.jsx to open a controller window for the script (**Figure 12.22**).

3. Inspect the first field, "Panorama angle." This is how much of a panoramic photo you have. In this example, 360 is correct.

4. In the second field, "Number of sides," enter a number to specify how many pieces to split the photo into. It will be broken into a cylinder. More sides mean a smoother curve (but increased render time). We recommend entering the same number as the original number of exposures (in this case 24).

5. The Side Overlap field is optional. You should use this option to prevent gaps created when Motion Blur is enabled. If the camera is moved to the outside of the cylinder, set the value to 10. To use the field, you must click the mode pop-up menu and switch to Alt mode.

6. Click the Make Panorama button when you're ready. After Effects converts the image into a cylinder (**Figure 12.23**).

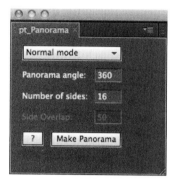

Figure 12.22 Scripts that use UI features can load into their own panel.

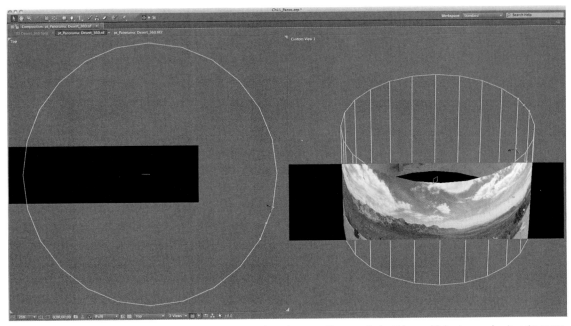

Figure 12.23 The large photo is split into several smaller panels and wrapped into a cylinder. Using multiple views makes it easier to see.

Integrating Panoramas with 3D Cameras

Once you've built a cylinder panorama, you need to decide where you want the action to occur. You can either shoot from the outside of the cylinder (like looking in on a carousel) or from within the cylinder (which can be scaled to a desired size). We find that shooting from within works best because it simulates the orientation of the camera when the photo was first shot. Simply add a 3D camera and try to match its properties to the lens used for the panoramic photo (**Figure 12.24**).

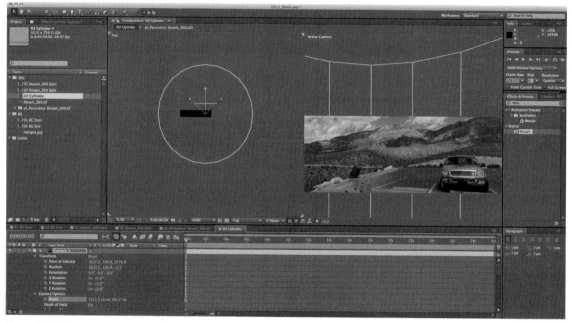

Figure 12.24 The camera's position was adjusted so it sits in the middle of the cylinder (the same position as the real camera that captured the scene). Adjusting the camera zoom allowed a better field of view. The entire scene was scaled larger by manipulating the null object.

TIP

You can make the Timeline cleaner by marking the panorama slices as shy layers.

The pt_Panorama script nests its results inside a precomposition. We find it easy enough to work with this new composition. Locate the precomposition in the Project panel and duplicate it (this way you can return to a clean copy if needed). Open the composition and design with it. To transform the cylinder, use the null object that is in the composition. The null object lets you scale or position the panorama.

We enjoy using the null object to place a green screen subject within the virtual set. You can animate the background or simply keyframe the camera to create useful camera angles and moves. Using the camera controls, you can adjust the relationship between the backdrop and subject (**Figure 12.25**). You can also continue to use the null object to tweak the background.

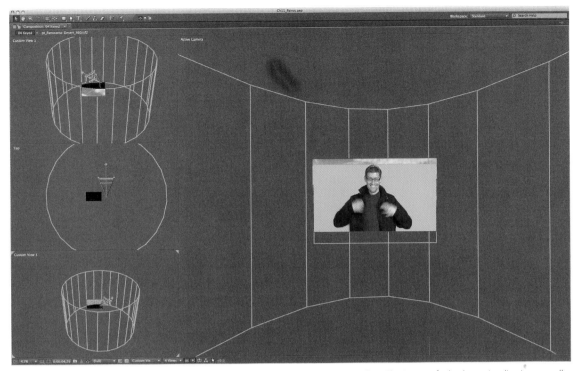

Figure 12.25 By placing a green screen subject into the scene, you can create a virtual set. This is great for both previsualization as well as completed projects.

Lighting the Scene

To get the most from your panoramic scene, we recommend adjusting the lighting. The photo you shot likely has a realistic lighting angle, so you'll want to match this. This allows inserted elements (whether they're footage layers or titles) to react to the scene in a realistic manner.

To start, adjust the ambient lighting level. For lights to build up, you first need to darken things a bit. Choose Layer > New > Light, and then choose Ambient as the Light Type. We recommend that you actually rename the light to ambient in the Timeline so it's easier to organize. Set the Intensity between 50–80% to create a slightly darker scene.

NOTES

If the Intensity value of all your lights totals over 100%, you may see a brightening in the scene. Remember that lights compound, so adjust the intensity accordingly.

You should then add a Point light to simulate the sun's position. Examining the photos you shot or any notes from the field, try to determine the sun's position. Choose Layer > New > Light, and then choose Point as the Light Type. Drag the light into position. Using multiple composition views (such as Custom View 1) makes it easier to see and position lights. If you'd like to add some directional lights, use Spotlights as needed (**Figure 12.26**).

Figure 12.26 Using three lights helps to create stylized lighting in the scene. The Spotlight is used to cast shadows from the text onto the actor. The Point light and Ambient light build the correct levels in the scene.

13

DVD and Blu-ray Design

As a child, my family's menu consisted of two choices: take it or leave it.

—Buddy Hackett

DVD and Blu-ray Design

Although Adobe Encore is included in the Creative Suite, you may wonder how it fits into a motion graphics workflow. The answer is easy, at the end. With Encore you can collect video and animation clips, and assemble them into portfolios and collections. The best part is that a single Encore project can be published as a DVD, Blu-ray Disc, or Flash (SWF) file.

We're sure that you'll find Encore easy enough to learn, but there's a special role for the motion graphics artist to fill. As the menu designer, you'll find opportunities for creating background loops, interactive elements, and typographic design. Why settle for built-in templates or stock backgrounds when you can create your own (**Figure 13.1**)?

By combining a camera, some junk around the office, and a little light, you'll be on your way to great backgrounds and interactive menus. The use of blending modes is a designer's secret, one you need to become initiated in. You'll quickly discover that healthy experimentation and organic design can lead to great results.

Figure 13.1 By combining photos, footage, and type, you can create a rich DVD or Blu-ray Disc menu.

Approach to Designing Menus and Interactive Projects

What's our secret to designing good menus? It's easy; function should drive the design (not the other way around). What we mean is that way too many menus for DVD and Blu-ray titles seem to be about designers showing off their design skills and not serving the needs of the greater purpose.

A menu for a Blu-ray or DVD piece is an informational graphic. It is meant to guide viewers in finding the material that they want to consume. We believe that menus should be tasteful and minimalist whenever possible. Always remember your purpose; let design be a servant to content (rather than making design into content).

Building a Design Brief

You know that frustration when a movie poster or trailer misrepresents what a film is really like? How about a really great cover for a very boring book? Keep in mind that you are essentially creating animated wrapping paper when you design a menu. Everyone will be much happier if what's on the outside directly relates to what's on the inside.

We recommend that you speak with others involved in the project to find out about the project's tone and style. Look at the pieces that will be contained within. If the menus you're designing are for a corporate project, seek out a style guide. The goal here is simple; figure out the "why" and "who" before you start to build the "what."

Organizing a Project

We can't stress enough the need to organize a DVD project. At the start of this book we discussed using a Common Media Folder. You should take the same approach here. DVDs often have several video tracks as well as audio clips, music, slide shows, and more. Get organized.

Another advantage to culling and sorting is that you may discover some great design sources, such as production stills taken by the crew, abstract shots buried in the B-roll, and so on. You never know what you'll find until you look.

Organizing Assets with Bridge

You've seen Adobe Bridge in use throughout this book. It's a very effective tool for organizing multimedia projects as well. Because of its diverse support for media types, Bridge can become invaluable as you organize a DVD. Here are several benefits of using Bridge:

- ▶ **Graphics.** You can quickly view Adobe graphic files such as Photoshop and Illustrator files. You can also see other formats without needing to open them. Press the spacebar in Bridge to quickly see a full-screen preview.

- ▶ **Audio.** Audio files can be auditioned from Bridge as well. As long as the files lack Digital Rights Management (DRM protection), they'll play within Bridge.

- ▶ **Video.** Video clips play in a preview window. As long as the format is supported by a QuickTime player or the Flash Player plug-in, it should play within Bridge (**Figure 13.2**).

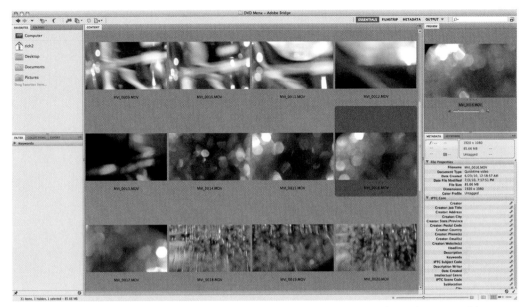

Figure 13.2 The ability to quickly browse footage and even preview clips in full motion makes Bridge quite useful.

▶ **Documents.** You can view PDF or InDesign files from within Bridge. This is a useful way to see style guides, notes, flowcharts, or other documents saved in the PDF format.

▶ **Slideshows.** Want to simulate a slide show? Select a series of assets in Bridge and choose View > Slideshow. You can then skip between slides and simulate the same experience you'll create in Encore.

▶ **Batch renaming.** If you want to keep your assets organized, you may need to rename them. Once you've isolated several images for a slide show, renaming them can ensure a consistent order. Simply drag the images into the order you want in the Bridge window (from left to right then top to bottom). Choose Tools > Batch Rename to give the files a consistent name and numbered order. When you import the files into Encore, slide shows will be easier to build.

▶ **Sorting.** A simple way to sort images is to take advantage of Bridge's ability to rank files. You can assign a star ranking to images or videos, and then use the sift features to only show files with a specified ranking or higher. Bridge's Review mode (**Figure 13.3**) makes it easy to analyze several images for comparison.

Figure 13.3 With a group of images selected, choose View > Review mode. You can then assign numerical rankings using the 1–5 keys. Use the left and right arrows to navigate through photos and the down arrow to deselect them. When you're finished, press the Esc key to exit or press Return (Enter) to open the files.

Identifying Connections and Creating Flowcharts

What's the secret to making great DVD and Blu-ray Disc menus? Know your purpose! How you design a menu will depend a lot on the number of buttons you need to fit as well as any branding or title elements you need to include. Be sure you have a cohesive design so your navigation is consistent. Here are a few questions you'll need to resolve to obtain a clear path to the functional limits you'll need to clarify:

▶ **How many tracks will you have?** Identify every element that you think will be on the DVD Oe BD. Is it a simple title with just one video track and a slide show? Or, is it a major compilation with hundreds of clips?

▶ **How will those tracks be grouped?** Give some thought to any organization that will need to occur. Portfolio discs are often grouped by topic or genre. Entertainment titles generally group subsidiary material to one or more menus while giving prominence to the feature.

▶ **Make a flowchart and know what you want (and where you want it).** Once all the tracks have been identified, you should group them and organize them using a flowchart or tree diagram. This can be created with an application like OmniGraffle (www.omnigroup.com) (**Figure 13.4**) or with the Organizational Chart Maker found in the Microsoft Office suite (www.microsoft.com). A flowchart is a useful way to identify which elements are grouped into each menu as well as to show the connections between menus and tracks. Taking the time to make an actual plan will speed up the design and authoring processes, and minimize unintentional errors.

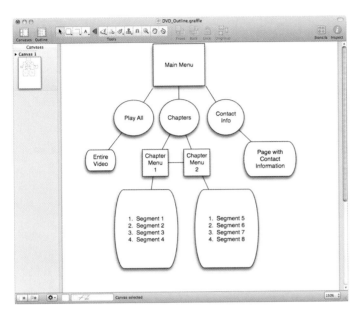

Figure 13.4 A flowchart is a quick way to identify the number of menus you'll need as well as how many buttons you'll need per page. This flowchart was created with OmniGraffle.

▶ **How many buttons will you have on each menu?** Are there any limitations for your design? We recommend identifying the menu that needs the most number of buttons and designing it first. By limiting yourself, you'll be certain to have enough room for navigation and won't have to make text too small to read. It's important to remember that menus become further compressed when discs are authored, so small text can break up and become illegible.

▶ **Will you have transitions between menu selections or your tracks?** Many designers build branching menus and use an animated transition to move between tracks. These short animations are often customized and heavily influence the design process.

▶ **Which menus will be motion menus and which will be still menus?** Not every menu needs to move (nor can every project afford this level of design). Be sure to identify which menus will benefit from animation and which will be simplified designs.

Preparing to Shoot Footage Plates for Menus

A staple of menu design is subtle motion. We're shocked at how many motion graphics designers have been trapped inside their computers, afraid to pick up a traditional design tool like a paintbrush or a camera. A favorite story of ours is about a designer posting to a support forum asking how to make fire. He expected a complex recipe involving particle effects. What he was told was a little more direct—"a match."

Why do we bring this up? Well, we encourage you to free your mind and actually shoot some footage plates. You'll learn how to turn everyday objects into beautiful motion graphics with just a little bit of light and some optical "squinting."

Creating the Studio

Truth be told, any room can work as a studio as long as you have a good free space to work in. We've pressed our conference room into service, shot in the basement, and even used a kitchen. The key is that you want a room that's dark and big enough to move in. If you don't have to spend time blocking out windows, choose that location (**Figure 13.5**).

Figure 13.5 You'll need a fairly dark room. The techniques in this chapter work best when the camera has lots of reflections to capture.

Because you're about to spend some time in the dark, there are a few things you can do to make the space highly productive. We recommend setting up two tables. You'll use one table for storage of the props you intend to shoot; the other will be your stage. Be sure your shooting environment is set up with what you need and that your props are handy.

To create an ideal (and simplified) shooting environment, we create a small cyc (a curved backdrop to avoid shadows). We use a piece of flexible, black plastic with a matte finish. For this example, we used an Infiniti Board from Cloud Dome (www.clouddome.com). These flexible boards are great and are priced between $40 and $90 depending on their size (**Figure 13.6**). You may also be able to create your own from materials at your studio or from materials at an art store.

TIP

Lots of options for turntables are available. We found searching under the terms turntable, turn table, and rotating display gave us good results.

Figure 13.6 The Infiniti Board creates a surface that appears infinitely deep. This works great for creating a perfect environment for tabletop shooting. The image on the right is what the camera captured (albeit purposely out of focus).

We use a motorized turntable to spin objects. By rotating objects, you get a nice animated pattern. This isn't a must, but it's not an expensive investment (**Figure 13.7**). You can invest in an actual photography model (prices vary greatly, but don't overspend). You can also get one from a hardware store or even press an old record player into service.

Figure 13.7 We use a turntable from Vuemore (www.vuemore.com) for our shooting.

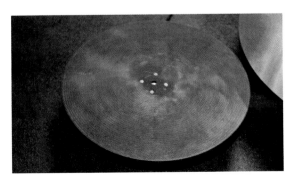

Lighting Equipment Needed

With lighting, the goal is to have bright lights that are easy for you to adjust. If you have them, you can use any professional video lights at your disposal. We favor cooler lights that are fluorescent based because they are cooler to the touch and safer to handle. But even big iron will do; just be sure to wear safety gloves and be careful when adjusting hot lights. You can even get away with cheaper shop lights from a hardware store if you're on a tight budget. All you're looking to do is create some bright directional light that you can shine on objects (**Figure 13.8**).

Figure 13.8 Very bright lights were pointed at a pile of coins and paper clips. Shooting through a colored gel knocked down the intensity of the lights and added color "in-camera."

Other items to get are small, handheld shop lights. These are essentially lights meant to hang in a workshop or construction site (**Figure 13.9**). One end has a lighting instrument (usually with a hook), and the other has a power cord that is similar to a professional-grade extension cord. We prefer the more modern styles with small fluorescent lights. These can produce enough light to create random lighting effects. By essentially "waving" or "floating" these lights above your subject, you can create subtle "motion" as the light moves across the surface of the images. The use of gentle rhythmic movement will give you the needed "motion" for your motion graphics.

Figure 13.9 Handheld lights let you create random patterns. By gently moving the light source, you can create organic hot spots and flashes in your background plate.

Another option is to use colored lighting gels to influence the subject. Although you can add additional color (or manipulate existing colors) in After Effects, you get a much more organic effect manipulating light during the shoot. Pick up some lighting gels, which you can easily purchase from professional lighting stores, at audio centers that cater to DJs, or from online vendors. We keep a "party pack" with our lights that contains several different colors (**Figure 13.10**). You can tape the gels around your handheld lights to create random color. You can hold pieces in front of the camera lens. You can also clip them with clothespins to the barn doors of your bigger lights. A little color goes a long way to improving design options.

Figure 13.10 Shooting with gels lets you colorize the background during the shoot. You can put the gel in front of the light or the subject. In post, you can keep this color or completely manipulate it to a new color.

Choosing a Camera

Our simplest advice is use the best camera you have. Don't use this as an excuse to rush out and plunk $30K down on new gear. We started shooting our own background plates more than a decade ago with the only camera we had lying around the office (a Canon ZR-10 DV camcorder).

Of course, if you have better gear at your disposal (or can call in a favor and rent or borrow), we offer this selection advice:

▶ **Use direct to disk format.** If you can avoid hitting tape, do so. Digital formats that allow you to transfer files to your system without the need of an expensive deck or hardware are beneficial.

▶ **Shoot progressive.** There is no reason to shoot background plates in an interlaced format. You'll want the smoothest motion as well as the ability to stretch or remap time. Trust us; go progressive (**Figure 13.11**).

TIP

If you have access to camera filters, a soft fx filter or pro mist can help soften your image.

Figure 13.11 Use the best camera you have at your disposal. We've become big fans of HDSLR cameras because they offer excellent lens choices and shallow depth of field.

NOTES

Before shooting, ensure that your lens is clean. Extra dust or smudges on the lens won't help you here.

▶ **Stick with HD.** We now shoot our plates at 1080p whenever possible. This gives us a large image that can be easily scaled or manipulated. If we want to slow down motion more (without longer processing times in After Effects), we might shoot 720p at 60 fps. In this case the footage is overcranked and recorded at a higher frame rate. In After Effects we can interpret the clip and set it to play back at a lower rate (hence slowing down the clip).

▶ **Try HDSLR cameras.** We enjoy shooting on HDSLR cameras for this style of shooting. The lens choice and short depth of field make it easy to get attractive blurring or Bokeh effects. Using a lens with a low f-stop can enhance the blurring.

▶ **Use a tripod.** The movement in the background plates
will come from moving the lights or objects, not the
camera. You want the camera to be locked off in place.
Using a tripod is key. This will make it easier to loop
the footage and creates a more fluid background plate
that's free from bumps and wiggles. Your best results
will often come from macro or extreme close-ups; camera movement will be too jarring when tightly focused.

▶ **Use a monitor.** Viewing your shots on a large monitor is
truly useful. If you have one at your disposal, a professional production monitor is ideal. You can also utilize
Adobe OnLocation to view clips on a laptop for certain
camera models. You may also find that your camera
offers an HDMI port that can directly connect to many
computer monitors or televisions. Go big here so you
can see your footage in all of its out-of-focus and soft-
light glory. When you're able to see your results, you
can readily make variations in the speed and type of
movement (**Figure 13.12**).

Figure 13.12 The camera was pointed down into shiny, decorative, glass stones. By using a large monitor, focus could be
tweaked to create the desired effect.

Finding Objects

It's important to find appropriate and appealing objects to
shoot. Anything that reflects light is an awesome candidate.
We usually put the word out a few days ahead of time so
employees can bring in their own objects from home. We
call our shoots "Shiny Stuff Day," and it becomes a matter
of pride to outdo each other.

Colorful objects that produce nice results are most helpful. Highly reflective surfaces like porcelain and metal can be very useful. Knickknacks and drawer contents can work as well. A spin to a local craft or hardware store can also bag some good finds. Just announce to your team to bring in items to shoot. You'll be surprised by the diversity of objects each person will bring in and even more surprised by the results you'll get (**Figure 13.13**).

Figure 13.13 We'll try anything to get results. Here you see liquid, crystal, broken computer parts, and even office supplies.

Here are some items we've used in the past:

- ▶ Crystal vases or stemware
- ▶ Glass objects of various shapes
- ▶ Metal objects like bowls and candleholders
- ▶ Plastic boxes or fish tanks
- ▶ Award statues (especially those made of acrylic or Lucite)
- ▶ Kitchen utensils and office supplies
- ▶ Dinner plates and porcelain fixtures
- ▶ Metal vents, springs, fasteners, and other hardware store items
- ▶ Jewelry pieces, beads, chains, pendants
- ▶ Liquids of various densities including soda, oil, water, seltzer
- ▶ Holiday lights and decorations
- ▶ Scientific flasks and beakers

Shooting Techniques for Footage Plates

Repeat after us: "I am willing to play for the sake of design." Did you say it? You need to free your mind enough to realize that great motion graphics doesn't mean you have to be a slave to keyframes and plug-ins. Creating great motion plates is really just figuring out fun ways to play with your camera and subject.

Trust yourself. As long as you are willing to experiment, you can achieve great creative results. It's our personal belief that creativity is an artist's ability to let go of fear and take chances.

In this section you'll learn how to create beautiful flowing textures and reflections of light. These simple footage plates can be layered and blended in After Effects. By employing simple footage, blending modes, and some optical trickery, beautiful backgrounds can be made.

Although you may be turned off by the time involved in shooting, don't be. In a very short amount of time you can build an immense library of footage. This raw material can be used not only for DVD backgrounds, but also for animated backgrounds, bumpers, lower third graphics, title sequences, and more. Take the leap and grab your camera; it's time to have your own "Shiny Stuff Day."

General Shooting Advice

In a moment we'll look at specific techniques. Here we offer general advice for all styles of subjects. When you start your camera rolling, be sure to get enough footage. We recommend that you roll for 1–3 minutes on each shot. This will give you plenty of variation to choose from and more than enough footage to make longer looping backgrounds.

Remember to experiment with focus and iris. We'll often rack focus to different positions because the deep blurring will take on a different look as you move the focus ring (**Figure 13.14**). If you're using a camera with Aperture controls, go ahead and experiment here as well. We'll often stack objects a few layers deep and play with the depth of field.

Figure 13.14 The same subject under the same lighting. We changed only the zoom and the focus.

Don't be afraid to try out an idea. Just watch your confidence monitor to make sure your shot is "working." Here's the deal; if you like it, it's working. If you don't, twiddle a knob, nudge a light, swap out the object for something else.

Be sure to keep an eye on your white level to ensure that the video is not getting too hot. These types of shots are prone to overexposure. Since you'll be combining multiple layers (and their brightness values often), you'll want to avoid blowing out the shot. While you're shooting, also consider capturing some still photos for use in high-resolution print projects.

Once you trigger the camera, it is okay to step away (provided it's on a secure tripod). By taking your hands off the camera, you'll minimize human vibration. Take advantage of your turntable or lazy Susan to create the movement. Even without rotating the object, the subtle motion of moving the handheld lights will give you great results. The goal is to create as much magic within the camera as possible. If it looks great while you're shooting, it will only get better when you take it into After Effects.

Liquid Pours

Fluids produce some of the most attractive footage you can shoot. There are several ways you can go about capturing a sense of fluidity, and we encourage you to discover your own techniques. We usually employ one of two methods.

Using a clear piece of Plexiglass, we place the camera so it shoots through the back as liquid pours across the front. To get a clean plate, you can place a white or black piece of fabric or foam core in the path of the lens. For your pours, be sure to use liquids that are viscous. We've found that milk, shampoo, paint, and syrups work well. Color can be achieved through the use of food coloring.

If we want more of a dispersion effect, a fish tank or glass mixing bowl works well. We generally fill the bowl with a colored liquid to begin (our favorites are generally diet soda). When you mix sugar with most diet sodas, you get lots of carbonation. We've also tried drink mix, which has both color and sugar in it (**Figure 13.15**).

Figure 13.15 We experiment with a wide range of diet sodas. Be sure to get several colors and brands. Try mixing in food coloring, sugar, or powdered drink mix in small quantities to get volatile effects. Remember to use small quantities, or you may get an explosive situation like the Mentos and Diet Coke Web video from several years back.

Perpendicular Shots

For a perpendicular shooting scenario, we typically place a reflective object (or group of objects) on a turntable. The camera is placed perpendicular to the turntable so it is shooting through the objects. The rotation of objects creates a sense of movement in the background.

Highly reflective objects work well, especially if they contain textures on the surface. It's also possible to shoot through clear or transparent objects to create refractions of the light (**Figure 13.16**).

Figure 13.16 Lock down the camera and let the objects move on the turntable. This will create very fluid movement.

For best results, use colored or mixed lighting to create irregularities and color variations. Be sure to experiment with different variations of focus because a subtle change in the lens can produce very different looks.

Spinning Shots

For variety, we'll use our turntables for a different style of shot. Loading up a turntable with small reflective objects (such as coins, paper clips, decorative glass beads, or shiny rocks) can create a pile of irregular reflections. Once the turntable begins to spin, you'll get great reflections.

The camera can then be angled and pointed at the turntable. If you're using a traditional video tripod, you'll shoot at an angle near 45 degrees. If you're using a photography tripod or using a camera stand, you may be able to get close to a 90 degree angle.

Vary the distance from the lens to the subject (you can use apple boxes or blocks to lift the turntable). Using lighting gels, you can colorize your lights or even just point the camera lens through them (**Figure 13.17**).

Figure 13.17 Lighting gels are very affordable and can be reused on multiple shoots.

Moving Lights

If you lack a turntable, don't worry; you can still make your own motion. By putting your lights into motion, you can create reflections and moving patterns. Either use both arms and reach around the objects or recruit another person for a second pair of hands. You'll want to make slow, gentle movement with the lights. We often use slow circular motions or oblong waves to create a flowing light.

Preparing with Premiere Pro

The footage you've captured could use a little culling. If you followed our advice, you probably rolled for 2–3 minutes per clip. Within those clips are starts and stops as well as changes in focus or camera settings.

Although you could just import the footage into After Effects and get to work, we recommend a quick swing through Premiere Pro. Why? Well, it's all about performance. With Premiere Pro you can play video clips in realtime (without having to invoke previews). You can also trim away parts you'd like to discard, split longer clips into multiple smaller clips, and strip away unwanted audio.

Loading Footage

We recommend you transfer your footage to a hard drive first before loading it into Premiere Pro. Ideally, you'll use a drive that spins fast enough for playing back video in realtime. Create a new project to hold your clips. Be sure to choose a preset that closely matches your acquisition format (**Figure 13.18**).

Figure 13.18 Premiere Pro has a wide variety of project presets that match most professional cameras (and even some common consumer cameras).

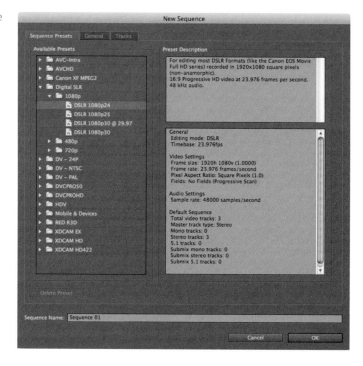

Load your footage by choosing File > Import. You can select a folder full of clips and click the Import Folder button. The clips are all added to the project (**Figure 13.19**). You can double-click an individual clip to load it into the Source monitor.

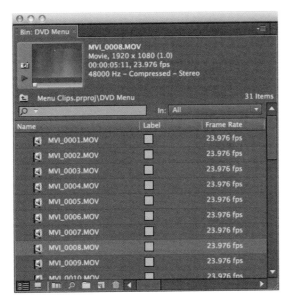

Figure 13.19 You can see a preview thumbnail for a selected clip at the top of the bin. Click the triangle to play a preview movie.

Making a Subclip

The next step toward organizing your clips is to trim them smaller. A subclip is a smaller part of a master clip. When creating a subclip, you can also rename a clip so it is more descriptive and easier to work with.

1. Load clips into the Program monitor (double-click or drag and drop).

2. Locate a section of the clip that is free from unwanted camera movement or jitter. Mark the section by pressing I for In and O for Out.

3. Choose Clip > Make Subclip.

4. Enter a name and click OK (**Figure 13.20**).

TIP

We favor a duration of 33:00–35:00 or 63:00–65:00 so we have enough handles to make 30:00 or 60:00 backgrounds.

NOTES

If you need to remove the audio from your subclips, you can edit them into a Timeline first with only the video track active. Highlight the clip in the Timeline and choose Clip > Make Subclip to make new subclips.

Figure 13.20 Be sure to choose a distinctive name so you can easily find a clip and avoid media management issues caused by duplicate names.

413

Media Manage

Once you've narrowed down your clips to just the desired selects, you'll need to media manage them. The goal here is to actually create new clips and discard the parts of the clips you didn't subclip. This process is a little tricky but worth it because it makes it easier to move, back up, and share your After Effects project.

1. Select a subclip in the bin.

2. Choose File > Export > Media or press Command+M (Ctrl+M).

3. Choose an export format and then a preset from the Preset menu or customize your own settings (**Figure 13.21**).

Figure 13.21 We usually strip the audio from the backgrounds to make smaller clips and avoid unwanted wild sound being included in a motion graphics project. Normally, we'd recommend a less compressed format; we used H.264 to save space on the book's DVD.

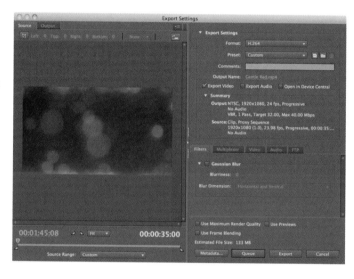

NOTES

By default, the Adobe Media Encoder may be set to start automatically. You can access the application preferences to adjust this setting.

4. Click the Output Name link and target a folder to hold the clips.

5. Click the Queue button to add the project to the Adobe Media Encoder queue.

6. Repeat steps 1–5 for the remaining clips that you'd like to export.

7. When you're ready, switch to Adobe Media Encoder and click the Start Queue button.

8. When the files are done, you can import them into After Effects.

Designing Menu Backgrounds in After Effects

Now that you've prepped clips, you're ready to move forward (even if you didn't shoot your own, we'll share some here and others via download). The techniques you'll use are extensions of those covered in Chapter 7, "Designing Backgrounds." This time you'll composite moving footage plates together using blending modes and colorization effects to produce backgrounds. Elements can interact in new and exciting ways thanks to blending modes.

Creating the First Composition

Switch to After Effects and create a new project. Be sure to save and name the file. You can then load your footage into After Effects like any other asset (choose File > Import or drag them into the Project panel). If you want, you can pre-organize elements into folders by shooting style to ease project management (**Figure 13.22**).

Be sure to clearly label the clips with a descriptive name and a proper file extension to make working with them easier.

The easiest way to learn blending modes is to just try them. The keyboard command Shift+– or Shift+= will cycle you through modes in Adobe applications.

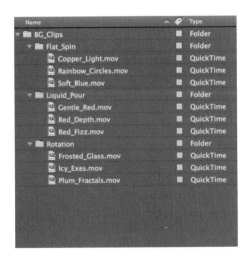

Figure 13.22 Nested folders from the organization on your hard drive will carry into After Effects.

You now need to create your first composition to serve as the basis for your menu. This composition will create the compound texture (containing two or more footage layers blended together). It should be slightly longer than your intended final duration to allow overlap to create a loop point. For example, set the first composition to 34:00 if you intend the final menu to be 30:00 (**Figure 13.23**).

Figure 13.23 When designing for HD, we prefer to stick with square pixels for maximum image quality.

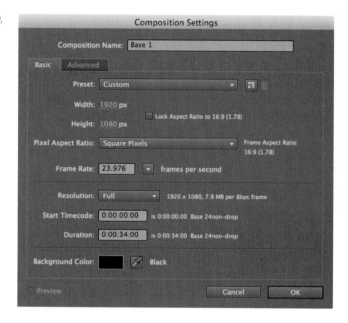

Depending on the project you intend to make, your menus may be built at different sizes (**Table 13.1**).

Table 13.1 Formats, Sizes, and Aspect Ratios

Format	Size	Pixel Aspect Ratio
NTSC DVD 4:3 Aspect Ratio	720x480	0.91
NTSC DVD 16:9 Aspect Ratio	720x480	1.21
PAL DVD 4:3 Aspect Ratio	720x576	1.09
PAL DVD 16:9 Aspect Ratio	720x576	1.46
Blu-ray 720p	1280x720	1.00
Blu-ray 1080p	1920x1080	1.00
Flash Interactive	1280x720 (recommended)	1.00

Stacking Footage

Now that you're ready to create a new texture, it's time to select clips. You'll need two to four footage layers for the technique to work (although you *can* use more, it tends to be overkill, like too many toppings on a pizza). If you'd like to preview a loaded clip in realtime, just Option+double-click (Alt+double-click) to open it in the appropriate media player software.

1. Load two or more footage layers into the base composition you created. This first composition is purely created for generating a texture. Color and looping will happen later.

2. Make sure your footage layers are long enough to fill the entire duration (if they run short, you can stretch them by choosing Layer > Time Stretch).

3. Turn off all layers except the bottommost two. Adjust the blending modes on the upper layer until you find a look that you like (**Figure 13.24**).

NOTES

For best results when stretching footage, go with even increments like 200%. Be sure to enable frame blending for all stretched layers to get the smoothest results.

Figure 13.24 Start by mixing two layers at a time so you can easily view the effect of changing blending modes and opacity.

You can use the keyboard shortcut Shift+- or Shift+= to cycle modes. Experiment with blur effects on the top layer or adjust opacity to your personal taste.

4. Activate RAM preview to see your results.

5. Repeat the blending technique on the remaining layers (**Figure 13.25**).

Try changing the stacking order and opacity to achieve additional results.

TIP

For greater visual impact, we recommend boosting the intensity of the bottommost layer. You can do this through a Levels or Auto Contrast effect.

Figure 13.25 Changing blending modes produces dramatically different effects.

You can press 0 on the numeric keypad as a shortcut to invoke RAM preview.

6. Activate RAM preview to see your results.

Looping the Background

Now that you've built a texture, it's time to create a seamless loop. To do this, you'll need to place the base composition inside a new composition (creating a nested composition).

1. Drag the base composition onto the Create a new composition button at the bottom of the Project panel (**Figure 13.26**).

Figure 13.26 Nesting one composition inside another makes it easier to create a looping background.

2. Select the newly created composition and access its settings by pressing Command+K (Ctrl+K).

3. Name the new composition **Menu 1** and set its duration to **30:00** (four seconds shorter than the base composition) (**Figure 13.27**).

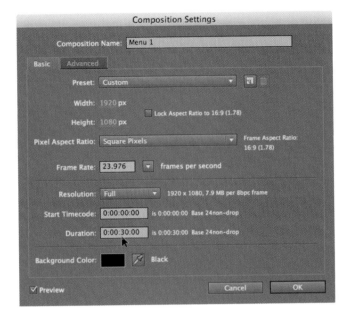

Figure 13.27 Shortening the composition creates a region for overlap.

4. Open the new composition and drag your current time indicator to the middle of the Timeline (near 15:00).

5. Split the layer, which will create the loop point. Select the layer and press Shift+Command+D (Shift+Ctrl+D) (**Figure 13.28**).

Figure 13.28 Be precise when you split a layer. Be sure the current time indicator is at the exact time you need.

You now have two layers, which need to overlap.

6. With Layer #2 active, jump to the end of the composition by pressing the End key. Press the right bracket key (]) to move the layer's Out point.

7. Select Layer #1, and then press the Home key to jump to the start of the composition. Press the left bracket key ([) to move the layer's In point (**Figure 13.29**).

Figure 13.29 The split points become the new In and Out points for the layer.

8. Activate Layer #1 and press O to jump to the layer's Out point. Add an opacity keyframe by pressing Option+T (Alt+T). Set the first keyframe to **0%** opacity.

Now let's create the transition.

9. Jump forward four seconds by pressing Option+Shift+J (Alt+Shift+J) and entering **+ -4:00**. Set a keyframe for **100%** opacity (**Figure 13.30**).

Figure 13.30 A dissolve between 3–5 seconds is long enough to create a gradual transition that hides the seam in the loop background. If you can't solve it, dissolve it.

10. Activate RAM preview to see your results.

Colorizing the Background

Now that you have a seamless background, you can stylize it for your DVD menu. There are no hard and fast rules here; just use your design abilities and well-chosen effects to get results (**Figure 13.31**). Here are a few of our favorite techniques to use:

▶ Place an adjustment layer on top of your footage with Hue/Saturation and Levels effects. These two can work well to create the proper contrast. We typically strip the color and then adjust the black and white points to get the right balance of darks and lights. You can also use the new Black & White effect to create a grayscale image.

TIP

Instead of a simple opacity change, you can also try the Gradient Wipe effect to create a more organic blend. Export a freeze frame from your composition and use that as the source layer.

Figure 13.31 By combining multiple effects, you can create complex, customizable effects.

For a great comparison on blur effects, check out Stu Maschwitz's blog at http://prolost.com/blog/2006/3/2/a-tale-of-three-blurs.html.

▶ Adjust the Output Levels with a Levels effect to clamp the whites and knock down the intensity of a background.

▶ Add an adjustment layer to create the soft bloom. Apply the Gaussian Blur, CC Radial Fast Blur, or Fast Blur effect and adjust the layer's blending mode and Opacity settings.

▶ Apply a colorization effect such as Colorama, Tritone, or Tint to an adjustment layer.

▶ Apply the Broadcast Colors effect to spot problem colors (use the Key Out Unsafe option). You can then tone down a brightly colored background with Color Correction effects. Most video compression methods prefer broadcast-safe video levels.

▶ Add a vignette layer to draw the viewer's eye toward the center of the menu.

Rendering the Background

When the looping background is complete, we recommend rendering two files. Create a reference frame that you can use in Photoshop to design buttons and any overlays. To export a still, move the current time indicator to a representative frame and choose Composition > Save Frame As > File. You should also render out a high-quality movie file. We recommend sticking with a lossless or very high-quality codec. When the rendering is complete, you can reimport the file.

Photoshop Design

The next jump in the DVD menu design process is to Photoshop. You could certainly stay in After Effects, but we find that it's a lot easier to manage the interactive sets that Encore needs for buttons within Photoshop. Plus you'll have faster and more precise control over text as you design.

Loading the Reference Frame

Photoshop offers comparable document presets to match your After Effects composition. Choose File > New, click the Preset list, and choose Film & Video (**Figure 13.32**). Select the preset that most closely matches your desired menu. Although Photoshop offers frame rates with its presets, don't worry about them because they're easy to change.

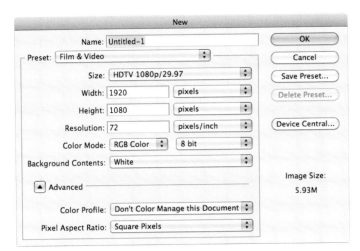

Figure 13.32 Stick with Photoshop's presets when designing menus.

TIP

If you're using Photoshop Extended, you can also place the movie file you rendered. Using a still background requires less RAM and is faster to design with. Encore requires you to import the video layer separately and connect the menu and background within Encore.

Load the reference frame you made by choosing File > Place. A navigation box opens so you can select the background layer. Locate the file and click Place. The file is added to your document as a Smart Object (**Figure 13.33**). The file should fill the screen because its dimensions match your menu background.

Figure 13.33 A reference frame can serve as a design proxy to speed up your workflow.

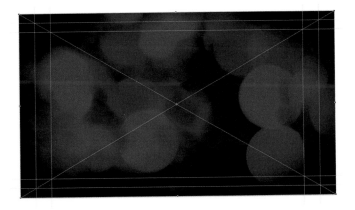

Adding Additional Imagery

When designing DVD menus, we prefer to combine abstract textures with a little reality. A well-composed image (or even a scaled and properly positioned one) can create a nice visual frame for your design. In Photoshop, choose File > Place and select any image.

Using the Place command adds the image as a Smart Object, so you'll be able to adjust and reposition it (all the way to its original pixel dimensions) with no quality loss (**Figure 13.34**). Try blending modes as well as reducing opacity to create a nice mixture of image to background (**Figure 13.35**).

Figure 13.34 Smart Objects are treated as flattened pixels when working in other Adobe applications.

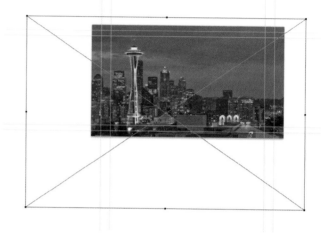

If you want to desaturate a Smart Object, you'll need to rasterize it. Right-click on a Smart Object in the Layers panel and choose Rasterize Layer.

Figure 13.35 Mixing photographic sources creates a nice balance. Experiment with both color and grayscale images.

Working with Text and Logos

Now that you have a great background, you should turn your attention to your foreground. Add any title elements to the menu page, as well as logos or artwork you need to include. We generally place these first before any buttons to create a usable frame.

Since the background will be moving and has a pattern to it, you'll need to create some separation. Try using layer styles, such as drop shadow, glow, or bevel to add a contrasting edge (**Figure 13.36**).

Figure 13.36 Don't overdo the layer styles; a little can go a long way toward separating the foreground from the background.

Although you don't have to worry about being broadcast safe, stay away from overly saturated colors like bright reds and yellows. Also, remember the concept of safe areas. Keep all major design elements inside the action safe area (the innermost 90 percent of the menu). For text that needs to be read, keep it within the title safe area (the innermost 80 percent of the menu).

Designing Buttons

The menus created by Encore are essentially layered Photoshop files. What this means in a practical sense is that you can easily create menus in Photoshop and bring them into Encore for linking. Here are some general design guidelines to follow:

▶ When designing your DVD or Blu-ray buttons, lean toward a sans serif font, which is easier to read and less prone to pixelation after compression.

▶ Create buttons at least 70x60 pixels in size. Designing buttons too small makes it hard to read them on a television.

▶ Encore limits you to 36 buttons for a 4:3 menu and 18 for a 16:9 menu. We personally try to stick to five or less per page (what you can count on one hand). Too many buttons means too many choices and too much thinking for the audience.

▶ Avoid lines that are thinner than three pixels and fonts that have thin lines. Both can cause unwanted flicker on television screens (especially in Standard Definition).

Buttons are essentially layer groups (also called sets). Every layer that you create and place in the group will properly import into Encore as a layer. If you name your layers correctly, you can even create interactive rollover states for buttons (**Figure 13.37**).

TIP

If you'd like to add a clearer area for text, just use a soft fill. You can draw a rectangle and fill it with white or black. Reduce the opacity or change its blending mode to create a screened area for your text or buttons. Gradient fill layers also work well.

Figure 13.37 A little effort in naming your layers will make the menu easier to work with in Encore.

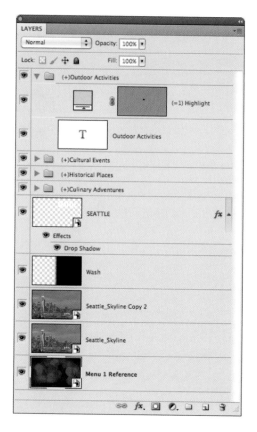

Encore recognizes certain naming structures for subpicture highlights, replacement layers, and more (**Table 13.2**).

Here are the basic steps to create a simple button for use in Encore:

TIP

You'll find an update to the Photoshop Video Actions in the Chapter_13_Media folder. Included is an action for making a new Encore button to speed up layer naming.

1. Work with a Photoshop document that's sized for a menu.

2. At the bottom of the Layers panel, click the Create a new group button.

3. Enter a name from the group. Be sure to prefix the name of the group with (#) in order for Encore to see the group as a page. For example, to name the page Play All, enter (#) Play All.

TABLE 13.2 Button Naming Styles

Menu Item	Photoshop Component	Layer-name Prefix	Sample
Button Name	Layer set that contains button components	(+)	(+)Play All
Chapter Button	Used for a layer set that links to a chapter in a Timeline or a slide show when a chapter index is created	(+#)	(+#)Chapter 1
Next Button	Used with a layer set that links to the next submenu	(+>)	(+>)Next
Previous Button	Used with a layer set that links to the previous submenu	(+<)	(+<)Previous
Main Button	Used with a layer set that links to the main menu	(+^)	(+^)Main Menu
Button Text	Text layers within the button layer set		Play
Button Image	Image layers within the button layer set		Graphic image
Button Subpictures (optional)	Single-color image layers. Each layer represents one color of the three-color button subpictures:	(=2) (=3)	(=1)Text highlight (=2)Text outline (=3)Underline
Video Thumbnail (optional)	Image layer within the layer set that serves as a placeholder for video	(%)	(%)Open thumbnail
Replacement Layer	Layer that acts as a drop zone for images	(!)	(!)Placeholder 1

4. Add text for the main button. You can also use shapes for buttons. No special naming is needed for this part of the button.

5. Create a highlight effect or subpicture overlay. Be sure to prefix the name of the group with (=1) in order for Encore to see the group as an overlay.

6. Repeat steps 2–5 to create as many pages as you require (**Figure 13.38**). When you're finished, save the menu as a layered Photoshop file (.psd).

TIP

Once you've built one button, just duplicate its group to make more. You can right-click a layer group and choose Duplicate Group. Modify and reposition the contents to taste.

Figure 13.38 By naming layers with the correct prefixes, subpicture highlights will work as soon as you import the menu into Encore.

Assembling Menus in Adobe Encore

Now that you have all the pieces ready, you can assemble your motion menus in Adobe Encore. A menu in Encore can include motion and sound. A video can serve as a background, or it can have all elements except for the button subpicture highlights.

There are two major approaches you can take:

▶ **Build entirely in After Effects and render a movie.** You'll then want to enable only the layers that need highlights. Choose Composition > Save Frame As > Photoshop Layers. This file can then be cleaned up so it only contains highlight layers.

▶ **Build in Photoshop and After Effects (the workflow we've used in this lesson).** Import a layered Photoshop file and a movie file. Reassemble in Encore. We prefer this workflow because it allows maximum flexibility to edit and reposition buttons during the authoring stage.

Importing Menu Assets

When you're ready to assemble your motion menu, you'll need to launch Encore and import your assets. When you first launch Encore (or choose File > New Project), a dialog box opens. The important thing here is to name the project and choose a delivery standard.

▶ For the Name and Location fields, give the project a descriptive name and target your project's Common Media Folder. Encore projects tend to have a lot of asset linking, so minimize moving elements and breaking file paths.

▶ Choose an authoring mode: Blu-ray or DVD.

NOTES

To learn more about authoring DVD, Blu-ray, and Flash menus with Adobe Encore, you have several choices. Extensive coverage is available in the Adobe Community Help Center (www.adobe.com/support/encore/) and video tutorials are offered on Adobe TV (tv.adobe.com).

▶ Choose a Television Standard of NTSC or PAL. You can also customize the settings by clicking the Default Transcode Settings button to open the dialog box in **Figure 13.39**.

Figure 13.39 Be sure to adjust frame rate, screen dimensions, and bit rate to your specific needs.

▶ You can import your menu assets by choosing File > Import As > Asset or press Command+I (Ctrl+I). This is how you should import the background movies or audio beds.

▶ To import a layered Photoshop file as a menu, choose File > Import As > Menu or press Shift+Command+I (Shift+Ctrl+I). Select a layered file with properly named groups and a menu is created.

Adding Backgrounds

Once you've imported assets, you can connect them together to build a motion menu. Double-click a menu in the Project panel to open it. In the Properties panel, the Motion tab should be selected by default. Drag the pick whip for the Video property to the motion menu background you created in After Effects (**Figure 13.40**).

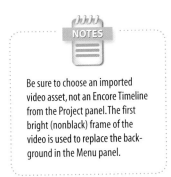

Be sure to choose an imported video asset, not an Encore Timeline from the Project panel. The first bright (nonblack) frame of the video is used to replace the background in the Menu panel.

Figure 13.40 When you use the pick whip to choose a background, Encore swaps out the video for the background layer and adjusts the duration of the motion menu to match the selected file.

You now need to remove the placeholder still from the menu. Locate the reference file you used in the Layers panel. Select it and press the Delete key. The menu uses a frame for the background movie; however, it won't appear to move until you render the menu (**Figure 13.41**). Before you invoke render time, let's finish the menu.

Figure 13.41 It may appear at first that nothing has changed when you replace the static background with a motion background. The menu will look different once it is rendered.

NOTES

Although you can't see or change them in Encore, any Opacity settings or blending modes you used in Photoshop do carry over. This means that the mixture of background layer with foreground photos and color washes will be preserved in the motion menu. If you need advanced controls, select the menu and choose Edit > Edit Menu In Photoshop.

Setting Button Order

When you import a menu, Encore assigns a number to each button to specify the order for selection. For example, the button numbered one will be selected first. When a user presses the forward or down arrow on the remote or keyboard, the button numbered two is selected. This seems straightforward enough, but Encore won't always label buttons in the order you want. However, this is a very easy fix.

1. Open a menu and select the button in the Menu Viewer.

2. Choose the desired number from the Number menu in the Properties panel (**Figure 13.42**).

3. Repeat until all buttons are in the desired order.

Figure 13.42 When you change a button's order, Encore automatically renumbers the other buttons after it.

Previewing Motion Menus

Now that you've assembled the menu, it's time to test it. Right-click on the first menu you want to use in the Project panel and choose Set As First Play (if you only have one menu, it should be marked by default).

To see a motion menu in action, Encore needs to render the menus. Choose File > Render Motion Menus. A dialog box opens to track progress of the rendering. Select the Preview When Complete check box to automatically preview the menu when rendering is done.

A new window opens and previews the menu set as the First Play option. If you have only one menu, it will open by default. Use the navigation controls to move between buttons and check your button highlights.

When you're finished, click the Exit Here button. If you want to preview a different menu, you can right-click it in the Project panel and choose Preview from Here.

NOTES

You can change how Encore automatically numbers buttons using the routing preferences. Open the Preferences menu by choosing Encore > Preferences > Menus (Edit > Preferences > Menus). Click to choose routing preferences such as circular or left to right. You can also change routing preferences to specify how to handle a jump when the end of a row is reached. When you're satisfied, click OK.

Index

WATCH
READ
CREATE

Meet Creative Edge.

A new resource of unlimited books, videos and tutorials for creatives from the world's leading experts.

Creative Edge is your one stop for inspiration, answers to technical questions and ways to stay at the top of your game so you can focus on what you do best—being creative.

All for only $24.99 per month for access—any day any time you need it.